POLITICAL THEORY AND CHRISTIAN VISION

POLITICAL THEORY
and
CHRISTIAN VISION

Essays in Memory of Bernard Zylstra

JONATHAN CHAPLIN
PAUL MARSHALL
Editors

UNIVERSITY
PRESS OF
AMERICA

Lanham • New York • London

Copyright © 1994 by
University Press of America®, Inc.
4720 Boston Way
Lanham, Maryland 20706

3 Henrietta Street
London WC2E 8LU England

Co-published by arrangement with the
Institute for Christian Studies, Ontario, Canada

Library of Congress Cataloging-in-Publication Data

Political theory and Christian vision : essays in memory of Bernard
    Zylstra / Jonathan Chaplin, Paul Marshall, editors.
                    p.   cm.
        Includes bibliographical references and index.
1. Christianity and government.   2. Political science—Philosophy.
I. Zylstra, Bernard.   II. Chaplin, Jonathan.   III. Marshall, Paul A.
    BR115.P7P553   1994   261.7—dc20   94–8990 CIP

            ISBN 0–8191–9529–4 (cloth : alk. paper)
            ISBN 0–8191–9530–8 (pbk. : alk. paper)

Contents

v

Contributors

Joan O'Donovan is a theologian and political philosopher based in Oxford. Her publications include *George Grant and the Twilight of Justice* and *Theology of Law and Authority in the English Reformation*. She is currently compiling a two volume anthology of Christian political thought.

John Witte, Jr., is Director of the Law and Religion Program and is Professor of Law at Emory University, Atlanta. He has numerous law journal publications and has edited and contributed to *Christianity and Democracy: Past Contributions and Future* and *The Weightier Matters of the Law: Essays on Law and Religion*.

James W. Skillen is Executive Director of the Center for Public Justice, Washington, D.C. Among his numerous publications are *The Scattered Voice: Christians at Odds in the Public Square* and *Political Order and the Plural Structure of Society*, co-edited with R. M. McCarthy.

Jonathan Chaplin is Tutor in Politics at Plater College, Oxford, and a member of the Steering Group of the British Movement for Christian Democracy.

David T. Koyzis is Assistant Professor of Political Science at Redeemer College, Ancaster, Ontario, Canada.

Justin Cooper is Vice-president of Academic Affairs at Redeemer College, Ancaster, Ontario, Canada.

Paul Marshall is Senior Member in Political Theory at the Institute for Christian Studies. His publications include *Thine Is the Kingdom* and *Human Rights Theories in Christian Perspective.*

Sander Griffioen is Professor of Social Philosophy at the Free University of Amsterdam, and a Fellow of the Institute for Christian Studies, Toronto. His most recent English publication, co-authored with Richard J. Mouw, is *Pluralisms and Horizons.*

John L. Hiemstra is Assistant Professor of Political Science at The King's College, Edmonton, Alberta.

David S. Caudill is Assistant Professor of Law at Washington and Lee College, Lexington, Virginia. His publications include *Disclosing Tilt: Law, Belief and Criticism.*

Bruce Clemenger is Research Coordinator for the Evangelical Fellowship of Canada and a doctoral student at the Institute for Christian Studies.

David S. Woods has worked in the British Government Economic Service.

Johanna Selles-Roney is a Research Fellow at Yale Divinity School.

Bernard Zylstra

1934-1986

The Editors thank the Stichting Zonneweelde of Amsterdam
for a grant to assist in the publication of this book.

Preface

Paul Marshall

Bernard Zylstra was born in the Netherlands in 1934. His family moved to North America after the second world war and settled in Grand Rapids, Michigan, the mecca of Dutch Christian Reformed folk. He studied in Christian schools and entered Calvin College in Grand Rapids in 1951. While there he came under the influence of H. Evan Runner, a philosophy professor who, perhaps because of his Irish Presbyterian background, was more captivated by Dutch Calvinist philosophy than were many of his colleagues of Dutch stock.[1] He exposed his students to a tradition of Christian thought rooted in the work of John Calvin and Johannes Althusius, revived by the nineteenth century Dutch statesmen Guillaume Groen Van Prinsterer and Abraham Kuyper, and which flowered as a twentieth century philosophical school in the work of Herman Dooyeweerd and D. H. Th. Vollenhoven. This school emphasizes that all knowledge, including academic knowledge, is rooted in faith and, hence, that every dimension of the academy, indeed every dimension of life itself, needs to be reformed in a Christian way.

One consequence of Runner's influence was to pull Zylstra away from his earlier interest in the ecclesiastical ministry and towards the study of law. He graduated from college in 1955 and received a Master of Divinity degree from Calvin Seminary in 1958. He then moved to law school at the University of Michigan, completing an LL.B. in 1961. With these preliminaries out of the way he travelled to the Free University of Amsterdam to commence studies with Herman Dooyeweerd, then Professor of Philosophy of Law. Zylstra was somewhat unusual in this choice of mentor since, although Dooyeweerd is the best known (often the only known) exponent of this philosophical school on this side of the Atlantic, most of its North American students in fact worked with Vollenhoven, whose field was the history of philosophy.[2] While studying in Amsterdam, Zylstra also served for two years as head of the Institute of Philosophy at the Free University. In 1968 he graduated with an S.J.D. cum laude for a dissertation on the British socialist Harold Laski.[3]

Shortly thereafter he returned to North America to teach political theory at the newly-formed Institute for Christian Studies in Toronto. The Institute was established as a philosophically-oriented graduate school to continue the approach of an "inner reformation of the sciences" developed in Calvinist philosophy. In 1978 Zylstra became its Principal and in 1983 its President, relinquishing this position in 1985 when it was evident that his health was failing. He died less than a year later.

These are the principal facts of his life. Out of the many facets we could explore, I will simply make some comments on his academic work. The theoretical framework of his study was shaped by what has been called "the inner reformation of the sciences." In this he claimed no great originality. His colleague Hendrik Hart describes this approach as follows:

> Scholars in [this] tradition believe that conversion in Jesus Christ is in principle total, radical and integral; that nothing in the life of the convert can be left outside of the scope of allegiance to Jesus as Lord of creation. Since all humans have both beliefs and concepts, these scholars argue that both the beliefs of faith and the concepts of reason ought to be subjected to the rule of the gospel.

. . . As a result these adherents believe that Christians active in scientific disciplines ought to celebrate their conversion by letting their faith have its effect in those disciplines. They should work in science for continuing reformation, changing science radically from within, pulling its roots out of its traditionally idolatrous soil and transplanting them in the soil of the gospel. . . .

At the same time people who support the inner reformation tradition affirm that science must maintain its own nature. An inner reformation does not seek to destroy science or make it unrecognizable. The need for reformation arises when science departs from its own nature and pretends to take on the structures of final truth and authoritative revelation. Science is certainly necessary in our culture, but in a radically reformed fashion.[4]

In elucidating this perspective as a teacher, Zylstra was always warm, alive and expressive; he was moved and moving. He struggled with the direction of the world, of his own neighborhood and of his own studies, and he never saw them apart. He could deal with abstract dimensions of Hegel or of systems theory and show how, for Hegel and von Bertalanffy, they were never merely abstract: hence we his students learned something of how to relate them to the pattern of the world. He saw ideas and beliefs in their relation to movements and powers: they were matters of life and death which had religious roots and touched our religious core. He would summarize a position so succinctly that it would be easy to miss the detailed textual analysis on which it had been built. This simplicity could then be mistaken for superficiality, and it was often only in face to face discussion, as the exegesis was unravelled, that it became plain that the points were innovative, textually solid and precisely put.

Despite these scholarly virtues the remarkable feature of Zylstra's expositions was not their depth but their breadth. Because of his own broad vision and this focus on the religious depth of theoretical questions, he always expanded the horizons of his readers and, especially, his listeners. He read widely and catholicly and continually labored to weave the most various strands together. He would aspire to see each part in the pattern of world history and the coming of the Kingdom of God in Jesus Christ.

When we presented seminars on theories of autonomy in liberalism, or the place of nature in Marx, or the underlying relativism of conservatism, his questions always pushed us, with the utmost kindness, beyond our own student parochialisms into their relations to fundamental questions of the political world. On reflection we found that our thinking had been cramped, not only channelled by the necessary tunnels of specialization, but all too often trapped in those tunnels. We felt that our eyes had previously remained only inches from the ground. If we discussed behavioralism we were encouraged to do so in terms of philosophical anthropology and the growth of technological society. A discussion of Eric Voegelin would lead to meditation on the place of the (late) Soviet Union in the world. Luther's two kingdoms were a path to understanding how to live in a world beset by sin.

In this way political questions became spiritual ones and spiritual ones became political ones, not in the sense of a politicized gospel but in the realization that all fundamental questions were at root religious questions. The route to this realization was not via biblical illustration or theological veneer but by uncovering the religious choices and commitments that lay at the heart of the theorists, theories and movements we studied.[5]

Zylstra was a *political* theorist: not in the all-too-common contemporary sense of a practitioner of a virtually autonomous discipline with its own texts and norms and who studies political theories. Political theory meant thinking about the basic questions of political reality in a systematic and rigorous manner in dialogue with political theorists past and present. Perhaps this contrast is put too strongly, so let me say that it meant that we were encouraged to write on European integration as well as Plato, on Canadian aboriginal policy as well as Machiavelli. Given this range of interests he actively discouraged students from doing doctoral work with him: instead he encouraged us to study international relations, or

American politics or comparative politics elsewhere. The goal was not to unite theory and practice but to learn the practice of theory. He would echo Simone Weil's view that, when properly shaped, "clear thinking can save human lives."

Although also trained in theology, Zylstra was a Christian political theorist, not a political theologian. His purpose was not to study the Bible or to study theology for political principles. Rather, in common with what he referred to as the "reformational" movement, he stressed that the object of political study was the world of politics. Of course, such study was never neutral but was inevitably shaped by a worldview, and so our task was to seek to conduct our studies in the light of a biblically shaped view of the nature of the world. Yet our purpose was not to study Christianity per se, but to study the world itself, the world that God has given us.

Such political thinking is a genuine searching, an ongoing, open-ended, continuing inquiry which attempts to understand the political dimensions of our existence. This inquiry is to be grounded in the word of God but, with that anchor, is to reach out freely and openly to whatever continuities, discoveries and changes this fecund creation will produce.

Zylstra's wide vision could be a problem as well as a virtue. He wanted to shape institutions and so sought administrative positions; he wanted to shape movements and so was involved deeply in community work. He always struggled with the combination of theoretical work and the maintenance of a community that would make that work feasible and fruitful. In the middle of these struggles he was diagnosed as having cancer. He died nine months later, but not before having again seen four seasons, something he asked of God.

He did not die full of years with the fruit of an academic life spread abroad. Studies with him had been truncated rather than completed. But his teaching, his training, his writing and his influence touched many lives, in the academy and beyond it. The essays that follow are by people whose studies were shaped by Bernard's life, and they are offered as a small testimony to him and to the work in which he lost his life.

Notes

1. See his "H. Evan Runner: An Assessment of His Mission," in H. Vander Goot, ed., *Life is Religion: Essays in Honor of H. Evan Runner,* (St. Catharines, Ont.: Paideia Press, 1981), 1-14.

2. Zylstra co-edited two works which have served as influential introductions to the thought of Herman Dooyeweerd. They are: Herman Dooyeweerd, *Roots of Western Culture*, B. Zylstra and M. Vander Vennen, eds., (Toronto: Wedge, 1979), and L. Kalsbeek, *Contours of a Christian Philosophy,* (Toronto: Wedge, 1975).

3. Published as *From Pluralism to Collectivism: The Development of Harold Laski's Thought,* (Assen: Van Gorcum, 1968; 2nd ed., 1970).

4. Hendrik Hart, "The Idea of an Inner Reformation of the Sciences" in P. Marshall and R. VanderVennen, eds., *Social Science in Christian Perspective*, (Lanham, MD.: University Press of America, 1988), 13-14.

5. Examples of Zylstra's publications illustrating the range and depth of his interests are: "Hegel, Marcuse and the New Left," *The Gordon Review* 11 (no. 5, 1970): 267-81; "Voegelin on Unbelief and Revolution" in W. F. de Gaay Fortman et al., *Een staatsman ter navolging (A Statesman to Follow: Groen Van Prinsterer Commemorated*), (The Hague: Antirevolutionary Party, 1976), 155-65; "Philosophy, Revelation and Modernity: Crossroads in the Thought of George Grant" in L. Schmidt, ed., *George Grant in Process*, (Toronto: Anansi, 1978), 148-57; "Daniel Bell's Neoconservative Critique of Modernity" in J. Kraay and A. Tol, eds., *Hearing and Doing: Philosophical Essays Dedicated to H. Evan Runner,* (Toronto: Wedge, 1979), 15-38; "Using the Constitution to Defend Religious Rights" in L. R. Buzzard, ed., *Freedom and Faith: The Impact of Law on Religious Liberty,* (Westchester, Ill.: Crossway Books, 1982), 93-114.

Introduction

Jonathan Chaplin

The essays in this volume are intended as contributions to the enterprise of Christian political theorizing to which Bernard Zylstra devoted his life's work. As Paul Marshall explains in the Preface, this is a multifaceted enterprise, with large and somewhat audacious horizons. Its aim is to investigate systematically, and on the basis of a clearly articulated religious and philosophical vision, the full range of dimensions of political reality, and to do so in close correspondence with related disciplines such as sociology, economics and law. Such a vision is "architectonic," to employ a term from Sheldon Wolin's book *Politics and Vision* (to which the title of this volume alludes), a book which was, rightly, required reading for all Zylstra's students. It is a vision "wherein the political imagination attempts to mould the totality of political phenomena to accord with some vision of the Good that lies outside the political order."

Bernard Zylstra's particular interests lay, for good strategic reasons, in the philosophical and methodological questions that underlie the study of empirical political systems. In his view, the neglect of rigorous critical reflection on the presuppositions of the discipline left many of its current practitioners lacking direction and their output lacking coherence. Even where the discipline had, in spite of such vulnerabilities, struck upon fundamental insights into political reality, these were at risk of being either exaggerated or misplaced on account of the discipline's underlying religious and philosophical disorientation. It was his aim to demonstrate the necessity for and the potential fruitfulness of an integrated, philosophically self-conscious and inter-disciplinary practice of political theory.

It is appropriate, therefore, that the essays in this book, all written by former students or colleagues, are illustrative of this concern with issues arising at the foundations of the discipline. Those in Section One address questions immediately related to the normative character of those foundations. According to influential Christian traditions such as Thomism and Calvinism, such normative foundations will be rooted in a conviction of the divine ordering of the cosmos. Joan O'Donovan's analysis of the Canadian political philosopher George Grant brings to the fore the conception of a lawful ordering of the created world which frames human experience and yet is expressive of the love and grace of God. She discloses how differences in such fundamental conceptions of world order generate significantly different readings of crucial historical and societal developments.

A conception like that outlined by O'Donovan must lie at the foundation of a vision of society and politics which claims to be rooted in biblical revelation. John Witte's essay on Dooyeweerd examines how one influential Christian philosopher worked towards the construction of an innovative theory of rights on the basis of just such a conception of divine world order. Dooyeweerd's philosophical articulation of the idea of creation order is highly distinctive and sophisticated. Witte shows how a sound legal—and by implication, political—theory needs to aspire to this level of philosophical sophistication if it is to account adequately for the complexity of actual legal experience.

James Skillen's wide-ranging analysis of the current state of political science reaches a similar conclusion by a different route. The discipline as a whole is differentiating, though in certain respects unhealthily so on account of its lack of an integrated theoretical perspective. Only by articulating such a perspective can it achieve clarity about its distinctive object and methods. The "comprehensive science of politics," towards which he urges political theorists and scientists to direct themselves, needs a coherent philosophical foundation which will furnish the conceptual apparatus necessary to identify what is unique about the political community (the state), to distinguish its multiple dimensions, and to grasp the subtle interlinkages among these dimensions.

James Skillen's essay also proposes a particular characterization of the unique nature and dimensions of the state, and so usefully prepares the ground for the three essays in Section Two, each of which presupposes a characterization of this kind. These essays consider further the nature of the political community (the state) from diverse angles. Jonathan Chaplin explores the relationships between the political community and other kinds of community in the light of the Catholic principle of "subsidiarity." The essay raises questions about the adequacy of the traditional formulation of this principle as a political norm, and proposes a reformulation which tries to avoid the problems of the concept of hierarchy which subsidiarity has traditionally presupposed.

David Koyzis raises the question of the obsolescence of the idea of the nation-state as this is posed in the thought of Hannah Arendt. He finds her critique of the modern attachment to the nation-state a powerful one, and suggests that the notion of a federal distribution of government powers comports well with a Christian conception of the political order.

Justin Cooper's assessment of an influential functionalist theory of international relation, developed by David Mitrany, concurs in expressing scepticism about the supposed perpetuity of the nation-state. Mitrany himself displays such scepticism, a point to which Cooper pays tribute, while calling attention to an uncritical technicism which has the effect of denying the inescapably normative character of political processes and institutions.

Section Three brings to view a contemporary problem of mounting urgency which is straining the capacity of western states to fulfil their distinctive task. The problem is that of "the plural society," the term used by political scientists (and before them, sociologists and anthropologists) to denote the co-existence within the same territory of incompatible social, cultural or religious communities.

Paul Marshall's essay approaches the problem by examining the dominant liberal responses to such pluralism. Liberalism's aspiration to establish a neutral framework within which such diverse communities can flourish unhindered is, he concludes, incapable of realization. A Christian pluralism will, he argues, prove more hospitable to diversity than will liberalism.

The same issue is addressed by Sander Griffioen by way of the current North American debate over the idea of a "public philosophy." He points out that in its dominant forms this idea has similarly proved unable adequately to embrace a genuine pluralism. Pierre Trudeau's variety of liberalism shares the same hegemonic tendencies indicated by Paul Marshall, as John Hiemstra's detailed analysis of Trudeau's view of the French Canadians demonstrates. Hegemonic tendencies are also shown to be a feature of contemporary American jurisprudence in David Caudill's critical assessment of the Critical Legal Studies movement. Caudill suggests Christians must learn from the movement's critique of current jurisprudential ideology.

Section Four examines themes pertaining to political economy. Bruce Clemenger's discussion focuses on Ludwig Von Mises's diminished view of economic activity and points to some of the deleterious political consequences of such reductionism. Economic reductionism of a different kind, as revealed by Karl Polanyi's institutionalist methodology, is also the subject of David Woods' contribution. Woods' essay brings to light some of the beneficial insights within economics yielded by an institutional approach, one with which the social and political theory proposed in Skillen's article has definite affinities.

Johanna Selles-Roney's critical appreciation of Simone Weil returns to the fundamental theological and confessional concerns addressed in the first chapter. Weil's understanding of the spiritual value of human labour was the basis of a profound and critical social analysis which, Selles-Roney suggests, remains important today.

The essays in this volume were prepared as a tribute to the life and work of Bernard Zylstra. Zylstra was only too aware that the project upon which he had embarked, as others before him upon whose contributions he had built, was at its earliest stages. A continuing and widening community of Christian scholars, engaging in dialogue with those of other persuasions, would be needed to take it forward to the point at which it might shape the contemporary political mind, and thereby shape actual political practice. We hope that these essays may stimulate others to lend their support to that project.

The Primacy of the Will and the Problem of Law in the Thought of George Grant

Joan O'Donovan

Among the contemporary political thinkers that attracted the scholarly attention of the late Bernard Zylstra was the Canadian philosopher, George Grant, who died in 1988. In an essay published in 1978, Zylstra analyzed the relationship between biblical religion and modernity in Grant's thought.[1] He proposed that the link between them lay for Grant in the primacy of the divine will characterizing the Old Testament portrayal of a creating and history-making God. According to Zylstra, Grant saw this Hebraic primacy of divine willing and making revitalized in Reformation Protestantism, and subsequently transmuted by the secularizing forces of technological liberalism into the supremacy of human willing. Behind Nietzsche's apotheosis of the finite will, creating, destroying, and renewing the world of things, Grant detected the sovereign will of the creating and re-creating God of biblical Christianity.

Zylstra draws out the opposition in Grant's understanding of biblical revelation between the God who is creative and willing, and the God "who as the eternally lovable is the object of human contemplation and the end of man's desiring."[2] This is the Father of Jesus Christ, who for Grant is not only unchanging perfection but is also self-abandoning and suffering love. Zylstra summarizes this opposition in the theoretically suggestive observation that "[Grant] accepts the God who is love while he hesitates before a God who wills love, and who has the sovereign right to command love because he is the maker and redeemer of man."[3]

Zylstra's observation suggests the theoretical dilemma presented by Grant's antithesis of divine love and divine will for a theological account of law, as it functions in God's creation, preservation, redemption, and sanctification of the world. For the theological concept of law in each of these contexts is intimately connected with the concepts of God's sovereign will and command. In biblical revelation God summons the world into being by his free command; he preserves its order and integrity by delegating to his human creature the right to command and to be obeyed; he redeems people by summoning them to faith in their salvation by the death and resurrection of Jesus Christ; he sanctifies them by empowering them through the Holy Spirit to obey the example and commandments of their Saviour. Thus, the theological concept of law in the spheres of created order, of human government, of saving faith, and of sanctifying grace, is incontestably dependent on the sovereign operation of God's will. It follows, then, that if we, with Grant, hesitate "before a God who wills love, and who has the sovereign right to command love," we are putting in jeopardy the meaningfulness and validity of the theological concept of law.

To view the concept of law with suspicion and apprehensiveness is consistent with the dominant mood of theology today, which may generally be described as one of eschatological narrowness. Eschatological narrowness is a preoccupation with the impact of God's future on our present, as this is grasped by means of such dynamic concepts as freedom, transcendence, openness, transformation, and revolution. Such a dynamic point of view has little patience with the conceptual associations of law with exteriority, objectivity, subjection, and permanence. It prefers to see law as *overcome* by the reconciling power of divine love rather than as *renewed* by it, being out of sympathy with the psalmist's ecstatic extolling of the purity, goodness, perfection, and beauty of God's ordinances.[4] It interprets St. Paul's graphic depiction of the oppressive and enslaving burden of the law's demands on sinful mankind as a final theological indictment of law as such.[5] In its eschatological vision of human liberation, embodied in an anticipatory way in the believing community, human action has shed its law-abiding character. The rule of Christ over his people is still conceded, but only in the most attenuated metaphorical sense; for Christ is no longer the communal law-giver, as in the older theological tradition. He elicits loving action from those who love him without commands, directives, controlling and formative principles. In this vision of communal freedom, action is wholly spontaneous, interior, mysterious, and inexpressible in the conventional moral language of ought and should, law and obligation.

It would appear that Grant's antithesis of will and love issues in a similar conception of loving action as beyond the operation of law. But there is much in his thought to counter the impression that the undermining of law belongs to his theoretical intention. For, while he criticizes the primacy of the will in the technological ontology of modernity,[6] he equally criticizes the eclipse of the transcending and objective claim of the law on human action. In fact, the Promethean will that realizes itself in modern technological capabilities is precisely the arbitrary and irrational will unbounded by law. By contrast, loving action is in some sense for Grant lawful action, involving human obedience or conformity to a perceived excluding claim. Indeed, it is hardly an exaggeration to suggest that Grant's whole literary life's work has been devoted to holding before the liberal public, with unswerving constancy, the concept of unconditional moral restraint.

Thus, the deeper theological ambiguity of the concept of law is rooted for Grant in its relationship to divine will, rather than to divine love. The relationship of law to divine love is unproblematic in terms of his Platonic understanding of God as the Eternal Perfection and Unchanging Measure revealed in Jesus Christ. Increasingly problematic in his writings is the relationship of law to God's sovereign will and command. He never systematically discusses the subject of law after *Philosophy in the Mass Age* (1959),[7] where, under the sway of Hegel, he proposes to ground an "absolute morality" in the Kantian notion of law as self-legislated limit. Nevertheless, in the next two decades he distances himself from the Kantian notion through a protracted criticism of the Western "language of willing" as regards both human and divine being and action. A close inspection of his anthropological and theological criticisms will enable us to focus more exactly his reservations concerning the relationship of law and will, to which we can then respond with theological formulations that avoid the voluntarist pitfalls against which Grant warns us.

The Future and the Will to Mastery
It is revealing of modern Western man's self-understanding that the word "will" is used as an auxiliary for the future tense, and also as the word which expresses our determination to do," remarks Grant in *Time As History* (11).[8] For the human capacity for "differentiated doing . . . depends upon openness to an imagined future and the power to plan towards that future" (13). Moreover, modern man's unsurpassed efficacy in the doing that "make[s] happen novel events" depends on his heightened concentration on the future in the form of rational prediction. In the characteristically modern paradigm of "willing and reasoning," authoritatively summed up in Heidegger's term "technique," the method of prediction is oriented to the mastery of human and non-human matter through the overcoming of chance. Hence, the primacy of the will to mastery means for us moderns a diminished capability of "partaking in time other than as future" (14). It means a civilizational disengagement from those activities and pursuits in which our attention is claimed by the present or the past: the enjoyment of natural and spiritual goods, the thoughtful recollection of traditions, admiration and reverence, love, desire, and contemplation.

Grant especially sets the activity of willing over against those of thinking and desiring. Because willing is "that power of determining by which we put our stamp on events (including ourselves) and in which we do some violence to the world," it requires that "we close down on the openness of deliberation and decide that . . . this will happen rather than that" (15). Thus the act of willing severs us from the "uncertain and continuous openness to all that is" which is indispensable to the most profound thought. Willing is the motor of doing, of reforming action, whereas: "In thought about the most important matters there is nothing we need do, there is nothing we can wish to change" (15).

Thought of the highest philosophical order—contemplation of the eternal—has in common with desiring the dependence on a "lovable actuality" (19). The "erotic language of wanting or desiring," says Grant, "express[es] our dependence on that which we need—be it food, another person, or God" (16). By contrast, in "the modern era the language of will" has become "the assertion of the power of the self over something other than the self, and indeed of the self over its own dependencies" (16). Kant's insight that "To will is to legislate," ("it makes something positive happen or prevents something from happening"), which is inseparable from his conviction "that we cannot will a purpose without willing means to bring it about," perfectly expresses for Grant "the responsible and independent self, distinguished from the dependent self who desires" (16). As the "responsible self" shoulders an ever greater burden of "'creating' . . . goodness" in "the morally indifferent world," it loses touch with the goodness that meets it from without, preceding and transcending it, lying beyond its particular purposes (17). To understand ourselves as wills, then, is to understand human and non-human nature as the mere stuff, meaningless in itself, of our unlimited creative projects. It is to set over against blind and inert matter ourselves as the absolute self-transcending source of law and order.

The Calvinist God and the Modern Sciences

Grant perceives an historical affinity between the prevailing modern conception of humans as autonomous, legislating wills and the conception of God as sovereign and inscrutable Will typifying Calvinist Protestantism. He ponders the receptivity of Dutch and English Calvinists of the seventeenth century to "the new physical and moral sciences" given birth in the Renaissance, attributing this receptivity, on the theoretical side, to two fundamental convergences between Protestant theology and the "Baconian account of science."[9] Initially, there was the common hostility toward "the medieval teleological doctrine with its substantial forms": the scientists attacking its interference with dispassionate observation and understanding of the physical universe; the theologians, its mitigation of the "surd mystery of evil" by the argument of "final purpose" from the world, that led "men away from the only true illumination of that mystery, the crucifixion apprehended in faith as the divine humiliation."[10]

In addition to the united Protestant assault on Thomistic-Aristotelian "natural theology," there was a further positive convergence between Calvinist theology and English "empiricism and utilitarianism." Grant appeals to Troeltsch's elucidation of this convergence.

> Calvinism, with its abolition of the absolute goodness and rationality of the divine activity into mere separate will-acts, connected by no inner necessity and no metaphysical unity of substance, essentially tends to the emphasizing of the individual and empirical, the renunciation of the conceptions of absolute causality and unity, the practically free and utilitarian individual judgment of all things (21).

Just as Calvinism dissolved the cosmic unity and integrity of finite nature, so it dissolved the underlying "inner necessity" and "metaphysical unity" of the divine nature, leaving behind the stark encounter of the human and divine wills, unmediated by the concepts of absolute goodness and law. Grant describes the inevitable turn to the mastery of nature by the "lonely soul face to face with the transcendent (and therefore elusive) will of God:"

> This will had to be sought and served not through our contemplations but directly through our practice. From the solitude and uncertainty of that position came the responsibility which could find no rest. That unappeasable responsibility gave an extraordinary sense of the self as radical freedom. . . . The external world was unimportant and indeterminate stuff (even

when it was our own bodies) as compared with the soul's am-
biguous encounter with the transcendent. What did the body
matter; it was an instrument to be brought into submission so
that it could serve this restless righteousness (23).

The predestinating arbitrariness of God's inscrutable Will bred
the technological arbitrariness of mankind's unrestrained drive to
mastery, pursued through the instrumentality of the mathematical
sciences. The modern human's opaque and lawless relationship to
the natural world mirrors the relationship of the Calvinist God to
His creation.

In summary, Grant's criticism of the modern primacy of the will,
as expressed in anthropological and theological language, centers
on the violent self-assertiveness and arbitrariness of the will operating apart from love and law. Thus, it challenges us to find an
anthropological and theological language in which will, law, and love
are indissolubly wedded. As both Grant and Zylstra well understood, this language is not our invention, except in the archaic sense
of "invent," meaning "to come upon" or "find"; for it comes to meet
us out of the Christian theological tradition, to be appropriated
anew.

Our appropriation of this language will limit itself to two spheres
of theological conceptualization of the relationship of will, law, and
love: in the creation as divinely decreed order, and in the revelation
of Jesus Christ as God's law for mankind.

(1) Natural law as divine ordinance. The Western theological tradition, indebted as much to St. Augustine as to St. Thomas Aquinas
(and indeed to Calvin), has viewed the world as a lawfully ordered
totality, or cosmos, which, in its ordered goodness, articulates the
loving will of its creator. As God's love, even in his creation of the
world, is ordered to the goodness of his own being, so the beings
created by his love are ordered finally to participation in his goodness. Thus, finite good and finite order are teleologically dependent
on God's infinite goodness and perfection, rooted in the oneness of
his being, will, and love.

To know a creature as good is to know it as participating in God's goodness. But it is also to know it as a finite form, its form or essence being the mode of its participation in the divine perfection and, consequently, the basis of its immanent goodness. The essential form or "nature" of the creature is the law of its being, determining the operations proper to it. Every creature, then, is subject to a twofold ordering: to God as its transcendent end (to "tell the glory of God," as the Psalmist says in Psalm 19:1), and to the perfection of its nature as its immanent end (to flourish "according to [its] kind," as Genesis 1 puts it). The reality of creaturely "kinds" or "species," and the constant, predictable interactions among kinds, constitute an indispensable component of worldly structure. Our stable knowledge of kinds, that enters into our spontaneous and deliberative dealings with all creatures, is an abiding testimony to the lawful consistency and trustworthiness of the divine will. It mediates to us, on the plane of finite and conditioned being, God's infinite goodness and unbounded love.

Created goodness that meets us in the individual nature or substantial form of the creature is a law to human desiring and willing. For the creaturely form that we know is a truth to our minds, an object of our admiration, and a fulfilment of our felt need. As such, it is a constraint on our willing and acting toward it; but a lovable constraint, to which we freely conform. At the climax of Grant's criticism of modern willing, he admits the possibility of human resolution and action in accordance with nature that is neither violent nor arbitrary: "Greek heroes," he says, "were summoned to be resolute for noble doing, but their deeds were not thought of as changing the very structure of what is, but as done rather for the sake of bringing into immediacy the beauty of a trusted order."[11] Genesis 1 tells us that God, and not mankind, pronounces the goodness of the non-human creation, to which goodness mankind responds with grateful and obedient action.

But Genesis 1 also speaks of human lordship or dominion over the rest of the creation (v. 26), and of its service to mankind (v. 29), so as to suggest that non-human creatures are ordered to the perfection of the human community, as well as to the perfection of their own kind. The creation forms a teleological hierarchy in which the lower kinds serve the higher (v. 30), but in which all non-human kinds in some sense are at the disposal of their human ruler. The symbolism in Genesis 2:19-20 of Adam naming the animals at God's behest conveys the unique knowledge of the natural ends of non-human creatures imparted by God to mankind.[12] Included in the purposes of the lower orders of creation—animal, vegetable, and mineral—disclosed to Adam is their use by humans for their survival and enrichment; even though such use is frequently consumptive, involving the destruction of the lower creature's substantial form (as in the use of animals and plants for food, of vegetables and minerals for shelter and warmth). But as *naming* is not *making*, so human disposal over the non-human creation is not God's disposal; rather, it is limited by the intrinsic, divinely given goodness and meaning of other creatures, that is not exhausted by human uses for them. Adam's lordship, then, is not brutal and extravagant, but respectful and restrained: he is set in the garden to "till it and keep it" (2:15).

Even more so with its own kind is the human will restrained by the intrinsic worth and meaning of the other. The special divinely decreed sanctity of human life, proceeding from the unique vocation of love and service bestowed by God on each person, everywhere circumscribes each person's willing and acting toward his or her neighbor.[13] The good that is our neighbor demands not only to be respected, but to be nurtured and enhanced, and above all, for Christ's sake. For Jesus Christ, incarnate, crucified, and resurrected, is the measure of God's love for and estimation of his human creature, frail and sinful though that human creature be. The love of Christ is, therefore, the measure of each one's regard for their fellow: it restrains each from making into an object of use the other for whom Christ died. We are not only children of the same Father and Creator, but brothers and sisters in the blood of Christ (1 Cor. 8:11). Christ's love is the law of our willing and doing in respect of our fellow humans; and, moreover, because his kingdom of love and peace is the *telos* of all creation, his law passes into our dealings with non-human creatures, to increase our appreciation of their worth and needs.

(2) Christ does not depend on or presuppose another separate and prior disclosure of divine or human being as its qualifying condition.[14] Thus all people, even in their sinful rebellion against their maker, do not confront a remote, hidden and mysterious God. God's will does not encounter people as obscure and elusive command, terrifying in its unmediated arbitrariness. His sovereignty, that permeates the creation in its contingent dependence on his will, does not menace the human person as a naked, unlimited power of disposal. For Christ reveals the eternal form and purpose of God's creating and ruling will to be free, self-abandoning love.

It is God's free, self-giving mercy that constitutes every creature in being, according to its own law; for it is by, in, and through Christ that every creature comes into being and remains in being. Thus it is that the human person, created by, in, and through Christ in a unique way, being made in God's image, is not a sovereign will, a law unto himself. Rather, the essential form of the human will is free obedience to God's law of love, spontaneous conformity to the unquestionable good that claims him from without, but claims his innermost self. Human perpetual striving for ontological independence and self-sufficiency, expressed in our civilizational epoch as technological hubris—the drive for unlimited mastery by technique of human and non-human nature—signifies the essential disruption of the human will by sin. Sin blinds us to the deepest meaning of God's law for his creatures, both written in the order of nature and on tablets of stone: namely, the obedience unto death and exaltation to eternal life of his own Son who became flesh in the man Jesus. As Jesus alone has satisfied the law's demand, so he alone has manifested the whole content of its demand for human conduct. In sacrificing himself upon the cross for undeserving sinners, Christ has reconciled us to God, justifying us, and awakening us to life in faith. Thus, he has revealed the whole content of the law, articulated in its manifold commands, to be the demand for faith in his own saving mercy, for persevering confidence in God's everlasting faithfulness to his covenant promises, for thankful self-surrender to the Father's loving purpose. Christ, our saviour and law-giver, is himself the form of the law. His commandments, given for our guidance, reflect back on the pattern of divine and human love that he is. The form of the law, therefore, proclaimed by the Old and the New Covenants alike, little resembles the self-imposed, abstract and impersonal imperatives of the Kantian conscience, embedded in the numinosity of external, objective command.

In his concluding chapter of *Philosophy in the Mass Age*, Grant recalls us from the aspiration to unlimited freedom dictating our technological conquest of nature to the supernatural consent of the will to limit "in all its ambiguity," that "is the very negation of freedom and power, the acceptance of one's own death" (99). This is our consent to natural and historical necessity, to the apparently blind and meaningless configurations of matter and events beyond our control, amidst the resulting suffering and affliction for ourselves and our neighbours. But lest such *amor fati* turn out to be a species of pagan idolatry, we must take to heart its Christological centre, disclosed by Grant's affirmation that ". . . because this acceptance of death is in the mouth of Jesus Christ, it must be understood as an act of joy"(99).[15] As in our lordship of nature, still groaning under the wages of sin, we are summoned by the grace of Christ to conform our wills to his law of love, so in our abasement and humiliation by nature are we likewise summoned to testify to Christ's own lordship over all the powers and principalities of nature and history. The last word on the theological unity of will, love, and law belongs to Christ's assurance to St. Paul: "My grace is sufficient for you, for my power is made perfect in weakness" (2 Cor. 12:9).

Notes

1. "Philosophy, Revelation and Modernity: Crossroads in the Thought of George Grant" in Larry Schmidt, ed., *George Grant in Process*, (Toronto: Anansi, 1978), 148-56.
2. Ibid., 156.
3. Ibid.
4. E.g., Ps. 19:7-10; 119:1-176. The stance described by my term "eschatological narrowness" is most influentially exemplified by the theological writings of Jurgen Moltmann and is given a more radical, philosophical hue by Wolfhart Pannenberg in, e.g., *Theology and the Kingdom of God* (1969).

5. E.g., Rom. 3:19-20; 4:15; 5:12-14; 7:1-13; Gal. 3, 4.
6. Grant adopts Heidegger's interpretation of technology as modern man's ontology, that is, as his fundamental relation to "the whole" and to himself. Moreover, he develops his criticism of modern willing within the Heideggerian method of ontological analysis.
7. Toronto: Copp Clark, 1959, 1966.
8. CBC, Toronto, 1969, 11.
9. "In Defence of North America," *Technology and Empire: Perspectives on North America*, (Toronto: Anansi, 1969), 20-21.
10. Grant invokes Luther's theses of 1518:

> Thesis 19. He is not worthy to be called a theologian who sees the invisible things of God as understood through the things that are made (Romans 1:20).

> Thesis 20. But only he who understands the visible and further things of God through the sufferings and the Cross.

> Thesis 21. The theologian of glory says that evil is good and good evil; the theologian of the Cross says that the thing is as it is.

Luther, *Werke*, Weimar edition, vol. I, 354, quoted in *Technology and Empire*, 21, n. 2.
11. *Time As History*, 16.
12. My interpretation of Genesis 2:19-20 is indebted to Oliver O'Donovan's discussion of the interrelation between Adam's lordship over other creatures and his knowledge of them in *Resurrection and Moral Order: An Outline for Evangelical Ethics*, (Grand Rapid: Eerdmans, 1986), 81.
13. In the Old Testament the theological rationale for the unique sanctity of human life is mankind's creation in the image of God (e.g., Genesis 9:6). In the New Testament it is a person's election in Christ to be conformed to the image of God's Son (Romans 8:29).
14. The much celebrated theological disagreement between Karl Barth and Emil Brunner in the 1930s over the relationship of nature to grace concerns precisely this issue, namely, whether we may

formulate a theological anthropology (using the currently available intellectual tools) that is independent of and that qualifies our understanding of God's revelation in Jesus Christ. (See especially the articles published in English translation under the title *Natural Theology*, Peter Fraenkel, trans., London, 1946.) The issue is as timely in our present climate of conflicting and destructive political anthropologies as when it was so heatedly debated.

15. Grant is reflecting on Jesus' words to Peter after the Resurrection, to comfort him for his denial: "When thou wast young, thou girdedst thyself, and walkedst whither thou wouldest; but when thou shalt be old . . . another shall gird thee, and carry thee whither thou wouldest not" (John 21:18).

The Development of Herman Dooyeweerd's Concept of Rights

John Witte, Jr.

Among his many other achievements, Bernard Zylstra worked to disseminate to a wider audience the legal philosophy of his mentor Herman Dooyeweerd (1894-1977). He expounded Dooyeweerd's philosophy in numerous courses, lectures, and private letters. He explained them in popular pamphlets, chapters, and introductory texts. He extrapolated them in his own important writings on liberalism, marxism, and modernism. Through his efforts, and those of some of his peers and students, Dooyeweerd's legal philosophy has come to enjoy considerable currency in Western Europe, North America, and South Africa.

Zylstra's emphasis on Dooyeweerd's legal philosophy was well placed. For Dooyeweerd, despite his renown as a general philosopher and Christian apologist, was first and foremost a jurist. He studied law for five years at the Free University of Amsterdam and in 1917 completed his dissertation on the role of the cabinet in Dutch public law.[1] For three years thereafter he worked in the Dutch Department of Labour as a clerk and legislative draftsman.

From 1926 until 1965, he served as a law professor at the Free
University of Amsterdam, where he taught legal philosophy, legal
history, and legal science. He presided over the distinguished Society
of Legal Philosophy and numerous other legal symposia. He
engaged in ample and able debate with such leading jurists of his
day as Giorgio del Vecchio, Georg Jellinek, and Hans Kelsen and
filled his library with a vast array of legal tomes. Well over half of
his own 200 odd professional publications are on legal subjects.

This article, dedicated to the memory of Bernard Zylstra, focuses
on one small part of Dooyeweerd's legal legacy, his concept of
rights.[2] Dooyeweerd addressed the subject of rights several times in
his career, each time seeking to develop a comprehensive Calvinist
concept of rights. His initial efforts led him to a rather traditional
Calvinist concept of political liberties, rooted in simple theological
principles. His later efforts yielded an intricate modal concept of
legal competences and subjective rights, rooted in a complex
philosophical system. The analysis that follows will pay particular
attention to the analytical stages through which Dooyeweerd passed
to develop his concept.[3]

Dooyeweerd's Early Concept of Rights
Already early in his career, Dooyeweerd developed a method for
the formulation of a distinctively Calvinist concept of rights. "Every
concept of rights," he wrote in 1926, "must be part of a more general
legal philosophy." "Every legal philosophy must be built upon"
certain cardinal religious beliefs or "law-ideas" (*wetsideën*).[4] For a
concept of rights depends upon the views of law, authority, and the
state that are taught by legal philosophy. A legal philosophy depends
upon the views of humanness, being, and knowledge that are taught
by a religious "law-idea." Thus to develop "a distinctly Calvinist"
concept of rights, Dooyeweerd felt required (1) to identify the core
beliefs that comprise the Calvinist "law-idea"; (2) to elaborate a
philosophy of law, authority and the state on the basis of these
beliefs; and only then (3) to analyze the origin, nature, and purpose
of rights.[5]

Accordingly, in the later 1920s, Dooyeweerd isolated a number
of religious beliefs that would become the core of his "Calvinist

law-idea" and the cornerstone of his legal philosophy. Neither his emphasis upon these beliefs, nor his formulation of them strayed far from the traditional views of John Calvin, Herman Bavinck, or Abraham Kuyper. Unlike his predecessors, however, Dooyeweerd was able to derive direct and dramatic legal implications from these religious views. Although he vacillated in the formulation of his early religious views, they can be reduced to four propositions.[6]

(1) All human laws, rights, and authorities, whether past or present, are ultimately rooted in the creation of God. In creation all organic and inorganic things and all human persons and institutions were separated "after their own kind" and given their distinctive form and function.

(2) God is the absolute sovereign over all creation—both at its inception and in its unfolding. Through his Word, he called creation into being. Through his providential plan, he guides its becoming. His sovereignty is absolute and constant. No creature and no activity is ever exempt from his authority.

(3) God exercises this sovereignty through the natural laws of creation. The laws of creation command the constant will of the Creator. They provide order and constancy, not chaos and indeterminacy. Because God's sovereignty is absolute and constant, his law is comprehensive and continually obligates all creatures in all their activities. The laws of creation, therefore, assume a plurality of forms. Some govern the activity of inorganic and organic things. Others govern the multiple activities of human beings, such as their language and logic, their social and legal activities, their morality and faith. Still others govern the formation and functioning of human institutions, such as the family, church, and state.

(4) Under the laws of creation, each person and each institution has both a "legal right" to exist alongside others and a "legal duty" to discharge the unique calling or responsibility that God has prescribed for it. The laws of creation, therefore, make possible a plurality of persons and institutions, each with a measure of "autonomy" or "sovereignty" vis-à-vis all others. The autonomy or "sovereignty" of any person or institution, however, is limited by the sovereignty of co-existing persons and institutions, and to the task or function to which it is called. Moreover, this limited sovereignty

of the creature is always subservient to the absolute sovereignty of the Creator. These four religious beliefs—in the created order, the absolute sovereignty of God, the laws of creation, and the created sovereignty of institutions and persons—recur as a constant refrain in Dooyeweerd's early writings on law, politics, and society.

On the basis of these religious beliefs, Dooyeweerd, *inter alia*, developed the rudiments of his legal philosophy. Like his early religious views, his early legal philosophical views drew heavily upon traditional Calvinist learning—particularly as formulated by the late sixteenth century jurist Johannes Althusius and by Dooyeweerd's contemporary Josef Bohatec.[7] "A truly Calvinist legal philosophy . . ." he argued, "must naturally be based on a *natural law* foundation. It must seek to base both statutory law and customary law on godly legal ordinances. Without this foundation, the problems of legal authority, responsibility, right, fault, and punishment will remain choked in a net of irresolvable antinomies."[8]

Dooyeweerd distinguished two types of "godly natural law" that govern legal and political life: (1) a primary or formal natural law, which delineates the office and authority of the state; and (2) a political or material natural law, which defines and undergirds the positive laws formulated by the state. The primary natural law establishes that the state is a distinctive office created by God, that it represents and reflects God's political authority and sovereignty, and that it is called to appropriate and apply God's law for the governance and the good of the community. The political natural law establishes that the positive law "is in essence not a human creation, but an ordinance of God" and thus that the state must predicate its laws on "explicit natural law principles."[9] Such principles, Dooyeweerd believed, were both "absolute" and "relative" (*hypothetisch*) in character. On the one hand, it was "absolutely indispensable" that the state seek to protect the person and property of its citizens, to punish crime and other misconduct, and to protect and respect social institutions like families, churches, unions, and others. On the other hand, the particular application of these absolute principles had to be tailored to the "individual circumstances" and to the "level of social differentiation" of the community.[10]

Dooyeweerd's early concept of rights grew out of these basic philosophical and religious views. Rights, for him, were simultaneously *liberties* of political subjects and *limitations* on political authorities.

The liberties of political subjects stemmed from their created "sovereignty." Each person and institution, Dooyeweerd believed, was created by God with a unique character and calling. Each was inherently "sovereign in its own sphere" and "competent" to retain its character and pursue its calling. This created "sovereignty" did not depend upon the state. It did not dissolve when the person or institution became subject to the state's authority. All political subjects enjoy "a fundamental social freedom" (*principieele maatschappelijke vrijheid*), regardless of the form of political authority that governs them.[11] On the basis of these assumptions, Dooyeweerd condemned vehemently undue state intrusions on the person or property of citizens or on the formation and functioning of families, churches, universities, labor unions, and other social institutions. He likewise endorsed traditional freedoms of contract, property, and association and traditional liberties of conscience, speech, and assembly.[12] Such rights, Dooyeweerd believed, were not only consistent with Calvinist beliefs, but in fact had been catalyzed by them. "Calvinism has, in its historical development, stood in the breach for human freedom," he wrote. "The declaration of human and civil rights in the American constitutions, though influenced in part by the ideas of the French Revolution, were grounded primarily in Puritan Calvinism."[13]

The liberties of political subjects were also rooted in the limitations on political authorities. The doctrine of political liberty, Dooyeweerd insisted, cannot be viewed simply as "a doctrine of the freedom of personal arbitrariness," (*willekeur*).[14] The doctrine of "*sphere* sovereignty cannot be seen as [a doctrine of] *personal* sovereignty of the individual or institution against the state."[15] These doctrines speak, instead, to "the inherent limitation on the competence of the state . . . prescribed by God in his natural law."[16] Institutions and persons enjoy political liberty because God has limited the sphere, the authority, the jurisdiction of the political authorities. "The state can thus . . . never possess the competence

to intervene in the internal structure [and government] . . . of
non-state associations [or to dictate] the legal substance of private
contracts, . . . trusts, or testaments."[17] Such matters lay beyond the
province of the state.

Dooyeweerd's Mature Concept of Rights

The limitations of Dooyeweerd's early concept of rights soon became readily apparent. His early formulation provided no criteria to
define concretely the class of subjects which could lay claim to
liberties. It offered no clear delineation of the boundaries between
and among the spheres of states, social institutions, and persons. It
offered only vague principles to govern the promulgation and enforcement of positive law.[18] It offered no account at all of a subject's
positive rights or entitlements to things, services, or other goods.
Without a greater degree of specificity and elaboration,
Dooyeweerd's natural law concepts could easily be adduced to
rationalize any number of legal and political forms. They could easily
be reduced, as he once put it, to "the vague political slogans of a . .
. Christian political party."[19] In the mid-1930s, therefore,
Dooyeweerd abandoned many of his early formulations. He maintained his basic religious views of the sovereignty of the Creator and
the sphere sovereignty of creatures. He also insisted that God ruled
his creation by law and that such a law assumed a variety of forms
to govern the multiple functions of creatures. Dooyeweerd disavowed, however, his earlier views of a formal and material natural
law and criticized sharply both Christian and secular theories of
natural law and natural rights.[20] He dropped his earlier references
to "fundamental social freedoms" and grew increasingly sceptical of
the historical connections between Calvinism and constitutional
rights and liberties.[21] He dissociated his views sharply from the many
Rechtsstaat and *Machtstaat* political theories that had gained
prominence on the Continent.[22]

Vestiges of his earlier concept of rights occasionally appeared in
his writings thereafter—particularly in his popular articles written in
the shadow of World War II. Appalled by Nazi and fascist travesties
against human rights, for example, he offered an unusually benign
assessment of liberal theories of rights. "The eighteenth-century

Enlightenment and the French Revolution were indeed renewing and progressive forces in historical development," he wrote. For they gave rise to "the idea of human rights and the idea that the state is a republican institution serving the common good. . . . Freedom and equality in a civil-legal sense were clearly not just hollow slogans of the French Revolution. . . . Under Nazism we have experienced what it means when civil-legal freedom and equality are abolished and man's legal status depends upon the community of 'blood and soil'."[23] Appalled by the rapid rise of state absolutism and the levelling of social structures during the war, he argued that "the differentiated life spheres of disclosed culture possess an *original right* [to function on] their own," free from state intrusion or interference.[24]

These sentiments, however, were more aberrational than exemplary. In much of his other writing—both before and after World War II—Dooyeweerd strove to develop a more philosophically sophisticated and politically viable concept of rights.

Philosophical Preconditions

Dooyeweerd's mature concept of rights emerged out of a more refined method of "legal concept formation" (*rechtsbegripsvorming*).[25] As before, Dooyeweerd insisted that any legal concept, including a concept of rights, must proceed out a broader legal philosophy. But such a legal philosophy, he now argued, must be drawn not out of simple religious beliefs, but out of a systematic philosophy of the created order. "Fundamental legal concepts can be fruitfully formed only if they are understood in their proper relationship to . . . the fundamental concepts of other aspects of reality."[26]

Accordingly, Dooyeweerd embarked on a lengthy effort to develop a systematic philosophical account of the created order. In his seminal work *The Philosophy of the Law-Idea* (1935-1936), and a variety of shorter works published thereafter, he explored at great length the various aspects and laws of the created order and the unique nature and function of individuals and institutions. Much of this general philosophy cannot concern us, save those doctrines and terms that shaped his general philosophy of law and specific concept of rights.[27]

The created order, Dooyeweerd believed, reveals a number of distinct aspects or modes of being. He distinguished fifteen such aspects, each with a core meaning, which he arranged hierarchically—the numerical (discrete quantity), spatial (extension), kinematic (motion), physical (energy), biotic (organic life), psychic (sensitive or feeling), logical (analytical distinction), historical (cultural formation), lingual (symbolic meaning), social (associational), economic (frugality), aesthetic (harmony or balance), juridical (just recompensing or retribution), moral (love), and pistical (faith) aspects, respectively.

Each modal aspect is distinct and irreducible. Dooyeweerd now called this the sphere sovereignty of the modality—a phrase which he had earlier used to describe the created independence of individuals and social institutions. With this phrase, he expressed the inviolable and irreducible status of these various modes of being which creatures display. A living thing, for example, cannot be understood simply as matter in motion—that is, the biotic aspect cannot be reduced to the physical or spatial aspects. The justice of a person's act cannot be understood simply as a product of economic, logical, or mathematical calculus—that is, the juridical aspect cannot be reduced to the economic, logical, or numerical aspects.

Each modal aspect, though distinct, builds on those below it. Spatial extension, for example, cannot be understood without a concept of numerical multiplicity. Beings that are alive do move in space and can be counted—that is, they have physical, spatial, and numerical functions. For a thing to be symbolic presupposes that its symbolic character has previously been formed in an analytically discernible manner which can be perceived by living beings—that is, it has underlying historical, analytical, psychic, and biotic aspects, which, in turn, presuppose the lower aspects. This relationship Dooyeweerd called the necessary "analogical relationship" among the modalities.

Each modal aspect, Dooyeweerd argued, has both a normative dimension (a "law side") and a functional dimension (a "subject side"). The modes of being remain distinctive and ordered because they are governed by a group of specific laws that God has created and commanded for that mode of being. Thus there is a hierarchy of modal laws that are part of, and help to define, each of these modes of being—laws of counting and arithmetic, geometry, dynamics, energy, life, feeling, logic, history, language, society, economics, aesthetics, juridical matters, ethics, and theology. These laws are not derived from special scientific inquiry. They are discovered by scientists in each of these fields and given positive form. They are "ontic aprioris" which provide order and constancy in the creation and make these distinctive modes of being and disciplines of study possible.

These modal laws, Dooyeweerd believed, govern the function of all creatures. All inanimate things, living beings, cultural things and associations are *subject to* all modal laws; this Dooyeweerd called the law-subject relation. But not all creatures function *as subjects* in all modal aspects; this Dooyeweerd called the subject-object relation. Creatures can thus be classified, in part, by the laws which govern them as subjects. The subjective functions of inorganic things are governed by the first four modal laws of number, space, motion and energy; plants, by the first five laws through the biotic modality; animals, by the six laws through the psychic modality. The subjective functioning of human beings themselves is governed by all fifteen modal laws, but the subjective functioning of social institutions is governed by only a select number of higher modal laws.

The highest modal aspect in which each creature functions as a subject renders it distinctive. It gives each creature its distinguishing character or purpose. Dooyeweerd frequently described this highest modal law as the qualifying modality or the internal law of the creature. Thus physical laws, for example, dictate that physical things move in space. Biotic laws mandate that the constituent parts of a plant not only move in space but that this motion be in service of and directed by a living process. The psychic laws prescribe that the animal feel or sense things or events around it and react in a way that preserves life. The juridical laws, which qualify the state, command that the institutions of government implement laws and policies of justice, peace, and harmonious balance. The moral laws obligate the family and marriage communities to serve the ends not only of justice but also of love, service, and cooperation.

Although organic things, plants, and animals function as subjects only in certain lower spheres, they function as objects in all modal spheres. Thus a piece of marble can be carved into a handsome statue and sold on the market—that is, it can become he object of a person's historical, economic, and aesthetic subjective functioning. Or the same piece of marble inscribed with the words of the Decalogue can be hung on the walls of a courtroom or church as a binding law—that is, it can become the object of a social institution's symbolic, juridical and pistical functioning.

In his famous *Encyclopedia of Legal Science* (1946) and several other books and articles, Dooyeweerd tailored these basic doctrines of general philosophy into specific concepts of legal philosophy and legal science. Legal philosophy and legal science, Dooyeweerd argued, are focused primarily on the juridical modality. Legal philosophy (*rechtsphilosophie*) treats the relationship between the juridical modality and all other modalities and the typical modal features of the juridical modality. Legal science (*rechtswetenschap*) treats the specific doctrines and concepts that are endemic to law, including the concept of rights.

Dooyeweerd's legal philosophical writings offer a profound analysis of the nature of positive law and its relationships with other modal aspects and disciplines. He described at length the distinctive norms of justice, retribution and equity that comprise the juridical modality. He defined in detail the nature of juridical functionality. He also used the analogical relationship between the juridical modality and other modalities to delineate and describe an array of interlocking legal concepts and subjects—the multiplicity and conflicts of laws (based on the numerical analogy); the jurisdiction or sphere of competence of the state (based on the spatial analogy); obligation and causation (based on the kinematic analogy); legal life or legal organs (based on the biotic analogy); legal will and legislative intent (based on the psychic analogy); legal analysis (based on the logical analogy); legal power (based on the historical analogy); legal meaning and interpretation (based on the lingual analogy); legal intercourse or association (based on the social analogy); legal economy or preservation (based on the economic analogy); and legal harmony or equity (based on the aesthetic analogy).

Mature Formulations.

It was in this broader philosophical context that Dooyeweerd elaborated his mature concept of rights. His concept drew upon more his now more refined definitions of (1) legal subjects; (2) legal competences; and (3) subjective rights.

Dooyeweerd first refined his definition of "legal subjects" (*rechtssubjecten*) or "legal persons" (*rechtspersonen*). Consistent with his earlier views, he insisted that legal subjects be viewed as "creatures of God . . . not creations of the state" and that they include both persons and institutions.[28] But he now limited the class of legal subjects to those creatures that "are competent (*hoedanig, bekwaam*) to operate on the subject side of the juridical sphere" in accordance with the norms that govern juridical functionality.[29] Dooyeweerd included in this class "legal individuals" (*rechtsindividueelen*) who have reached the age of majority, are lucid, able, and unencumbered by criminal or civil sanctions or restrictions.[30] He also included various organized social institutions and natural institutions (*rechtsverbanden*) "that both function as subjective juridical unities in their internal legal spheres and . . . are recognized as organized legal subjects in their external commercial and social interactions."[31] Such institutions can be qualified by the juridical modality itself (like municipalities, cabinets, or agencies) or by other modalities (like corporations, clubs, or churches), provided they are sufficiently well-organized and independent entities.[32]

Such legal subjects, Dooyeweerd argued, are vested with both legal competences or capacities (*rechtsbevoegdheden*) and legal rights or subjective rights (*subjectieve rechten*). These two categories originate respectively in the law side and the subject side of the juridical modality. They are thus ontically distinct and cannot be conflated in practice.[33]

A *legal competence* is the capacity of a legal subject to assume a legal status and to perform the appropriate legal actions that accompany that status.[34] Individual legal subjects, he argued, have the capacity to assume the legal status of a parent, priest, trustee,

testator, plaintiff, property owner, and so forth and to perform a
variety of acts in compliance with the rules that govern that status.
Groups of legal subjects have the capacity to organize themselves
into churches, corporations, clubs, families, labor unions, or universities, and to perform a series of acts in compliance with the rules
that govern that institution.[35]

The rules that govern legal subjects in each legal status
Dooyeweerd called "private laws" or occasionally "non-state civil
laws"—though he does not always use these terms consistently.
Private laws are produced both by the state and by the legal subjects
that are bound by them. On the one hand, Dooyeweerd insisted that
"the *original* competence" to determine the *form* of private law
"cannot belong to any other organized community but the state,"
which assures that such private laws respect the "juridical norms" of
"inter-individual justice, legal security, and equity."[36] The state thus
defines basic rules for the formation of contracts, the disposition of
property, the litigation of a tort, or the formation of a corporation,
club, or church. On the other hand, Dooyeweerd insisted that the
competence to determine the *content* of these private laws lies not
with the state but with the legal subjects that will be bound by them.
"The internal spheres of these kinds of private law, qualified by the
non-juridical leading function of the societal relationships to which
they belong, remain exempt from the competence of the State."[37]
Thus the individual legal subject determines for himself the content
of his contract, the character of his property, or the gravamen of his
tort suit. The corporation, club, or church determines for itself the
rules for selecting members, electing officials, or disciplining the
wayward. So long as the legal subjects abide by the basic norms of
the judicial modality which are positivized by the state, they "have
power to form their own private law . . . and have it obeyed."[38]

The state must respect and protect the legal competence of legal
subjects. It cannot generally obstruct the individual legal subject
from entering a valid contract, litigating a valid claim, or devising
legally held property. It cannot prevent the church from holding
unobtrusive religious assemblies, the family from adopting rules of
discipline, or the business from specializing in certain types of legal
commodities. Such interference in the internal competence of legal

subjects generally lies beyond the state's competence (except, perhaps, in times of war or emergency). The state must also protect legal
subjects against similar interference with the exercise of their competence by third parties and provide appropriate legal or equitable
remedies in the event of such interference.[39]

The state can intervene, however, when a legal subject exceeds
its sphere of competence or obstructs the competence of another
legal subject. Thus the state can invalidate a contract induced by
fraud or duress, forestall a law suit designed only to harass or
bankrupt a defendant, or invalidate a testament designed to disin-
herit illegally a family member. The state can prevent the church
from performing obtrusive or dangerous ceremonies, the family
from abusing or neglecting the child, or the corporation from trading
in illegal or top secret commodities. For, in each case, the legal
subject is operating in excess of its own competence, in derogation
of another's competence, and in violation of basic social norms.[40]

Dooyeweerd's concept of legal competences thus encapsulated
and elaborated his earlier concept of political liberties and limitations. As before, he coupled the liberties of political subjects with
the limitations on political officials. Now, however, he offered a
more refined principle for determining which individual and institutional subjects could claim such liberties. He also tied their claims
to political liberties to their created callings and responsibilities.
Simultaneously, he offered a more refined principle for determining
the boundaries of state responsibility and for differentiating public
law and private law.

While legal competences involve the capacity of the subject to
engage in certain actions, *legal rights* involve the claim of the subject
to certain objects.[41] Legal rights, Dooyeweerd argued, are comprised of both legal entitlements and legal interests. On the one
hand, the right vests in the legal subject (1) an entitlement to have
the object of its right in hand or at his disposal (*beschikkingsbevoegdheid*); and (2) entitlement to enjoy and benefit from the
use or control of this object (*genotsbevoegdheid*).[42] Legal entitlements thus define the relation between the legal subject and the legal
object.[43] On the other hand, the right vests in the legal subject "a
retributive interest" to prevent third parties from interfering in the

use and enjoyment of the object of its right.[44] Legal interests thus define the relationship between the legal subject and third parties.

The exercise of a legal right is neither automatic nor autonomous. First, the legal subject can exercise its rights only if it is legally competent to do so.[45] Second, even if competent, the legal subject can exercise her rights only if the legal object is at her disposal. Third, the legal subject must always exercise that right "within the context of both a legal community and inter-individual relations."[46] The legal subject can thus, in the exercise of his right, neither violate the general norms of "inter-individual justice, legal security, and equity," by which the state governs the legal community, nor interfere in the competences or rights of other legal subjects.[47]

The content of a legal right, Dooyeweerd insisted, must be determined by the nature of the legal object. Dooyeweerd was not content with the traditional distillation of rights into "life, liberty and property" or the traditional divisions of rights into "natural and civil" or "real and personal." Such formulations, he believed, were inherently focused on the nature of the legal subject and provided no "strict scientific boundary on the [subject's] right."[48] By shifting the focus from the nature of the legal subject to the nature of the legal object, he was able to find such a "scientific boundary."

To define the nature of the legal object, Dooyeweerd embarked on a rather intricate and involved modal analysis. Two modal criteria appear to be most critical to his definition and delimitation of the objects of legal rights.[49]

First, an object of rights must be qualified by the juridical modality or one below it. Numerous objects meet this criterion and can (if they also satisfy the second modal criterion) be included in the class of legal objects. The class of legal objects can include animals, plants, and concrete physical things, for they are qualified by the psychic, biotic, and physical modalities respectively.[50] It can include many forms of "performance owed by other persons" (*dienstverrichting*), based on debt, custom, or contract, for these obligations are qualified by the juridical, social, and economic modalities respectively.[51] It can also include rights themselves, as in the case of a mortgage, secured transaction, or claim to subrogation, for they are qualified by the juridical modality.[52] These classes of legal objects correspond rather closely to the classes of real rights, personal rights, and incorporeal rights that are adopted by many rights theorists still today.

Dooyeweerd's first modal criterion, however, excludes other objects in which many contemporary theorists would readily vest a right. It excludes a right to performance of moral and religious obligations, for these objects are qualified by the moral and pistical modalities, which stand above the juridical sphere. Thus a legal subject cannot insist on performance of another's promise made in good faith or without the usual formalities of contract formation. A spouse has no right to the other spouse's performance of connubial duties. A parent has no right to a child's obedience, nor the child to a parent's care. A parishioner cannot insist on receiving from the church the administration of a sacrament, the consecration of a wedding, or the rite of ordination to the clergy.[53] A cleric has no right to the parishioner's faithful payment of tithes or attendance at services. Such morally and pistically qualified claims cannot be the objects of subjective rights.

Dooyeweerd's first modal criterion also excludes a variety of personality and civil rights. For every person perforce functions as a subject in all modal spheres and thus cannot serve as the legal object of a subjective right. The parent has no right to her child. One spouse has no right to the other. The master has no right to his servant. The creditor has no right to the debtor. In each case, the claimant may have competence to perform legal actions with respect to the other person and may also demand that they perform certain obligations (so long as they are not qualified by morality or by faith). But the claimant has no right to the other person per se. Likewise, the individual has no rights to her own life, limb, or liberty, or her own reputation, dignity, or honor. All these are qualities inherent in the person, not objects to which rights can be attached.[54] They, too, are matters of competence, not of right.

Earlier in his career, Dooyeweerd also used this first criterion to exclude so-called immaterial property rights, such as copyright, patent, and trademark. Each of these objects, he argued, is neither a material thing nor a legal duty owed by a third party. It is, in effect, the "brain child" (*geestesprodukt*) of the person, an extension or manifestation of an individual's personality. It cannot, therefore, become the object of a right.[55] Near the end of his career, Dooyeweerd disavowed this position and argued that copyrights, patents, and trademarks be considered a special class of things to which real rights can attach.[56]

Second, the objects of legal rights must not only be qualified by the juridical modality or one below it. They must also function as an object of the modalities below the juridical. Some of these analogical relationships, such as those with the logical, psychic, and aesthetic modalities, are innocuous enough. That a thing has been subject to psychic feeling, logical analysis, or aesthetic harmonization does little to delimit the class of legal objects. The analogies with the cultural, economic, and lingual modalities, however, have more impact.

Based on the cultural analogy, Dooyeweerd restricted the class of legal objects to those things that have been "the object of legal formative power (*juridische beschikkingsmacht*), exercised either by the legal subject itself or by some other legal subject."[57] "Things which in the present state of human culture are not controllable by cultural activity cannot function as legal objects of human rights."[58] Thus there can be no right to natural things like wild animals, open seas, undiscovered lands, or hidden minerals (though there may be a right to an exclusive license to locate or pursue them). There can be no right to natural conditions like rain, sunshine, clean air, or open views (though, perhaps, one can have an easement or prescriptive interest in them enforceable against third parties).[59] There can be no right to natural processes like "breathing or sleeping, which are altogether beyond human cultural formation."[60] Legal objectification of a thing requires prior cultural formation.

Legal objectification, Dooyeweerd believed, also requires prior economic valuation. Based on the economic analogy, he further restricted the class of legal objects to "relatively scarce goods, serviceable to human needs, whose value can be objectified by law." "Nothing can be the object of a subjective right," he wrote, "that is not now, no longer, or not yet subject to economic valuation."[61] In later years, Dooyeweerd softened this requirement somewhat. The value of the thing, he argued, need not necessarily be financial, so long as it is capable of "legal objectification."[62] Yet Dooyeweerd offered no method by which such "objectification" should proceed. He did not appreciate sufficiently that any judicial enforcement of a right to such an object would invariably result in financial calculation by the court. He also did not relax his requirements that legal objects be "relatively scarce" or "serviceable to human needs."

Finally, based on the symbolic analogy, Dooyeweerd restricted the class of legal objects further to those that "have a legal significance that can be defined through juridical interpretation."[63] This restriction effectively eliminated all claims to "inherent" or "natural" rights that have not yet been positivized by state law. "There is no subjective right that is not regulated by legal norms," Dooyeweerd wrote. "The imperative (*gebiedende*) and prohibitive (*verbiedende*) norms" promulgated by the state "define the . . . positive forms [and] boundaries of rights. . . . Natural subjective rights, that fall outside the positive legal order have no actual *juridical* content."[64]

Critical Reflections

Although forged in the context of his polemics with continental jurists and in the contours of a civil law system, Dooyeweerd's concept of rights offers many valuable insights even for a contemporary common lawyer like myself.

Dooyeweerd's concept of *legal competences* (as well as his early concept of political liberties) illumines our understanding of "rights" at public or constitutional law. Dooyeweerd's theory provides clear criteria to determine the class of subjects who have standing to claim competences or liberties. It recognizes that competences or liberties belong to both persons and institutions alike. It argues that each person's and institution's exercise of this competence or liberty cannot be defined simply by political precept or personal predilection but by created callings and mandates. It recognizes that liberties of political subjects and limitations on political authorities are inextricably tied.

Dooyeweerd's concept of *subjective rights* provides important insights for our understanding of "rights" at private or common law.

Perhaps his most brilliant insight was that no legal right can exist without a legal object, and that the nature and scope of rights should be determined by the nature of the legal object. On that basis, he was able to distinguish a variety of different rights of property, contract, tort, and inheritance. He was also able to provide principled arguments against "rights" that are rooted in moral or religious claims or in the "personality" of the legal subject or another party.

Some of Dooyeweerd's formulations can be easily extended to address current rights issues. Dooyeweerd, for example, could consistently endorse current theories of welfare rights and benefit rights to public education, social security, unemployment compensation, police protection, and the like. The distribution of such benefits lies within the competence, if not the mandate, of the state. The objects of such rights are tangible social goods, that have been subject to cultural formation, economic valuation, and legal positivization.[65] Dooyeweerd could also consistently embrace the efforts of those who are seeking to protect animals, plants, and other natural resources from human exploitation and abuse, although he would reject the terms these advocates use. His argument would not be based on the rights of these natural resources, for they are incapable of the subjective juridical functions which rights presuppose. His argument would be based on the competence of the state. Just as the state is called and competent to respect and protect *human* creatures and their activities regardless of their qualification, so it is called and competent to respect and protect *natural* creatures and their activities, regardless of their qualification.

Despite its many virtues, Dooyeweerd's mature concept of rights is not free from difficulty. This is not the place to recite a litany of criticisms, but a few points merit mention.[66]

First, although Dooyeweerd purported to provide a comprehensive Christian concept of rights, there are several gaps in his treatment. His analysis of rights is decidedly "Western," even "European" in orientation. He offered few reflections on the theory and law of rights in "primitive," southern, and eastern cultures, and drew most of his legal examples from Roman-Dutch, and occasionally Anglo-American, law. Despite his desire to develop a comprehensive Christian concept of rights, a skeptic could see in his formulations more of an apologia for the status quo than Dooyeweerd recognized. Moreover, in his mature formulations Dooyeweerd omitted from analysis several classes of rights (or competences), which were firmly in place in Western law when he wrote and which he had enthusiastically embraced in his early concept of rights. For example, he touched only lightly in his discussion of competences on the subject of criminal rights, such as the rights to be free from illegal searches and seizures, to have a fair trial, to face one's witnesses, to defend oneself, and to be free from cruel and unusual punishment. He made only passing references, in later editions of the *Encyclopedia of Legal Sciences,* to civil procedural rights to have standing, to sue, to cross-examine witnesses, to appeal. He took virtually no account at all of the large cadre of constitutional and political rights and liberties that emerged in Europe and North America after World War II. Whether these "rights" are classified as subjective rights or legal competences, they need to be analyzed.

Second, Dooyeweerd offers little direction to resolve conflicts between the rights and competences of different legal subjects. He describes at length the various rights and competences which both persons and institutions can claim. He also describes the competence and power of the state to intervene when a person or institution exceeds its sphere of competence or claim of right. Yet the complex disputes that his broad system raise require more specific principles of decision than he offers. Dooyeweerd describes well enough the resolution of simple disputes between the rights of two persons. He also touches lightly on disputes between the competence of one person and the rights of another. But he largely ignores the legal resolution of disputes between the competences of two persons or two institutions, between the competence of a person and the rights of its individual members, and between the competence of the person and the rights of an institution. Failure to provide such principles has been the bane of many modern theories of institutional rights.

Third, Dooyeweerd's insistence that to be legitimate all rights must be positivized by state law vests too much confidence in the state. Dooyeweerd was understandably averse to natural rights theories that placed the source of rights beyond state law. He had, after all, dismissed his own early natural law concepts because of their indeterminacy. Yet leaving the definition, or positivization, of rights to the state alone is both indeterminate and dangerous.[67] What happens if the state breaches its created mandate and becomes totalitarian and repressive? What happens if an individual or group is prejudicially excluded from certain rights and privileges? Paradoxically, Dooyeweerd's aversion to natural rights theories drove him dangerously close to the theories of legal positivism and political absolutism that he so sharply criticized throughout his career.

Finally, to my mind, Dooyeweerd circumscribed the class of subjective rights far too narrowly by insisting that they be restricted to (1) relatively scarce goods, (2) serviceable to human needs, and (3) subject to economic valuation and administration. If taken literally this requirement would effectively preclude rights to anything that exists in abundance, is idle, or has no present market value. Yet there are many objects in modern culture, from cows to cars, that are not at all "relatively scarce," but should, nonetheless, be subject to claims of right. There are innumerable objects, like luxuries and playthings, that serve no obvious "human needs," but should clearly be included among objects of rights. There are innumerable objects and opportunities that have no inherent economic value (or legal objectification), but cannot be so readily precluded. Surely, Dooyeweerd did not mean to preclude rights to objects that have only sentimental value (like a worn family album), heuristic value (like an unpublished manuscript), aesthetic value (like a well-manicured lawn), or potential economic value (like a product in progress). Surely, he did not mean to preclude rights to opportunities to vote, to travel, to work, and the host of other civil and political rights currently in vogue. This part of Dooyeweerd's modal analysis of subjective rights requires considerable amendment and emendation.

Despite its difficulties, Dooyeweerd's mature concept of rights offers a formidable challenge to both adherents and antagonists. Adherents are challenged to refine Dooyeweerd's formulations still further and apply them afresh to the myriad rights controversies currently besetting legal academies and courts. Antagonists are challenged to offer alternative concepts of rights that partake of the same methodological rigor and intellectual acuity as Dooyeweerd's formulations.

Notes

This essay is based in part on remarks made at the 50th Anniversary Symposium on Herman Dooyeweerd, hosted by the Institute for Christian Studies, Toronto in June, 1985. In developing these remarks, I have drawn in part on my Introduction to H. Dooyeweerd, *A Christian Theory of Social Institutions*, M. Verbrugge, trans., J. Witte, Jr., ed. (La Jolla, CA: The Herman Dooyeweerd Foundation, 1986), 7-30. I wish to thank Frank S. Alexander and Johan van der Vyver for their comments on earlier drafts of this essay.

1. H. Dooyeweerd, *De ministerraad in het Nederlandsche staatsrecht*, (Amsterdam: Van Soest, 1917).
2. Bernard Zylstra also wrote on the subject of rights. See B. Zylstra, "Using the Constitution to Defend Religious Rights," in L. Buzzard, ed., *Freedom and Faith: The Impact of Law on Religious Liberty*, (Westchester, IL: Crossway Books, 1982), 93; also "The Bible, Justice, and the State," in J. Skillen, ed., *Confessing Christ and Doing Politics*, (Washington, D.C.: Association for Public Justice, 1982), 39.
3. For other treatments of Dooyeweerd's concept of rights, see J. van der Vyver, "The Doctrine of Private-Law Rights," in S. Strauss, ed., *Huldigingsbundel vir W A Joubert*, (Durban: Butterworths, 1988), 201, 208-14, 224-27; P. Marshall, "Dooyeweerd's Empirical Theory of Rights," in C. T. McIntire, ed., *The Legacy of Herman Dooyeweerd*, (Lanham, MD: University Press of America, 1985), 119; H. van Eikema Hommes, *De samengestelde grondbegrippen der rechtswetenschap*, (Zwolle: W. E. J. Tjeenk Willink, 1976), 115-276.
4. H. Dooyeweerd, "Lectures Notes on Law and Politics—December, 1926," (unpublished; in the personal library of H. Evan Runner), 17-18.

5. Ibid. See also H. Dooyeweerd, *De beteekenis der wetsidee voor rechtswetenschap en rechtsphilosophie*, (Amsterdam: J. H. Kok, 1926), 63; id., *De structuur der rechtsbeginselen en de methode der rechtswetenschap in het licht der wetsidee*, (Amsterdam: N. V. Dagblad en Drukkerei De Standaard, 1930), 223.

6. See generally, H. Dooyeweerd, *Calvinisme en Natuurrecht*, (Amersfoort: Referaat voor de Calvinistische Vereeniging, 1925), 11-32; id., "Twee-rlei Kritiek om de principeele zijde van het vraagstuk der medezeggenschap," 2 *Anti-revolutionaire staatkunde* 1 (1926) [hereinafter *A. R. S.*]; id., "Het oude probleem der christelijke staatkunde," 2 *A. R. S.* 63 (1926); id., *De beteekenis*, 60f. (cited in note 5 above); id., "De oorsprong van de antithese tusschen christelijke en humanistische wetsidee en hare beteekenis voor de staatkunde," 3 *A. R. S.* 73 (1927). This summary is adapted from my introduction to Dooyeweerd, *Social Institutions*, 15-17 (cited in the introductory note above).

7. For the following discussion, see generally Dooyeweerd, *Calvinisme en natuurrecht*, 15-32 (cited in note 6 above); id., *De beteekenis*, 70-72, 110-11 (cited in note 5 above); id., "Calvinisme contra neo-Kantianisme. Naar aanleiding van de vraag betreffende de kenbaarheid der goddelijke rechtsorde," 20 *Tijdschrift voor Wijsbegeerte* 29 (1926); id., *De universaliteit der rechtsgedachte en de idee van den kultuurstaat*, (Amsterdam: Almanak van het Studentencorps aan de Vrije Universiteit, 1927); id., "De bronnen van het stellig recht in het licht der wetsidee. Een bijdrage tot opklaring van het probleem in het inzake de verhouding van rechtsbeginsel en positief recht," 4 *A. R. S.* 1, 3-15 (1930) and 8 *A. R. S.* 57-94 (1934). See also the excellent discussion in J. Skillen, "The Development of Calvinistic Political Theory in the Netherlands, With Special Reference to the Thought of Herman Dooyeweerd", (Ph. D. Diss., Duke University, 1974), 307f.

Unlike some commentators, I see in Dooyeweerd's early writings more of the residue of a traditional Calvinist natural law theory than the rudiments of his later, philosophically sophisticated view. For contrary interpretations see, e.g., O. Albers, *Het natuurrecht volgens de Wijsbegeerte der Wetsidee: een kritische beschouwing*, (Nijmegen:

Janssen, 1955), 3f.; H. van Eikema Hommes, *Een nieuwe herleving van het natuurrecht,* (Zwolle: W. E. J. Tjeenk, 1961), 238f.

8. H. Dooyeweerd, *De beteekenis,* 70 (emphasis added) (cited in note 5 above).

9. Id., *Calvinisme en natuurrecht,* 16, 29 (cited in note 6 above).

10. Ibid., 27-29.

11. H. Dooyeweerd, *De crisis der humanistische staatsleer in het licht eener calvinistische kosmologie en kennistheorie,* (Amsterdam: Ten Have, 1931), 182.

12. See H. Dooyeweerd, "Het vraagstuk der gemeentemonopolies in het belang der volksgenzondheid, beschouwd in het licht van de nieuwe opvattingen inzake de bedrijfsvrijheid," *Rechtsgeleerd Magazijn Themis* 126 (1920); id., "De band met het beginsel. Inzake het vraagstuk der medezeggenschap," 7 *Nederland en Oranje VIII,* 2, 33 (1926); id., "Tweeërlei kritiek," 15-17 (cited in note 6 above); id., *De crisis,* 136f., 170f., 181f. (Cited in note 11 above); id., "Het Amsterdamsche rapport inzake de medezeggenschap van het personeel in de gemeentebedrijven en -diensten," 8 *A. R. S.* 71, 121, 157 (1932).

13. Dooyeweerd, *Calvinisme en natuurrecht,* 31 (cited in note 6 above).

14. Ibid., 29.

15. Ibid. (Emphasis added).

16. Ibid.

17. Dooyeweerd, *De Crisis,* 181 (cited in note 11 above).

18. Dooyeweerd was painfully aware of this defect. Already in 1925, he wrote: "The burning question is now, where does the state find God's normative principles, which form the political natural law?" Dooyeweerd, *De beteekenis,* 27-28 (cited in note 5 above). His answer—they must be found in scripture, conscience, and history—was not too satisfying. Ibid.

19. The phrase is from H. Dooyeweerd, *In de strijd om het souvereiniteitsbegrip in de moderne rechts- en staatleer,* (Amsterdam: H. J. Paris, 1950), 51, where Dooyeweerd comments on such use of his early teachings.

20. See, e.g., Dooyeweerd, "De bronnen," 8 *A. R. S.* 57 (cited in note 7 above); id., "De wetsbeschouwing in Brunner's boek 'Das Gebot

und die Ordnungen'," 9 *A. R. S.* 334 (1935); id., "Das natüerlichen
Rechtsbewusztsein und die Erkenntnis des geoffenbarten
göettlichen Gesetzes," 13 *A. R. S.* 157 (1939). See also his later
sentiments in id. "Een nieuwe studie over het Aristotelische begrip
der gerechtigheid," *Rechtsgeleerd Magazijn Themis* (1958), 3, 60f.
21. See H. Dooyeweerd, *De christelijke staatsidee,* (Rotterdam:
Libertas, 1936), translated as *The Christian Idea of the State,* J. Kraay,
trans., (Nutley, N.J.: Craig Press, 1978), 26-27.
22. See, e.g., id., 44f. and H. Dooyeweerd, *De Wijsbegeerte der
Wetsidee,* (Amsterdam: H. J. Paris, 1935-1936), 3 vols. translated as
A New Critique of Theoretical Thought, D. Freeman and W. Young,
trans., (Philadelphia: The Presbyterian and Reformed Publishing
Company, 1969), 4 vols., 3:425f [hereinafter referred to as *NC*].
Dooyeweerd's criticisms are elaborated in the work of a student, J.
Mekkes, *Proeve eener critische beschouwing van de ontwikkeling der
humanistische Rechtsstaatstheorieen,* (Utrecht-Rotterdam: Libertas
Drukkerijen, 1940).
23. H. Dooyeweerd, *Roots of Western Culture: Pagan, Secular, and
Christian Options,* J. Kraay, trans., M. Vander Vennen and B.
Zylstra, eds., (Toronto: Wedge Publishing Foundation, 1979), 185-
86. See also id., pp. 156-70. This volume contains a translation of a
series of articles that first appeared in the weekly *Nieuw Nederland*
in 1945-1948 and that were published in edited form as H.
Dooyeweerd, *Vernieuwing en bezinning om het reformatorsich
grondmotief,* (Zutphen: J. B. van den Brink, 1959).
24. Id., at 89 (emphasis in original). See further discussion in Marshall, "Dooyeweerd's Empirical Theory of Rights," 125f. (cited in
note 3 above). Unlike Marshall, however, I see Dooyeweerd's statements in *Roots* and other popular writings as vestiges of an earlier
concept of rights that he had largely abandoned, not as indicia of a
second concept of rights separate from his mature modal theory,
discussed below.
25. Dooyeweerd addressed these methodological concerns
throughout the 1930s and 1940s. See, e.g., Dooyeweerd, *De structuur,* 223-66 (cited above in note 5) and his introduction to the
various editions of the *Encyclopaedie der Rechtswetenschap*
[hereinafter *Encyclopaedie*]. (The *Encyclopaedie* was first drafted in

the mid-1930s, first published in Amsterdam by Drukkerei D. A. V. I. D. in 1946, and subject to numerous revisions thereafter. I have used the 1946, 1958, and 1967 editions; all references hereafter are to the 1967 edition, unless otherwise indicated.) Among later writings, see particularly H. Dooyeweerd, *Wat is rechtwetenschap?* (Amsterdam: Vrije Universiteit, 1950), 33-53; id., "Over de methode van begripsvorming in de rechtswetenschap," *Rechtsgeleerd Magazijn Themis* 298 (1953).

26. *Encyclopaedie*, 1:6

27. The cryptic discussion of Dooyeweerd's ontology that follows is a distillation of the rich discussion in *NC*, 2:1-413. To do justice even to the highlights of that discussion requires more space than is available here. Dooyeweerd provides a more comprehensive introduction to his ontology in his *In the Twilight of Western Thought: Studies in the Pretended Autonomy of Theoretical Thought*, (Nutley, NJ: Craig Press, 1980), 1-26. See also L. Kalsbeek, *Contours of a Christian Philosophy: An Introduction to Herman Dooyeweerd's Thought*, (Toronto: Wedge Publishing Foundation, 1975), 76-159; C. Seerveld, "Dooyeweerd's Legacy for Aesthetics: Modal Law Theory," in C. T. McIntire, ed., *The Legacy of Herman Dooyeweerd*, (Lanham, MD: University Press of America, 1985), 41.

28. *Encyclopaedie*, 3:116.

29. Ibid., 3:103-104, 112-13.

30. H. Dooyeweerd, "Perikelen van een historische rechtstheorie. Een critische beschouwing van de Inleiding tot de studie van het Nederlandse Recht door Prof. Mr. L. J. van Apeldoorn, *Rechtsgeleerd Magazijn Themis* 25, 44 (1954); *Encyclopaedie* (1958 ed.), 2:59-60

31. *Encyclopaedie*, 3:155. "The juridical unity of the legal person," Dooyeweerd continues, "lies in the actual juridical organization of the legal associations, which is regulated by statutes and rules." Id., 155-56. For further discussion, see Dooyeweerd, *Social Institutions*, 70-107 (cited in the introductory note above).

32. Id., 3:113-14. See also Dooyeweerd, "Perikelen," 44 (cited in note 30 above); *NC*, 3, 278-80, 549-56.

33. *NC*, 2:402-403.

34. On the concept of "legal competence," see H. Dooyeweerd, "Grondproblemen in de leer der rechtspersoonlijkheid: een critische beschouwing naar anleiding van H. J. Wolf's standaardwerk 'Organschaft und juristische Person'," *Rechtsgeleerd Magazijn Themis* 199, 367, 401, 409 (1937); *Encyclopaedie*, 3:170f.; *NC*, 2:402f. Those legal subjects that devise their own rules and government exercise "active" subjective competence. Those that adopt or submit to existing rules exercise "passive" subjective competence. *Encyclopaedie*, 3:103-104.

35. See *Encyclopaedie* 3:104, where Dooyeweerd describes this competence as "the legal power to perform valuable legal transactions, . . . a competence to promulgate (or participate in the promulgation) of just statements of will which have juridical existence as actual legal relationships, and eventually from this position function as positive legal norms."

36. *NC, 3:451*.

37. See Dooyeweerd, "Rechtspersoonlijkheid," 401, 409 (cited in note 34 above). See similar discussions in *Encyclopaedie*, 3:170-71, 220-21; *NC*, 2:402-403; id., *The Christian Idea of the State*, 28-29 (cited in note 21 above).

38. H. Dooyeweerd, "Rechtspersoonlijkheid," 409 (cited in note 34 above). See further discussion of "private law" and the competence of the state to define it in Dooyeweerd, *De Crisis*, 171-82 (cited in note 11 above); Dooyeweerd, *Roots*, 25-28 (cited in note 23 above); Dooyeweerd, *Social Institutions*, 92-93 (cited in the introductory note above); *NC*, 2: 402-403, 3:278-80, 451, 549-55; *Encyclopaedie*, 3:169-71, 6:76-78, 94-96. Though Dooyeweerd distinguishes between the private law of inter-individual relationships (e.g., the law of contracts, torts, or property), and the private law of institutions (e.g., the internal laws of churches, families or business associations), the state seems in his view to have the same competence with respect to each of them.

39. Ibid. See also *Encyclopaedie*, 3:170-71.

40. Ibid. See also H. Dooyeweerd, *De strijd*, 50-61 (cited in note 19 above).

41. Dooyeweerd, "Rechtspersoonlijkheid," 408 (cited in note 34 above); *Encyclopaedie*, 3:168-69, 188.

42. Ibid. The terms "beschikkingsbevoegdheid" and "genotsbevoegdheid" are translated in *A New Critique* as "the power of use and enjoyment," but this translation is, to my mind, neither nuanced nor broad enough. See *NC*, 2:402. However translated, these terms do not speak to the entitlement to acquire or alienate a legal object. Acquisition and alienation, Dooyeweerd believed, were matters of competence, not right. See Ibid. where he speaks of the "competence to transfer subjective rights," a maxim which I assume applies to transfers both to and from the legal subject.

43. For the sources of this view in Dooyeweerd's theory of the "Gegenstand" relation between subject and objects, see *NC*, 2:391, 398. See also the fine discussion in Marshall, "Dooyeweerd's Empirical Theory of Rights," 131-35 (cited in note 3 above).

44. See *NC*, 2:130-40, 407.

45. See Dooyeweerd, "Rechtspersoonlijkheid," 401-402 (cited in note 34 above); *Encyclopaedie*, 3:175-76; *NC*, 2:402-403. See also the excellent discussion in van der Vyver, "The Doctrine of Private-Law Rights," 212-13 (cited in note 3 above) on the distinction between competence and right. While legal rights depend upon legal competence, legal competences do not depend upon, nor can they be conflated with, legal rights. The parent may be competent to raise and discipline a child but has no right to the child's obedience. Likewise a state may be competent to govern, but it has no right to the conformity of its citizens. That conflation, Dooyeweerd argues, "promotes a legal duty to the rank of a legal object," and "paradoxically renders the doctrine of rights a pillar of power-state (*Machtstaat*) theories." *NC*, 2:402; *Encyclopaedie* (1958 ed.), 2:98-101; *Encyclopaedie*, 3:221-28.

46. *Encyclopaedie*, 3:188. See also 3:169-71, where Dooyeweerd argues: "There is no subjective right that is not regulated by legal norms. . . . Every subjective right has its juridical form of existence inside the juridical order of time. . . . Subjective rights receive a positive form through regulative legal norms."

47. *NC, 3:451.*

48. *Encyclopaedie*, 3:172-73, 217-20.

49. Ibid., 3:169-235 and the summary in *NC*, 2:406-408, 411-l3. See also Marshall, "Dooyeweerd's Empirical Theory of Rights," 135-36 (cited in note 3 above).

50. *Encyclopaedie*, 3:173-74.

51. Ibid., 3:174. In the same passage, Dooyeweerd also included among objects a catch-all category of "generally, any social goods . . . [that are] amenable to subjective legal power" but offered no further elaboration of this point. For a possible inference, see below note 65 and accompanying text.

52. Ibid. See also id., 3:170-71, 182-88; *NC*, 2:408-11.

53. *NC*, 2:407-408.

54. See Dooyeweerd, "Rechtspersoonlijkheid," 406-407 (cited in note 34 above); *Encyclopaedie*, 3:172-73, 197-98, 208-209, 217-20; *NC*, 2:412-13.

55. *Encyclopaedie* (1946 ed.), 2:87; *NC*, 2:412-13.

56. See *Encyclopaedie*, 3:178-79, 208-209. See also discussion in van der Vyver, "The Doctrine of Private-Law Rights," 226 (cited in note 3 above); Hommes, *De samengestelde Grondbegrippen*, 219f. (cited in note 3 above).

57. *Encyclopaedie*, 3:174.

58. *NC*, 2:407.

59. *Encyclopaedie*, 3:176-77; *NC*, 2:407, 412-13.

60. *Encyclopaedie*, 3:176. But cf. *NC*, 2:407, where Dooyeweerd argues that such natural organic functions cannot be objects of rights because they lack an "economic" (rather than a "cultural") analogy.

61. *Encyclopaedie*, 3:177-80. See also Dooyeweerd, "Rechtspersoon-lijkheid," 405-406 (cited in note 34 above); *NC*, 2:406-407.

62. *Encyclopaedie*, 3:180-81.

63. Ibid., 3:177-78.

64. Ibid., 3:169, 171 (emphasis in original).

65. This perhaps is what Dooyeweerd meant when he included in the class of legal objects "social goods . . . that are amenable to subjective legal power." See note 51 above.

66. See my introduction to H. Dooyeweerd, *Encyclopedia of Legal Science*, J. van der Vyver, trans., (forthcoming), where I offer broader criticisms of Dooyeweerd's legal philosophy, including his concept of rights.

67. In defense of Dooyeweerd, it can be argued that he recognized that other non-state social institutions also are competent to define and positivize the subjective rights of their members. Nonetheless, legal subjects invariably must turn to the state for the enforcement of their subjective rights, thereby rendering critical the state's definitions or positivizations of enforceable rights.

Toward a Comprehensive
Science of Politics

James W. Skillen

Introduction

The study of politics is as old as the existence of polities, originating most distinguishably in Greece when Plato and Aristotle began to reflect systematically on the nature and meaning of the polis. Up until late in the nineteenth century, the study of politics was guided by competing visions of what a polis, or an empire, or a feudal estate, or a state ought to be and of how it *ought* to function. Whatever the differences between classical Stoics and classical Aristotelians, between Catholics and Protestants, between Machiavellians and Lockeans, the primary object of study was "government" or "the state," and the primary functions under examination were "law," "ethics" and the "use of force." Up until the Renaissance and Reformation, the integrative frames of reference were, in turn, the polis-centered view of life and human nature articulated by Plato and Aristotle; the empire-wide Stoic view of power, human rights and reason; and the Church-guided view of lower governments serving the moral, legal, and rational ends of a Holy Roman Empire and its Canon Law. The growth of political theory following the Reformation was due, in large measure, to the historical differentiation of states themselves, and the primary concern was to obtain knowledge for the purpose of governing or of overcoming war and establishing peaceful order.

Until late in the nineteenth century, therefore, one could describe the study of politics in the West as a subfield of moral philosophy having the practical aim of understanding how the monopolization and use of force by governments could achieve lawfully accepted or governmentally necessary ends. After the American Revolution this discipline came to focus increasingly on constitutional questions—that is to say, on questions of how the existing variety of state institutions could be defined, legitimated, and coordinated according to a basic or fundamental law.[1]

The attempt to synthesize all empirical and moral knowledge of politics into a special discipline was not characteristic of moral philosophers. From Machiavelli to Comte, however, various attempts were made to show how a certain angle of vision could explain or account for the entire landscape of politics and the rest of society. Hobbes and Locke stand out among early modern moral philosophers as ones who offered new arguments For what a state ought to be—both men doing so in a manner that was individualistically reductionistic. Moreover, with Hobbes we see the first of many science-inspired, reductionistic attempts to explain all diversity in terms of one or two functional characteristics of life. For Hobbes, "matter in motion" accounted for life in general, and the competition of "passions" explained political life in particular. As Kenneth McRae puts it:

> By this procedure the cultural specificity of behavior is reduced to insignificance, if it does not disappear altogether. Hobbes made politics a science, but a science that suppresses or subordinates every major source of human variation: ethnic identity, social orders and classes, individual temperament. Moreover, Hobbes does not merely enunciate a new doctrine; he initiates a major philosophical tradition that remained without serious challenge until the eighteenth century.[2]

A more complex attempt to synthesize empirical studies of politics is to be found in Montesquieu who tried to show how the intricate pattern of climatic, geographical, social and political inter-relationships is linked to the central governing principle underlying the three main types of political system: republican, monarchical, and despotic.[3] Nineteenth-century Europe manifested the growing spirit of nationalism against the backdrop of the recovery of community ideals in the eighteenth century. Within a few decades after Rousseau and Burke, says McRae, the idea of community "was to be placed wholly and without hesitation at the service of the nation and the nation-state, as nationalist writers and nationalist movements multiplied throughout Europe."[4]

In August Comte we meet the most important influence behind the quest for a social science which could be as solid and integrative as the natural sciences. But Comte's societal universalism did not actually inaugurate the systematization of political science. Comte's ideal of a comprehensive, explanatory social science is truly one of the greatest influences on the ideal of an empirically complete, behaviorally focused science of society, but his influence also had a diffusing effect since it tended to drive political scientists to explore different functions of society in general rather than to distinguish clearly what is political from what is not. If society becomes everything, and everything becomes a part of society, then what place is there for political science in distinction from sociology?[5]

American Endeavors
In American experience, the academic differentiation of political Science from moral philosophy seems to have begun at Columbia University late in the 1800s when first Francis Lieber and then John Burgess headed up a new department for that purpose. Yet even there, the focus of attention was on "the state" and the approach was largely institutional and constitutional. The differentiation of the academic discipline nonetheless reflected the sense that a more focused study of political reality was needed, given the growing complexity of that reality and the need for more specialized knowledge on the part of those who govern.[6]

Beginning in the 1920s at Chicago, Charles Merriam called for a new science of politics that would go beyond historical, juridical, institutional, and comparative studies of government and bring in the contributions of geographers, ethnologists, statisticians, psychologists, sociologists, biologists, and economists.[7] From that time forward, American political scientists began to specialize in studies of political life that tried to take seriously these different characteristic human *functions*. Yet in the absence of a commensurate strengthening of critical political philosophy, and in many respects based on faulty positivistic assumptions, this differentiation of empirical studies soon led to a diffusion that could no longer be integrated.

Merriam, after all, did not simply mobilize students for specialized functional study; he did so with a certain philosophical and scientific bias. In 1921, fifteen years after the founding of the American Political Science Association and its journal, the *American Political Science Review*, he wrote,

> Within relatively recent times, the theory of politics has come in contact with forces which must in time modify its procedure in a very material way. The comparatively recent doctrine that political ideas and systems—as well as other social ideas and systems—are the by-products of environment, whether this is stated in the form of economic determinism or of social environment, constitutes a challenge to all systems of thought. It can be ignored only under the penalty of losing the *locus standi* of a science.[8]

Merriam and many influenced by him, in other words, not only began to trace out the multiple functions of Western political institutions and civic behavior, they did so under the dominant conviction that a more naturalistic and positivistic method would be needed to make political science a true science. Merriam, Harold Lasswell, William Foote Whyte, and eventually a flood of students after World War II, laid the basis for what became the behavioral revolution in the 1950s. The 1940s ended, says Gunnell, quoting a 1949 article by William Anderson, "with the growing conviction of many political scientists that there was a definite need for more work in the "field of scientific method" that would yield "a body of testable propositions concerning political nature and activities of man that are applicable throughout the world" and "at all times" and that in the end would make possible a science of "human political behavior. . . ."9

What we find in the development of American political science by the 1950s, therefore, is both the continuing differentiation of studies aimed at the multiple functions of institutions and individuals, as well as the differentiation of competing views of science and philosophy of science. With respect to the study of diverse functions or modalities of political life, we can point to those who were convinced that the "environmental determinants" of political life are primarily economic. Others considered the primary determinants of politics to be psychical, or social, or geographical, or even biotic conditions or functions.

The general tendency was toward "functionalism," that is, toward an attempt to explain or predict all political behavior by reference to one such modal function. Both human beings and political institutions were reduced in theory to a determinant of that function. But these different functionalist views displayed additional contrasts and conflicts depending on whether the political scientist was a behavioralist, or a Marxist (or neo-Marxist), or one of the newly emerging "systems" thinkers. In other words, one's view of social science oriented one differently toward even the same functions and phenomena of political life.

From the point of view of Andrew C. Janos, the differentiation of specialities until very recently occurred within the general Western paradigm which sought to explain political institutions and behavior in terms of societal differentiation which is prompted by technological and economic dynamics. Even so, within that wide "paradigm" considerable differences in viewpoint and specialization have existed.

Systems theory in the 1960s, for example, was much more like Marxism than earlier behavioralism in the sense that it wanted to gain a comprehensive explanation of social interaction and interdependences. But systems analysts and neo-Marxists stand far apart in their views of history, economic determinism, and the legitimacy of political institutions in the capitalist West. Talcott Parsons, Karl Deutsch, David Easton, and others looked with optimism in the 1960s to a general systems theory of political life that would finally validate "a science of politics modeled after the methodological assumptions of the natural sciences."[10]

This brings into view my thesis that most of the "sciences" or "methods" adopted by political scientists have been reductionistic in character. In other words, a particular function or characteristic of political life—social, economic, psychic, cybernetic, or some other—has been abstracted and then adopted as the factor by which to explain, in causal fashion, everything from voting habits to institutionalization, everything from congressional lawmaking to Supreme Court decisions, everything from war to peace. In the final analysis, however, the meaning of the *political* is either lost from view or explained away.[11]

Within the circles of those who have taken natural scientific models as their guide, the assumptions and presuppositions of political scientists are quite similar to those of other social scientists who have accepted the same models. The assumptions are that human beings are primarily creatures of habit and behavior shaped by an environment in which their natural drives and passions of self-preservation lead them to seek mastery over nature and over one another through technology. Technological inventiveness both prompts and is prompted by modes of social cooperation and organization, concentrated most importantly in the economic arena. Explanations of political institutions, laws, voting habits, elite decision-making, and countless other features of political life are then sought by means of a scientific map or model that will account for specific predictable behaviors caused by a variety of "environmental" or "passionate" forces.[12]

William Riker's interpretation of the progress of political science, for example, goes like this. Until 1948 when Duncan Black published his "On the Rationale of Group Decision Making" there was no "deductive and testable theory about political events."[13] But between 1948 and the 1970s, when the discipline came of age, says Riker, such a scientific theory finally emerged. According to Riker, "the content of political theory is the authoritative allocation of values, following Easton's (1954) definition of politics, in that it involves the amalgamation of individual preferences into a social choice and the subsequent enforcement of the result. At this quite general level, the goal of political theory is to identify the conditions for an equilibrium of preferences. . . . The history of political theory over the last forty years has consisted largely of increasingly precise specification and increasingly deeper analysis of equilibrium conditions."[14]

Other Currents

In contrast to this behavioralism and systems analysis, which continues to dominate the academic discipline of American political science, more recently a revival of critical and classical social theory has been taking place. Self-critical reflection on the very process of political science was sparked in the 1960s by debates over the nature of science and theory. The argument gained ground "that theory is actually an element in the practice of science, and more than an analytical [sic] specifiable element; that political theory is a concrete activity with a past and future; and that theorizing is a distinct endeavor."[15]

Influential figures such as Sheldon S. Wolin began to look at the positivistic revolution in political science as "a serious deviation from the historical role of theory and theorizing and its relationship to politics," producing on the whole a "sterilization of political theory."[16] Neo-Marxist thinkers focused on the uncritical and instrumental character of the pretended "scientific" social sciences. Neo-classical thinkers Eric Voegelin, Leo Strauss, Hannah Arendt, John Hallowell, and others, some of whom had been publishing as early as the 1930s, began to gain new influence among students looking for deeper roots for political science in Western history, in philosophy, and in biblical revelation. The historically oriented hermeneutical philosophers began to have an impact on those who were stepping back from behavioralism and systems analyses.[17] And even within the main streams of behavioral and systems analysis, a reorientation was taking place toward useful knowledge, toward public policy expertise, and away from "scientific knowledge" for its own sake.

In each case, a different view of science, of politics, and of human nature shows up. What Eric Voegelin helps to show, for example, is that science itself is historical and rational, subject to canons of historical and rational judgment about the meaningfulness of the enterprise. From Voegelin's point of view, a naturalistic, behavioral, or systems-theory quest for a predictive map of discrete social phenomena must come to grips with its own presuppositions. If David Easton, for example, wants to claim scientific validity for his approach, he cannot simply continue his quest on *the faith* that one day he will be able to construct an adequate map. He must account for his *faith* in that kind of scientific approach. He should be required to explain why he discards or ignores so much of the historical, moral, legal, and social reality of political life that others have taken seriously for centuries in the study of politics. And ultimately, any student of politics has to account for the full reality of political life, not just for certain patterns of behavior or particular political outcomes. But how can that be done without an articulated notion of what the state or political community is and ought to be?

The point to be made here is that diversity in the discipline has to do not only with the fact that different functional specializations and reductions are at work, but also with the fact that different basic presuppositional orientations have been adopted. "By the early 1970s," says Gunnell, "it was not easy to find coherence among the trends or to bring the discipline together into a common notion of theoretical endeavor."[18] In his 1970 presidential address to the American Political Science Association, Karl Deutsch tried to argue that political science could still be considered an integrated discipline with multiple levels of theory. But in trying "to give all sides a place while to some degree maintaining the priority of the behavioral vision of theory," Deutsch ended up conveying such "an amorphous notion of theory that the very thing that was to be identified became still more elusive."[19]

As I will argue at the end of this essay, it is important for Christian scholars to make the most of present insights while avoiding the chaos of competing reductionisms if we are to chart a course of integrative political science. Despite the incoherence of the discipline today, one positive feature of our time is that many political scientists have become increasingly conscious that they disagree over fundamentals, that they must account for their standpoints, their tools, and their methods. A growing number of political scientists recognize that they must be able to explain the reality and meaning of politics as a whole. Thus, we could be approaching a creative moment for more vigorous debate across traditions and among competing schools of thought over the very meaning of politics, government, science, philosophy, and human nature. John Dryzek's brief summary of the history of political science in the twentieth century suggests just such a pregnant moment.

The idea that political institutions have autonomous influence on collective outcomes formed a major organizing principle of early twentieth century political science. In mid-century this tradition was thoroughly displaced by approaches which stressed methodological individualism and saw political life as under the influence of forces originating elsewhere in society. Political institutions came to be viewed as arenas for the pursuit of interest, their structure reflecting social influences, and politics itself came to be defined in terms of resource allocation. However, the 1970s and 1980s witnessed a "new institutionalism" which again treated institutions as independent variables in their own right and individual political action in terms of role and obligation rather than pursuit of preference.[20]

If Dryzek is correct that there is a new appreciation for the reality of political institutions in their own right, then perhaps we are set for a new round of constructive debate among different schools of thought about the nature and meaning of those institutions. If so, and if Christian political scientists find the assumptions and presuppositions undergirding behavioralism, or systems analysis, or critical theory, or classical theory inadequate or even illegitimate, then we will have to challenge them at the most basic level—at the level of fundamental assumptions about human nature, history, philosophy of science, social organization, and so forth. At the same time, however, many of the functional elements and institutional characteristics which these different approaches have abstracted and even absolutized are certainly part of reality. Thus, Christian scholars will have to challenge the foundations of political science today in ways that can recover or re-encompass the functions and dimensions of political life which have been examined by other schools of thought. And if Christian scholars are going to reject various reductionistic approaches, as I think we must, then these reductionisms themselves must be accounted for. In other words, we will have to show what is mistaken in a particular reductionistic explanation or "model" and show how that political function or characteristic is accounted for more properly in some other non-reductionistic interpretation.

Issues of Strategic Concern for a Christian Orientation in Political Science

1. What is the "Political"?

The first and most obvious concern that should occupy political scientists today, especially if we want to chart a course for Christian scholarship, is to know *what* this science is a science *of*. The acts of description, analysis, synthesis, and theoretical judgment all presuppose that some object of analysis is under consideration. What is the "object" of study in political science? What is the "political" that is being distinguished from everything else for the purpose of examination? This question springs from, and leads to, a host of other epistemological concerns, but this is the most immediate point of departure.

Obviously in order to distinguish the analyzable, one must assume many things about the kind of analysis that should be used and about the meaning of reality of which the "political" is a part. A disciplined study of "politics" cannot proceed very far without some self-critical reflection on the nature of the analytic process and on the meaning of the "whole" of reality from which the "political" is being abstracted for special analysis. Political science, just as every other science, must be rooted in (or take for granted) philosophical considerations of a most fundamental sort. We will return to this point below.

For the moment, however, it is enough to concentrate on this first question concerning the identity of the political. What is being distinguished for study by a science of politics? If one says that politics is "the authoritative allocation of values," or that political science is "the study of power," or that the object of study is "political institutions" or "political behavior," to what is one referring? What kind of authority is allocating what kind of values? What kind of power? How can we distinguish political from non-political institutions and behaviors?

The fracturing of political science as a discipline is due in part, as we've shown, to the fact that those calling themselves political scientists find no agreement in answering these questions. And if there is no agreement on *what* the object of study is, then we should not be surprised to find that a coherent discipline does not exist. For Christian scholarship, therefore, the immediate question of what constitutes the "political" is of utmost concern. Said another way, the first concern of Christian political scientists should be to orient themselves in such a way as to be able to delimit or circumscribe the proper object of study.

Answers to questions about the object of political study cannot be arrived at abstractly because we do not find ourselves in an abstract situation. Late in the twentieth century we confront a field of nearly chaotic incoherence called "political science" where most students of politics have picked up different and competing scientific "tools" from graduate schools which represent and pass on that diversity. Thus, any attempt to reach agreement about the object of study will have to be conducted not only by way of a close look at political reality, but also by way of a critical assessment of classical theory, systems theory, functional analysis, behavioralism, neo-Marxism, and much more.

The constructive or "thetical" proposal I would put on the table for discussion in this regard is one that is deeply indebted to the school of thought growing from the work of Herman Dooyeweerd and sympathetic to recent work in political science calling for a re-focus on the identity of the state and for a communitarian critique of liberal individualism and functional reductionism.[21] The object of political study, I would argue, should be the state (or political community) and inter-state relations, of which all the "political" institutions mentioned above are a part (legislatures, executives, courts, etc.). States and inter-state relations can, I believe, be shown to be distinguishable from other kinds of communities, institutions, and relationships such as churches, families, industrial corporations, colleges, and many more. These distinctions exist not because theoretical thought has created them but because different structural entities have actually differentiated in the course of history—as expressions of the historically unfolding order and drama of creation. States and interstate relations which now exist have not always existed, and they may not remain for many more decades or centuries. That is part of what constitutes the historical dimension of a science of politics. The focal purpose of a Christian approach to political science today, therefore, should be to obtain a precise historical delimitation and comparative account of all diverse states and international political institutions and relationships in the context of a normative Christian anthropology, social philosophy, political theory, and philosophy of history.

States, inter-state relations, and transnational institutions do function in numerous ways, in close interconnection with the rest of human and non-human reality. Thus, the study of states will require numerical, physical, historical, psychical, social, economic, moral, juridical, and other functional analyses. But other institutions and communities also display these same functions, so the distinguishing feature of political science will have to be its integral, synthetic account of states and their relationships.

Political science, I would argue, is a multifunctional entity science, not a *mono-functional* or *modal* science. That is to say, it is a science aiming to understand things (entities) called states (or political communities) which are distinguishable from other kinds of "things." We cannot succeed in explaining political reality if we insist on abstracting a single function or "mode" of political life such as the social or moral or biotic function and then try to explain political entities by reference to one of their functions.[22]

To state this hypothesis or proposition is, of course, not to answer most of the pertinent questions connected with it. For example, what is a state? What is the "entity" to which I am referring? My preliminary description would be that

A state is an organization of citizens under a government with general public law-making authority over a particular geographical realm by virtue of its constitutional claim to legitimacy which entitles it to enforce its laws and protect its domain by the use of force.

The very people who are organized as citizens in a state are also members of families, churches, schools, and business enterprises, and thus the characteristic shape of any particular state or set of inter-state relationships will depend, in part, on how the state's public laws deal with non-state reality. Governments aiming to create totalitarian states generally violate the non-political spheres of society by attempting to apply public law where it should not intrude. Governments aiming to create libertarian states generally fail to shape or protect the public trust adequately.

These statements in turn raise further questions: Am I not making normative claims about what a state *ought* to be rather then merely describing reality objectively? If so, is that not a violation of what science ought to do?

Here, of course, we enter the arena having to do with the nature and limits of science. We will turn to that in a moment. For now, it is sufficient to say that the way in which one distinguishes *what* is to be analyzed will indeed circumscribe the scope and limits of what can and may be discussed. If, as I hypothesize, the state takes shape historically and functions ethically and juridically as well as geographically and physically, then there is no way to eliminate normative considerations without making the science of politics impossible. Or to put it another way, if someone insists that only the measurement of positivized behavioral functions is legitimate in a science of politics, then that person's preconception of science has already predetermined the limits of political study without having begun to assess what I am claiming is a broader reality of political life. If, as I contend, political reality *does* include multiple normative characteristics, how can one "distinguish the analyzable" (i.e., politics) without also entering into normative considerations of political reality?[23]

Recognizing that political institutions are related to non-political institutions and that political institutions express functional dimensions similar to other institutions certainly means that a study of politics will have to be closely related to other social sciences. Moreover, all social sciences ought to display or make overt their philosophical presuppositions and assumptions since all analysis of the "political" takes for granted a wider horizon of human social life from which the political is being abstracted for study. Not to be conscious of that from which one is abstracting the political, and not to be conscious of what one is presupposing about the nature of reality in the process of performing that abstraction, is to be involved in a very uncritical "science."

2. What constitutes a science of politics?

The questions just asked about the nature of the "political" lead directly to a second issue of urgent concern for our Christian scholarship: How do we achieve a true science of that reality? This is the point at which we simply cannot avoid the matter of critical reflection and philosophy. If one objects by saying that philosophy is not an empirical science and that ethical and juridical concerns, for example, belong to philosophy but not to science, then one has already made a number of pre-judgments about what a science is. Perhaps such judgments are correct, but if so they need to be defended. If the "defense" given is simply a recitation of Comte's view of history, namely, that the development of human consciousness has moved from a theological through a philosophical to a modern positive stage, then that "defense" needs to be examined on its own merit—as a philosophy of history and science, not as a set of empirical conclusions about politics.[24] Thus, we return inevitably to the philosophical foundations of science itself.

This is not to say that every political scientist must concentrate on philosophical questions to the exclusion of all else. Rather, it is to insist that since every science of political reality uses certain investigative tools, concepts, norms, and procedures, then those methods, tools, and assumptions must not remain unexamined or else that science risks its very validity as science. At least a few Christian political scientists will have to be busy with critical philosophical reflection on the foundations of political science in close cooperation with those who are preoccupied with the study of the variable details of legislation, voting habits, or something else. Short of such cooperation in the definition of the science itself— from its most fundamental assumptions on through to the widest synthesis of all researches into the diversity of political experience— it is hard to conceive of anything like a "discipline" or a "school of thought" actually functioning. How can Christian scholars make anything like a coherent contribution to the science of politics outside a shared discipline? Are we not at the point today where the very question of social science calls for a major restorative, reforming, reconstituting effort to which Christians should be making an integral and distinguishable contribution?

Once again, allow me to put forward a hypothesis for consideration and debate. In seeking to distinguish the analyzable, as I argued above, political scientists should recognize that they are focusing attention on a highly complex, multi-functional set of states and inter-state relations. "Political" is not a functional adjective like "social" or "psychological" or "juridical" but is rather an institutional or community adjective referring to, or qualifying an entity—the state. "Political" refers to something—to the political order, to a human communal "thing"—not to a functional modality of all human existence. The adjective "political" derives from the state, or originally from the polis. All state institutions, and all the citizens and officials of states, will express social, psychological, juridical, and other functions, but the political order cannot be reduced to any one of those functions.

Consequently, the *first level* of scientific abstraction involved in a science of politics is the abstraction of the state and interstate relations from all other things in the world. The first set of scientific questions has to do with how to perform such an abstraction. Thus, the first presuppositional concern of political science must be with its philosophy of human nature, human society, and historical institutional differentiation.

My philosophical hypothesis, in contrast to Weber, Marx, Almond, Janos, and many others, is that God has so ordered his creation that human responsiveness to God in the creation's historical unfolding leads necessarily to the differentiation of multiple institutions (whether well-formed or ill-formed), among which are states (and inter-state relations) which become the public-legal integrators of all socially differentiating reality. Political institutions, therefore, are not caused by, nor are they mere functions of, technological innovation and competition, any more than they are caused by, or remain the function of, economic institutions or family institutions or church institutions. States have come into existence, in their own right, as an expression of human beings responding to the very ontological character of the creation order.[25] If, as I've argued, states are public-legal integrators of society, they will necessarily reflect, in historically variable ways, the influence and character of the economic, familial, ecclesiastical, and technological institutions and communities in the societies they integrate and in the larger world of which they are a part. But the search for causal connections will always have to be multiple and multilateral, never monistic or unilateral.

Moreover, when one comes to study a particular political order such as the United States, with its highly amorphous and porous political identity, the study of the political influence of interest groups from nearly every sector of society will be very important. The state, particularly in the liberal tradition, does not exist as a self-enclosed monad. At the same time, however, even in the liberal case, all of the societal interrelationships and influences that give shape to the political order do express themselves in, and exert their influences on, a state. And the reverse influence is also true. As Beiner points out, the modern liberal state does complicate matters because it "prides itself upon lacking any basis in a substantive end or set of ends." This *itself* is its "end," namely, the provision of procedural conditions for the satisfaction of ends not determined by the state but by self-defining individual members.[26] Nevertheless, says Beiner, it is a mistake to identify this "absence of substantive ends" with the absence of a state. The liberal state may for this reason be stronger or weaker, better or worse, more just or more unjust than other states, but it is still a state.

The *second level* of abstraction involved in a science of politics is that of isolating and abstracting multiple functions of the state or political order. For a science of politics this means that a multi-functional science will be needed to "get at" the full object of study. At a functional level, comparative analysis will be essential—comparing, for example, the social or physical or cybernetic or juridical peculiarities of states with the social or physical or cybernetic or juridical peculiarities of families and business organizations and labor unions and ethnic communities, etc.

But this also means that political scientists will necessarily presuppose (and should articulate) a philosophy, a fundamental ontology, of the interrelationships of these functions. Just as it is essential to become fully conscious of one's philosophy of the institutional differentiation of society, one must also become fully cognizant of one's philosophy of the multi-functional character of human and non-human reality. Christians certainly should not take for granted the psychical, social, ethical, physical, biotic and other functions of life in this world as if they are arbitrarily interrelated conditions of existence in a world that makes no sense. Part of our political philosophy must be a wider human and creation-order philosophy that seeks out the meaning of the identity and interrelationship of all dimensions of God's created world.

My hypothesis is that the "modal functions" of the creation, as Dooyeweerd refers to them, are interrelated in a distinct hierarchy of complexity; that all human and non-human creatures and all human institutions function in all of these dimensions of the creation in different ways. Thus the state, the family, the church, and every other institution or community cannot be reduced to one of its functions—whether social, biotic, psychical, economic, or juridical. To understand the political order correctly, one must grasp it in all of its functions. We will discover upon close examination, in other words, that every person, thing, and institution in the world expresses itself differently in the same modalities—social, psychological, juridical, etc. Thus, the uniqueness of each institution must be uncovered both by internal analysis of its singular identity as well as by comparative analysis of the way it functions differently from other institutions and relationships in the same modalities.

The basis, then, for statistical studies of political behavior, and for comparative sociological analysis of political institutions, and for cybernetic analysis of information "flows" through government to society and back again, is that the "state" functions in all these ways. It would be a mistake *not* to examine contemporary political institutions, in all their variety, by means of well-constructed statistical, cost-benefit, sociological, ethical, historical, juridical, and communications methods. The mistake comes in starting with a false assumption that human behavior is constituted by nothing more than animal regularities which might one day be reduced to causal predictability as if normative human responsiveness were an illusion or a mere epiphenomenon. As Almond and others have acknowledged, there are many aspects of human behavior which simply cannot be grasped by scientific methods which assume that all of reality is "clock-like." This is another way of saying that human reality, including political reality, cannot be explained away in terms of "natural" functions. A single mono-causal scientific method will not be able to penetrate to, or open up the meaning of, the political order.[27]

A *third level* of abstraction necessary in a science of politics, I would argue, is one which distinguishes the acting subjects, the essential objects, and the defining norms (or response-demanding standards) of political life. The tendency of modern differentiated science has been to separate ethics or moral philosophy from empirical or positive science in a Kantian or Comtean attempt to get exact scientific judgments about the phenomena—the facts—while leaving the so-called noumenal world or the value preferences of people in the hands of others.

This mistaken prejudgment about what constitutes science, particularly social science, has not only led to various reductionistic attempts to explain (or explain away) political reality, but it has also kept hidden the integral identity of the political world. In contrast, I would argue that people (acting subjects), in a wide variety of capacities, from lords and commoners to colonial administrators and non-Western tribal subjects, using multiple *objects* from military weapons to legal codes, from computer technologies to electric chairs—have struggled (sometimes in revolutions and civil wars) to shape their political communities ("states," which I would identify as institutional *subjects*) in response to supra-arbitrary *norms* or *standards* which are creationally binding on such entities.

Toward a True Science of Politics

A true science of politics, then, must be one that studies closely the empirical reality of all states and inter-state relations, with the aim of understanding the characteristic similarities and differences of these political "phenomena" as expressions of the invariable "subject-object-norm" order of God's creation. The invariable "laws" which hold for bio-ecology, for geography, and for physical things may be laws to which human beings can only learn *subjection*—either to live or to die. But the ways in which different peoples shape their political institutions historically in response to "norms" of love, justice, stewardship, social differentiation, and so forth, have made, and will make, for a highly complex reality that demands multiple normative judgments about what is better or worse, historical or anti-historical, logical or illogical, just or unjust, economical or wasteful, ethical or unethical for political life.

Political science in this sense has to be a "moral" science, part of moral philosophy. But this is not to say that it can be separated from the study of states in their physical, historical, symbolic, and other functions. To the contrary, an exclusive concentration on the moral philosophy of politics would be as inadequate as an exclusive concentration on the statistical measurement of voting habits. Neither of these gets at the complex whole of political order in history which is constituted by multi-functional, multi-institutional human states and inter-state institutions characterized by subject-object relations organized in response to a diversity of obligatory, trans-subjective norms of justice, love, stewardship, and so forth.

The very nature of a state or of any inter-state relationship is that it is constantly struggling (whether through violence as in Northern Ireland, Afghanistan or South Africa, or through relatively peaceful means as in Holland, Canada or Japan) to articulate in law the legitimate rules by which all citizens can be compelled to act out of political obligation. To study the interests of various groups, the economic influences on politics, the voting opinions, or the privileges of the political elite without studying the juridical and

ethical principles by which the laws are being written or the government is being overthrown, is to make a scientific mistake of immense
proportions. Such a mistake either turns one away from the full
reality of political order or it leads one to attempt a reductionistic
explanation of that order.

Our concern as Christians, therefore, with the nature of science
must be a concern to discover or recover means of analysis and
theoretical synthesis that can truly do justice to political reality—in
all of its complexity. This requires, I am hypothesizing, a continuous-
ly self-critical synthesis of all researches on every institution and
functional dimension of all states and inter-state relationships with
a view to explaining the multi-functional, subject-object-norm characteristics of political order in history. To do this will require not
only a team approach of political scientists; it will also require close
cooperative work with other social and natural scientists as well as
with philosophical and humanities scholars in order to root the
science of politics in a wider and deeper social philosophy and
philosophical anthropology.

Notes

This is an abridged version of an article of the same title in
Philosophia Reformata, 50th year (1988): 33-58. Thanks are due to
the editors of this journal for permission to reproduce it here. A
number of political science colleagues—professors and scholars—
read and gave valuable suggestions for this paper. While they bear
no responsibility for the final product, I am deeply grateful for their
assistance. Thank you, Stanley Carlson-Thies, Justin Cooper, Clarke
Cochran, Robert Eells, William Harper, Jerry Herbert, Kerry Hol-
lingsworth, David Koyzis, Dale Kuehne, and Luis Lugo. An earlier
version of this paper was first presented at a conference entitled 'A
New Agenda for Evangelical Thought' at Wheaton College in
Illinois, June 26, 1987, sponsored by the Institute for Advanced
Christian Studies and the Institute for the Study of American
Evangelicals.

1. See Quentin Skinner, *The Foundations of Modern Political Thought: vol. I, The Renaissance; vol. II, The Age of the Reformation* (New York: Cambridge University Press, 1978).

2. Kenneth McRae, "The Plural Society and the Western Political Tradition," *Canadian Journal of Political Science,* vol. 12, no. 4 (December, 1979), 682. Cf. Eric Voegelin, *The New Science of Politics,* (Chicago: University of Chicago Press, 1952), 152-61; 178-89.

3. McRae, "The Plural Society," 682f.

4. Ibid., 683.

5. On Comte, see Janos, *Politics and Paradigms: Changing Theories of Change in Social Science,* (Stanford: Stanford University Press, 1986), 7, 21-22; Eric Voegelin, *From Enlightenment to Revolution,* John H. Hallowell, ed., (Durham, NC: Duke University Press, 1975), 136-89; Frank E. Manuel, *The Prophets of Paris,* (New York: Harper Torchbooks, 1962), 249-96.

6. John G. Gunnell, "Political Theory: The Evaluation of a Sub-Field," in Ada W. Finifter, ed., *Political Science: The State of the Discipline,* (Washington, D. C.: American Political Science Association, 1983), 6. On the development of American political science see Raymond Seidelman, *Disenchanted Realists: Political Scientists and the American Crisis,* (Albany, NY: SUNY Press, 1985); and A. Somit and J. Tanenhaus, *The Development of American Political Science from Burgess to Behavioralism,* (New York: Irvington, 1982).

7. Gunnell, "Political Theory," 6-7.

8. Charles E. Merriam, *New Aspects of Politics,* 3rd enlarged edition, (Chicago: University of Chicago Press, 1970), 65.

9. Gunnell, "Political Theory," 12, quoting William Anderson, "Political Science North and South," *Journal of Politics* vol. II (1949): 298-317.

10. Gunnell, "Political Theory," 19. See, for example, David Easton, *A Framework for Political Analysis,* (Englewood Cliffs, NJ: Prentice-Hall, 1965), and Karl Deutsch, *The Nerves of Government,* (New York: The Free Press, 1963, 1966). For a good introduction to the behavioral revolution leading to systems theory, see Alec Barbrook, *Patterns of Political Behavior,* (Itasca, IL: F. E. Peacock Pub., 1975). For a background to systems theory, see Ervin Iaszlo, *The Systems*

View of the World, (New York: George Braziller, 1972). David Easton's 1969 presidential address at the American Political Science Association convention was sharp in pointing to the shortcomings of behavioralism and calling for a "post-behavioral" turn. See Easton, "The New Revolution in Political Science," *American Political Science Review* 50 (1969): 1051-61.

11. On reductionism see Skillen, *International Politics and the Demand for Global Justice,* (Sioux Center, IA: Dordt College Press, 1981), 1-97; Theodore R. Malloch, *Beyond Reductionism: Ideology and the Science of Politics,* (New York: Irvington Pub., 1983).

12. See G. A. Almond and S. J. Genco, "Clouds, Clocks and the Study of Politics," *World Politics*, 29 (July, 1979), esp. 489-522; David B. Truman, "The Impact on Political Science of the Revolution in Behavioral Sciences," in Heinz Eulau, ed., *Behavioralism in Political Science*, (New York: Atherton, 1969).

13. William H. Riker, "Political Theory and the Art of Heresthetics," in A. W. Finifter, ed., *Political Science: The State of the Discipline*, (Washington, D. C.: American Political Science Association, 1983), 41.

14. Ibid., 47-48.

15. Gunnell, "Political Theory," 25.

16. Ibid., 26. See Sheldon S. Wolin, "Political Theory: Trends and Goals," in David L. Sills, ed., *International Encyclopedia of the Social Sciences*, vol. 12, (New York: Macmillan, 1965), 325-28; George J. Graham and George W. Carey, eds., *The Post-Behavioral Era*, (New York: McKay, 1972).

17. See Fred Dallmayer and Thomas A. McCarthy, eds., *Understanding and Social Inquiry,* (Notre Dame: University of Notre Dame Press, 1977); Richard J. Bernstein, *Beyond Objectivism and Relativism: Science, Hermeneutics and Praxis,* (Philadelphia: University of Pennsylvania Press, 1983).

18. Gunnell, "Political Theory," 29.

19. Ibid., 30. See Karl Deutsch, "On Political Theory and Political Action," *American Political Science Review*," 65 (1971): 11-27.

20. John S. Dryzek, "The Progress of Political Science," *The Journal of Politics*, 48, no. 2 (May, 1986): 314.

21. See Skillen, "The Development of Calvinistic Political Theory in the Netherlands, with Special Reference to the Thought of Herman Dooyeweerd," (Ph. D. Diss., Duke University, 1974; Skillen, "Herman Dooyeweerd's Contribution to the Philosophy of the Social Sciences," *Journal of the American Scientific Affiliation*, 31, no. 1 (March, 1979): 20-24; Skillen, "Societal Pluralism: Blessing or Curse for the Public Good?" in Francis Canavan, ed., *The Ethical Dimension of Political Life: Essays in Honor of John H. Hallowell*, (Durham, NC: Duke University Press, 1983), 166-72; Herman Dooyeweerd, *Roots of Western Culture*, (Toronto: Wedge, 1979); Dooyeweerd, *A Christian Theory of Social Institutions*, trans. Magnus Verbrugge, ed. John Witte, Jr., (LaJolla, CA: The Herman Dooyeweerd Foundation, 1986); David T. Koyzis, "Towards a Christian Democratic Pluralism: A Comparative Study of Neothomist and Neocalvinist Political Theories," (Ph. D. Diss., University of Notre Dame, 1986).

Regarding the recovery of focus on the state, see *Daedalus* (Fall, 1979), theme issue on "The State"; Peter Evans et al., eds., *Bringing the State Back In* (New York: Cambridge University Press, 1985).

For the communitarian critique of liberalism and functional reductionism, see Wilson Carey McWilliams, *The Idea of Fraternity in America,* (Berkeley: University of California Press, 1973); Clarke E. Cochran, *Character, Community and Politics,* (Tuscaloosa: University of Alabama Press, 1982); Michael Walzer, *Spheres of Justice*, (New York: Basic Books, 1983); Michael Sandel, *Liberalism and the Limits of Justice,* (New York: Cambridge University Press, 1982).

22. See Skillen, "Dooyeweerd's Contribution to the Philosophy of the Social Sciences," op. cit., and Dooyeweerd, *A Christian Theory of Social Institutions*, op. cit.

23. Note, for example, the contrast between discussions of international politics by those who take ethical and juridical considerations seriously and those who do not. The former includes Stanley Hoffman, *Duties Beyond Borders: On the Limits and Possibilities of Ethical International Politics,* (Syracuse: Syracuse University Press, 1981). The latter includes Karl Deutsch, *The Analysis of International Relations*, 2nd ed., (Englewood Cliffs, NJ: Prentice-Hall, 1978).

24. See Voegelin's critique of positivism, for example, in *From Enlightenment to Revolution*.

25. Cf. Cerny, "Structural Power and State Theory," 1-5.

26. Beiner, "The Classical Method," 472-73. Cf. Lowi, *The End of Liberalism*, and McWilliams, *The Idea of Fraternity in America*, esp. 170-79, 507-624.

27. See Paul Marshall, "Mathematics and Politics" *Philosophia Reformata* (Amsterdam), 44th year (1979): 113-36, and Marshall, "Some Recent Conceptions of Operationalism and Operationalizing," *Philosophia Reformata*, 44th year (1979): 46-68.

Subsidiarity as a Political Norm

Jonathan Chaplin

Introduction

A noteworthy characteristic of recent political thought—one of which Bernard Zylstra had a lucid understanding—is an emerging recognition of the inadequacy of a fundamental premise of the classical liberal tradition, namely that the central problems confronting political philosophy can be reduced to a singular relationship, that between the individual and the state. Philosophical reflection has for too long been preoccupied with a cluster of dilemmas arising from this relationship: how to derive the authority of the state from the individual, how to render the state accountable to individuals, or how to protect the individual against the state. It is being realised that these problems cannot adequately be answered so long as the vast terrain of social relationships and communities existing *alongside* the individual and the state is taken into account. The realization is dawning that we cannot grasp the nature of the political association unless we also understand the nature of the numerous *non-political* associations which frame the larger part of the social life of the individual; that human beings are social creatures not just in that they live in "society," but in that they live in multiple and diverse socie*ties*; and that if these diverse expressions of our sociality are not fostered and protected against deformations arising from an exaggeration either of state power or individual liberty, we shall be impoverished as citizens as well as in our other social roles.

This theme is attracting renewed interest across the ideological spectrum. Neo-conservatives in the U.S.A., attacking bureaucratic "megastructures" like the state and the large corporate institutions, urge a recovery of those "mediating structures" (Berger and Neuhaus's term) which shield the individual against them.[1] Neo-liberals, exposing the inefficiency and illiberality of the public sector, seek to shift the responsibility for economic coordination and welfare provision onto private organizations.[2] Neo-socialists, disillusioned by the failed promise of state-administered socialism, join with Greens and feminists in urging a new variety of decentralized, pluralistic socialism ("associationalist socialism," as Paul Hirst characterises it) which meets human needs by means of, rather than at the cost of, democratic participation.[3]

We may therefore be witnessing a rebirth of "pluralism" (strictly, of "normative" pluralism, as distinct from the supposedly purely "descriptive" variety of pluralism developed by American political scientists in the nineteen-fifties and sixties and still influential today.[4] While profound differences remain between these various strands of thought, there is at least a consensus that the modern state has overreached and thereby incapacitated itself, and needs to be refashioned in a way that respects the independent contributions of a plurality of associations, communities and institutions which have for too long either atrophied through neglect or collapsed under direct assault.

We have, of course, been here before. Among the many works voicing similar concerns in the early decades of this century was Pius XI's social encyclical *Quadragesimo Anno*, published in 1931:

> . . . things have come to such a pass through the evil of what we have termed "individualism" that, following upon the overthrow and near extinction of that rich social life which was once highly developed through associations of various kinds, there remain virtually only individuals and the State. This is to the great harm

of the State itself; for with a structure of social governance lost, and with the taking over of all the burdens which the wrecked associations once bore, the State has been overwhelmed and crushed by almost infinite tasks and duties (§78).[5]

Today the role of this "structure of social governance" is being rediscovered once again. The specific form of the structure recommended by Pius XI—a kind of liberal corporatism—may not be our guide today, but the broad contours of the social vision underlying it do indeed merit critical reappropriation and elaboration.

The purpose of this paper is to highlight the importance of this task by assessing critically the principle of subsidiarity together with the distinctively Catholic conception of associational autonomy which it presupposes and apart from which it cannot be fully grasped. In the first part of the paper I review the origins and meaning of the principle of subsidiarity, drawing both on papal statements and on interpretations of the principle by Catholic philosophers, especially those associated with Solidarism, such as Heinrich Rommen, Johannes Messner, and Oswald Von Nell-Breuning (author of the first draft of *QA*). In the second part I assess the adequacy of the principle of subsidiarity as a norm for the state.

Subsidiarity: Origins and Meaning
The term "subsidiarity" has recently entered European political debate because of its relevance to the future "federal vocation" of the European Community. Federalism is, however, but one specific application of the principle, one addressed to the question of the division of powers between different levels of government. The principle operates much more widely, as a basic norm for the distribution of functions as between the state and all other bodies. It holds that the state ought not to assume tasks which other communities can perform for themselves, and counsels that what Pius XI termed the "structure of *social* governance" should not be needlessly overridden by *political* governance from above. Traditionally these other communities are known in Catholic thought as "lesser" or "subordinate." The term in fact includes both *subordinate*

political bodies such as municipalities or provinces, and *non-political* bodies such as families, unions, or schools.

This political application of the principle will be my primary concern, but it is essential to note that subsidiarity also applies to fundamental relationship *between the individual and any community* (or "the community" in general). Subsidiarity has always been understood to apply comprehensively to all social relationships and thus lies at the heart of Catholic social philosophy.

Before briefly recapitulating the relevant themes of this philosophy, an outline of the history of the principle is necessary. The term "subsidiarity" does not appear in *Rerum Novarum*[6] but the idea is operative in it nonetheless. Although *RN* cannot be said to have actually "taught" the principle, as the *New Catholic Encyclopedia* claims, the principle is undoubtedly implied at several points in the document. It draws a careful distinction between lesser or "private societies" and the larger society, and affirms that the state has a duty to give legal effect to the natural right of individuals to join such "private societies" (§51).

In particular it endorses at length and enthusiastically the virtues of workingmen's associations (§§48-51). As Calvez and Perrin put it, for Leo associations like these could "help re-knit the connecting tissues of a society which individualism had reduced to isolated units."[7] Consistently with this *RN* also affirms the independent rights of both the family and religious orders against the state and urges that they must be vigilantly protected against unwarranted state intervention (§§14, 53). Further, where such intervention proves necessary, "the law must not be asked to do more nor to proceed further than is necessary to put right the wrong" (§29).

The principle of subsidiarity can therefore be said to be founded in *RN*. However, as is well known, it receives its first explicit papal formulation in *Quadragesimo Anno*:

> Just as it is gravely wrong to take from individuals what they can accomplish by their own initiative and industry and give it to the community, so also it is an injustice and at the same time a grave evil and disturbance of right order to assign to a greater and higher association what lesser and subordinate organizations

can do. For every social activity ought of its very nature to furnish help to the members of the body social, and never destroy or absorb them (§79).

On a number of occasions Pius XI's successors reaffirmed the principle explicitly. Pius XII did so on several occasions.[8] John XXIII reaffirms it and employs it at several points in *Mater et Magister*[9] (§§53, 117, 152), which also contains a lengthy section acknowledging the importance of the growth of "associations" (§§59-67). He also applies it to the international sphere in *Pacem in Terris*[10] (§140). Paul VI employs it, though without mentioning the term, in *Populorum Progressio*[11] (§33). Happily, subsidiarity also receives mention in *Centesimus Annus*[12] (§§15, 48), together with the complementary principle of solidarity. *QA* remains the classic explicit formulation, though other themes in subsequent social encylicals, especially elaborations of the meaning of the common good, clearly bear upon its interpretation and application.

So much for the history of the idea; what of its meaning? I shall take its general sense first, and then consider at greater length its political application. The term "subsidiarity" derives from the Latin word *subsidium*, meaning help or aid. It is in fact already implied in the conception of the relationship between the individual and society which is at the base of Catholic social philosophy. Humans are social creatures unable to realize their ends in isolation from others. They need the *subsidium*, the help, of society in order to be human. Society itself thus performs a "subsidiary function" in relation to persons; "all social activity is of its nature subsidiary," as Pius XII puts it. A "subsidiary" function is not a "secondary" one but rather an *indispensable auxiliary* one. Society performs a subsidiary function not simply when the individual meets a crisis, but as a matter of course.

The same point emerges from a consideration of the concept of the common good. The good of the individual cannot be realized apart from the good of the whole. The common good takes priority over all individual goods, but only in the sense that the individual needs what is contained in the common good in order to attain his individual good. The good of individuals is embraced within it, fulfilling it by offering those conditions, resources, opportunities, and securities without which the individual cannot realize his own ends. Whatever limitations are imposed by the common good upon the exercise of individual rights are imposed in order to guarantee conditions in which such rights may be effectively realized. In a radical sense, the meaning of the common good is already given in the meaning of personhood: "The right of society, the common good, is necessarily *within* the rights of the person which it guarantees. It transcends the person only because it is also indwelling in him."[13]

Now the help (*subsidium*) offered by society as such to the individual is nothing other than that which is contained in the common good. Hence, as Messner puts it: "The law of subsidiary function and the law of the common good are, in substance, identical."[14] The principle of the common good both legitimates collective action but at the same time limits such action to that which is necessary to help individuals in the realization of their own ends in responsible freedom. The common good authorizes the community no further than to the point at which individuals require its aid. Subsidarity is thus a inherent feature of the common good, not a qualification of it.

I now turn to the application of subsidiarity to the relationship between the state and lesser communities. A preliminary question is what falls under the heading of "lesser communities." Thomas himself discusses in any detail only the family and the household, but modern Catholic philosophers, such as Rommen and Messner, take cognizance of a much wider range of communities typical of a differentiated industrial society. Following the lead given by Leo XIII, who specifically acknowledged workingmen's associations as having a natural foundation, they have extended Thomas's Aristotelian argument for the organic evolution of state from household, to include not only lesser territorial groupings, but also professional and vocational organizations, religious, national, cultural and educational bodies.[15] Sometimes a distinction is drawn between communities directly ordained by nature (family, locality, occupational group, state, international society), and associations based on freely chosen ends (unions, employers' associations, charitable groups and so on).[16]

Human society is envisaged as a divinely ordered hierarchy of qualitatively different communities each ordered to distinctive, non-transferrable ends rooted in man's rational nature and governed by natural and divine law. The ranking of the communities is determined by the hierarchical arrangement of ends. Particular communities come into existence in the social process as expressions of particular aspects of human social nature. While man's supernatural end is his highest, he can only move towards it through this plurality of natural associations, each directed to fulfilling one partial end and possessing a unique character and range of rights and duties determined objectively by natural law. As John Paul II puts it in *CA*:

> The social nature of man is not completely fulfilled in the State, but is realized in various intermediary groups, beginning with the family and including economic, social, political and cultural groups which stem from human nature itself and have their own autonomy, always with a view to the common good. This is what I have called [in *Sollicitudo Rei Socialis*] the "subjectivity" of society. . . .(§14).

The subordination of lesser communities to those above them in the social hierarchy does not compromise their separate identity nor diminish their independent (relative) value. As Rommen puts it: "All organizational forms have their intrinsic values and their objective ends, the upper form does not make the lower form superfluous; it must never abolish it, nor may it take over its functions and purposes."[17] In the strict sense, *every* higher community performs a subsidiary function with respect to those below it, (but this point tends not to be pursued, for reasons I explore later).

It is the essential subsidiary function of the *state* with respect to the lesser communities which attracts the greatest interest. The general principle is that the state has a duty to offer lesser communities such help as is needed in order for the latter to realize their distinctive ends. All that was said above about the subsidiary function of society with respect to individuals also applies to the state's subsidiary function with respect to lesser communities.

The state is the supreme guardian of the common good of the whole society. As such it is empowered to act in a variety of ways in order to secure that overriding moral end. The state's authority is in principle as wide in scope as the attainment of the common good requires. But it is no wider. Just as the common good includes within itself the good of individuals, so it also includes the particular goods of the lesser communities. It is necessarily pluralistic in character. Hence the state cannot thrive at the expense of the rights of its citizens, nor of the rights of the lesser bodies within its jurisdiction. *The state must enable lesser communities to be themselves.* In practice this will mean that the acknowledgement of a substantial measure of autonomy on the part of lesser communities will be an essential ingredient of the common good.

It is true that Thomists employ the language of the "whole" and its "parts" when referring, respectively, to the state and the lesser communities. This is the basis on which some commentators have sought to portray the Thomist conception of the state as "organicist" or "universalist."[18] Their argument is that since the *telos* of the whole takes precedence over those of its parts, the autonomy of the parts is always precarious. What this argument overlooks, however, is the fact that for Thomas the state is a "unity of order" (*unitas ordinis*), not a "substantial unity." In a whole which is "unity of order," the parts retain their independent substantiality. The "unity of order" realized in the state thus establishes a structured relationship among the lesser communities, but in this relationship the independent purposes of these communities must be upheld; otherwise the common good itself will be impaired.[19]

This interpretation is borne out by Oswald von Nell-Breuning in an article commemorating the fiftieth anniversary of *QA*. As the principal author of this encyclical he may be regarded as a reliable interpreter. The document recommends the creation of vocational corporations whose aim was to mitigate the conflict of interests between employers and workers by establishing a structure of cooperation. Von Nell-Breuning insists that the intention of this section of the document (81-87) was in no sense to legitimate the state corporatism characteristic of the regimes of Mussolini or Salazar. What was envisaged, rather were autonomous voluntary bodies equipped with a right to self-government.[20]

The protection of the autonomy of lesser communities will safeguard individuals from the likely encroachments of a burgeoning centralized state. Individual freedom is extended by safeguarding associational freedom. Protecting this autonomy is, moreover, crucial to the proper functioning of the state itself, a point expressed in *QA*:

> The supreme authority of the State ought, therefore, to let subordinate groups handle matters and concerns of lesser importance, which would otherwise dissipate its efforts greatly. Thereby the State will more freely, powerfully, and effectively do all those things that belong to it alone because it alone can do them: directing, watching, urging, restraining, as occasion requires and necessity demands. Therefore, those in power should be sure that the more perfectly a graduated order is kept among the various associations, in observance of the principle of "subsidiary function," the stronger social authority and effectiveness will be [and] the happier and more prosperous the condition of the State (§80).

The autonomy of the lesser communities comes to legal expression in their possession of special rights. Messner is especially emphatic in asserting the principle of juridical pluralism, (and on this he acknowledges the contribution of late nineteenth- and early twentieth-century legal pluralists such as Gierke, Duguit, Hauriou, and Gurvitch). Corresponding to the plurality of communities, there is, he holds, a "plurality of categories of equally original fundamental rights, none of which can be derived from another."[21] These rights move in different orbits and are qualitatively different from, and irreducible to, each other. Although the state is responsible for establishing a legal framework within which lesser communities can securely exercise these particular rights, it is not itself the source of these rights. Such rights are essentially natural rights, rights which the state merely codifies and balances in positive law. The state affords lesser bodies the necessary legal recognition, but "it is their essence, their ends, that control the legal forms, not vice versa."[22] Such associations should therefore in general be left free by the state to adopt their own internal rules. On the other hand these must be conducive to realizing their natural moral purposes. The freedom of association is more than the individual's right to join an association. It also carries with it the duty to see that the association fulfils its morally legitimate purpose. If this duty is not fulfilled, it may be necessary for the state to intervene to ensure that it is. This would not be a violation but a restoration of the natural rights of the association.

The special rights of lesser communities constitute a major limit to the exercise of the sovereignty of the state. The possession of sovereignty is indeed an essential concomitant of the state's duty to the common good of the whole society. Since only the state has this duty, only it has this right. Although the state's rights and those of lesser communities are "equally original," they are not "equal" in the sense of being identical in content. But political sovereignty must be carefully defined. It emphatically does not mean legal omnicompetence, but only legal universality and finality. The state's writ certainly runs throughout its entire territory and takes precedence over the lesser authorities of other bodies, acting as final adjudicator in cases of conflict. But since the spheres of authority of the lesser communities are also original and rooted in nature, they may never be conceived as mere delegations of political authority.[23]

We must now explore further what the state may do as it acts subsidiarily towards the lesser communities. A very wide range of activities have been proposed as warranted by the principle, but three particular kinds of activity may conveniently be distinguished: enabling, intervening, and substituting.

1. **Enabling** activities will involve the creation of the necessary general legal, economic, social and moral conditions in which lesser communities can flourish. Legally, a just and stable order must be established in which the special rights of lesser communities are upheld. Economically, as *Centesimus Annus* puts it, the state acts by "creating favorable conditions for the free exercise of economic activity, which will lead to abundant opportunities for employment

and sources of wealth" (§15). Socially and morally, it is the task of the state to foster harmonious relations between individuals and between communities and to encourage those public virtues which foster healthy community activity.

2. **Intervening** activities, i.e, interventions in the internal affairs of a lesser community, are justified when there is some obvious deficiency or distortion within them which may affect the common good. These might include either negative interventions (restrictions) such as tightening the election procedures of a large, undemocratically run trades union or limiting the rights of corporate shareholders, or positive interventions (provisions) such as supplementing low incomes with welfare payments. Such intervention must always aim at restoring the ability of lesser communities to fulfil their own responsibilities to the wider community. That is, the intervention is justified not in terms of the benefits accruing to the particular communities themselves, but to those accruing to the common good. The state is only authorized to act in the interests of the common good, never solely in the interests of a lesser community. The warrant for and the limits of the right of intervention are contained within the right itself, which derives its content from the common good.

Not surprisingly, different authors, including different popes, interpret the scope of legitimate intervention differently, but let us take Rommen as an illustration. He envisages a program of social legislation protecting the worker, recognizing the rights of trade unions, abolishing child labor, defending agricultural holdings, imposing progressive taxation, curbing monopolies, granting privileges to farmers cooperatives, ensuring honesty in financial institutions, protecting the small saver, or imposing tariffs.[24] Such intervention must however be no more than a "reconstitution of the order of self-initiative."[25]

3. **Substituting** activities, in which the state directly assumes tasks specifically belonging to lesser communities, are in general ruled out. Direct responsibility for the "partial common goods" of lesser communities fall outside the political order. Hence comprehensive nationalization and a centrally planned economy are in principle excluded. But in exceptional circumstances, when a par-

ticular community is chronically deficient and incapable of performing basic functions, such substitution is justified, temporarily if
possible. Or, where activities performed by lesser bodies grow to the
point at which they become indispensable to the common good, then
the state must act to protect the common good, perhaps by bringing
certain natural monopolies into public ownership (cf *QA* §79; *CA*
§48).[26]

An Assessment of Subsidiarity

These, then, are the broad contours of the conception of the role of
the state generated by the principle of subsidiarity. It is a substantial
and distinctive conception, too frequently overlooked by Protestant
social and political theorists and, indeed, by Catholic writers
enamoured of more fashionable theologies of liberation (which have
yet proved unable to propose a substantive and authentically Christian account of what a just state would look like).

Nevertheless, the principle of subsidiarity encounters a significant problem which calls for a substantial reformulation. The
problem centers on the idea of a *hierarchical* arrangement of communities. The notion of hierarchical ordering is fundamental to
Thomist metaphysics. Whatever is made of its general merits, it
creates evident difficulties when applied to the social world. While
it is essential to acknowledge that human beings function within a
diversity of communities, it is problematic to view these as ranked
within a *hierarchy*. When we attempt to picture the multitude of
communities, institutions, and groups which populate a modern,
differentiated society in terms of an idea of graded hierarchy,
numerous questions arise. In what sense does the municipality rank
"above" the family? Is the corporation above the union, or vice
versa? Where are political parties or schools positioned in the
hierarchy? And perhaps most awkwardly, in what sense does the
church as the supernatural community crown the entire hierarchy?
It appears difficult to find a satisfactory single criterion according to
which a complete ranking could be achieved—which suggests that
the very idea of a ranking may be misplaced.

The problem with the idea of hierarchy can be seen by exploring
the question why, as Calvez and Perrin point out, "subsidiarity only

looks one way".[27] It is not difficult to see the initial plausibility of this with respect to the state. While the state fulfils a subsidiary function towards the lesser communities, these communities do not appear to fulfil a similar function towards the state. In an indirect sense, the lesser communities do assist the state in its task insofar as they effectively fulfil their own functions and thus make state aid unnecessary. Yet it is not part of their primary purpose to be responsible for the state in the way that the state is essentially responsible for them. However, it is more difficult to see why subsidiarity is only a one-way function with respect to the relationships between the various lesser communities themselves. It has already been noted that few interpreters of subsidiarity have much to say about how higher communities other than the state are supposed to aid those below it in the hierarchy. We can now see that this is partly because it is very difficult to determine whether some communities are above or below others. I suggest that it is also because aid evidently goes in both directions. Does the corporation aid the trade union or vice versa? Does a professional association aid a university, or vice versa? The appropriate conclusion to draw here is surely that *each community performs subsidiary functions towards all the others.*[28]

The point can be pressed further by noting that, in Thomist social philosophy (under the influence of Aristotle), the idea of one community being subordinate to another implies that a lesser community is somehow incomplete, lacks self-sufficiency. But if it is true that all communities perform subsidiary functions towards all others—that the family needs the corporation and the school as much as they need the family and each other—then *all* communities are equally lacking in self-sufficiency. In that case, it becomes redundant to speak of any of them being arranged according to a hierarchical subordination. Now it is true, of course, that Thomism posits *degrees* of self-sufficiency. All lesser communities lack self-sufficiency, but some lack it more than others. I suggest that it is exceedingly difficult to operationalize this essentially *quantitative* notion of self-sufficiency. Different communities, precisely because they are *qualitatively* distinguished from each other, just provide *different kinds of help* to one another. The corporation offers job opportunities to families, while the family offers mature adults capable of work to the corporation (at least when each functions properly). In other words, we need to distinguish between different *kinds* of subsidiary relationship. The general concept of subsidiarity needs specifying with respect to particular kinds of relationship between communities.[29]

If this is true then it is more appropriate to conceive of different communities as standing in horizontal rather than vertical relationships to each other; to speak of coordination, rather than subordination. Can the same also be said of the *state*, however? It may be that lesser communities stand in horizontal relationships to each other, but can the same be said of the state's relationship to such communities? Earlier it was suggested that the idea that "subsidiarity only looks one way" has an initial plausibility regarding the relationship between the state and the lesser communities. However, in view of the foregoing, there seems to be no inconsistency in saying that subsidiarity here is also a two-way process. Just as the family provides mature workers to the corporation, so it provides mature citizens to the state (of course it does many other things too). If we acknowledge that the family is in some sense the "basic" unit of society whose demise would imperil the future of society as a whole, there is no reason why we should not term the help it offers a "subsidiary function." Similarly, without the taxes provided by corporations, the state's revenue would be considerably reduced.

What then is distinctive about the state? To answer this we need to specify precisely its unique subsidiary function. Earlier it was acknowledged that the state's primary responsibility is *for* other communities, whereas their primary responsibility is not for it (or for each other). The state uniquely is charged with directly promoting the common good of the whole society. We might therefore say that the subsidiary character of the state is a primary aspect of its nature, whereas the subsidiary character of other communities is a secondary aspect of theirs. To put it differently, it is possible to specify the distinctive ends of the lesser communities without reference to what they can do for the state, whereas it is not possible to specify the distinctive end of the state without reference to what the state can do for other communities.

Is there then, after all, a hierarchical relationship at least between the state and other communities? There is, insofar as the state possesses authority over them, but the nature and limits of this authority needs carefully specifying. It is necessary clearly to distinguish between the different kinds of authority that attach to each different community. The nature of the authority is determined by the "end" of a community. This function determines not only the internal nature of the community but also, and as a consequence, the kind of "help" it can offer to other communities. The authority of the state is not essentially a spiritual, moral, social or psychological kind of authority but a *legal* kind. It performs *its* subsidiary function towards other communities by means of law, by establishing a legal framework, embodying norms of justice and the requirements of the common good, within which other communities can operate. This is *its* unique contribution to the promotion of the common good. (Thomist writers have in fact always recognized that everyone, not only the state, contributes to the realization of the common good). While each social relationship possesses original rights which may not be overridden by the state, with respect to public law the state does indeed stand above all other communities in a hierarchical relationship. This is not a general hierarchical priority, but only a functional legal, and hence a limited, one.[30]

The three kinds of state activity—enabling, intervening and substituting—which were distinguished above, can now be specified more precisely. First, the state *enables* other communities to realize their ends by recognizing and protecting the various rights and duties pertaining to each and, in the interests of the common good, by adjudicating between them when conflicts of rights or duties arise. Earlier it was suggested that the "enabling" role of the state has normally been understood to include "legal, economic, social and moral conditions." What is now being proposed is that the task of creating *legal* conditions is the definitive function of the state. The distinctive end of the state is the creation of a framework of public law embodying the norms of justice and the requirements of the common good.[31] The state's activities in other realms (economic, social, moral and so on) are thus to be pursued by means of the creation of such a framework of public law. For example, the state should foster favorable economic conditions not primarily by functioning itself as an economic agent (producing, consuming and so on) but by laying down a framework of law which embodies principles of economic justice. Second, the state will need to *intervene* (positively or negatively) in the internal affairs of other communities when any failure on their part to fulfil their duties bears consequences for the common good (which, of course, embraces the particular purposes of other communities). Where mere intervention proves insufficient to protect the common good, *substitution* may be necessary (as in the case of public utilities).

A reformulation of the principle of subsidiarity along these lines may help to avoid some of the problems arising from the way in which it has traditionally been articulated. The principle need not be abandoned, but it does need to be detached from its unhelpful association with the concept of hierarchy. And its applications need to be specified more closely by identifying the distinctive ends of each different kind of community and, thereby, the distinctive kind of "aid" each can provide to others. In the case of the state, the distinctive subsidiary function it performs towards other communities may be understood as the establishment of a framework of public law, embodying the norms of justice and the requirements of the common good, within which these communities can realize their own ends as fully as possible. Thus reformulated, the principle of subsidiarity can acquire a greater degree of precision and thus function more effectively as a substantive norm to guide the complex and multifaceted relationships between the state and other kinds of community.

Notes

This is a shorter, revised version of an article to appear in F. McHugh and S. M. Natale, eds., *Rerum Novarum 1891-1991. Four Revolutions: An Unfinished Agenda,* (Lanham, MD, and London: University Press of America, 1993).

1. P. L. Berger and R. J. Neuhaus, *To Empower People: The Role of Mediating Structures in Public Policy,* (Washington, D. C.: AEI,

1977). See also Michael Novak's discussion of "mediating structures" in his *Catholic Social Thought and Liberal Institutions: Freedom with Justice,* 2nd ed., (New Brunswick, N.J.: Transaction Publishers, 1989), 201f.

2. See, for example, R. Nozick, *Anarchy, State, and Utopia,* (Oxford: Blackwell, 1974), chapter 10.

3. See, for example, P. Q. Hirst, *Representative Democracy and its Limits,* (Cambridge: Polity, 1990), chap. 5; Hirst, *Law, Socialism and Democracy,* (London: Allen and Unwin, 1986); G. Hodgson, *The Democratic Economy,* (Harmondsworth: Penguin, 1984); M. Rustin, *For a Pluralist Socialism,* (London: Verso, 1985).

4. On descriptive pluralism, see G. Jordan, "The Pluralism of Pluralism: An Anti-theory?" in *Political Studies* vol. XXXVIII, no. 2, (June, 1990): 286-301. For a useful survey of normative pluralism, see J. W. Skillen and R. N. McCarthy, eds., *Political Order and the Plural Structure of Society,* Emory University Studies in Law and Religion, (Alpharetta, GA.: Scholars Press, 1992).

5. Section 78. In O. von Nell-Breuning, *The Reorganization of the Social Economy,* (New York: Bruce Publishing Co., 1937).

6. In E. Gilson, ed., *The Church Speaks to the Modern World,* (Garden City, N.Y.: Doubleday and Co., 1954). References to encyclicals are to *section,* not page number.

7. J-Y. Calvez and J. Perrin, *The Church and Social Justice,* J. R. Kirwan, trans., (Chicago: Henry Regnery, 1961), 408.

8. For example, in a Speech to the new Cardinals, 1946, cited in Calvez and Perrin, ibid., 122n.

9. In M. Walsh and B. Davies, eds., *Proclaiming Justice and Peace: Documents from John XXIII to Paul II,* (London: Collins, 1984).

10. Ibid.

11. Ibid.

12. London: Catholic Truth Society, 1991.

13. Calvez and Perrin, op. cit., 118.

14. J. Messner, *Social Ethics,* J. J. Doherty, trans., (St Louis, Mo: B. Herder, 1949), 196.

15. H. Rommen, *The State in Catholic Thought,* (St. Louis, Mo. and London: B. Herder, 1945), 301.

16. Messner, op. cit., 138.

17. Rommen, op. cit., 301.

18. Herman Dooyeweerd describes the Thomist conception as "universalist." See his *Roots of Western Culture*, J. Kraay, trans., (Toronto: Wedge, 1979), 122-23, 129-31; *A New Critique of Theoretical Thought*, (Amsterdam: H. J. Paris, 1953-8), 3: 208-209, 219, 221.

19. Dooyeweerd's concept of political "integration," as the relationship among citizens uniquely realized by the state, is closer in meaning to the Thomist idea of the state as a "unity of order" than he was ready to admit. See, for example, *New Critique* 3:438.

20. "50 jaar 'Quadragesimo Anno',", in *Christen democratische verkenningen* 12 (1981): 599-606. Von Nell-Breuning suggests that Pius XI may not have fully grasped the meaning of Nell-Breuning's first draft, and acknowledges that the choice of language used to describe the vocational corporations may have lent itself too easily to misinterpretation. On the other hand, he also notes that the pope's specific request to draw on the German *Genossenschaft* idea as found, for example, in Otto von Gierke, suggests that the pope did after all have a fairly clear idea of what he intended.

21. Messner, op. cit., 177.

22. Rommen, op. cit., 143.

23. This idea of juridical pluralism is elaborated in a sophisticated manner by Dooyeweerd. See, for example, *New Critique*, 3:664-93. Reluctantly, Dooyeweerd does at one point concede a certain convergence between the Catholic view and his own theory of "sphere sovereignty," though he immediately qualifies it as a "practical" rather than a "principial" one. See *Roots of Western Culture*, 126, 129. I suggest that Dooyeweerd's concern to demonstrate a radical difference between his Calvinist-inspired philosophical position and that of Thomism led him to misinterpret the latter at this point.

24. Rommen, op cit., 321-24, 351-52.

25. Ibid., 304.

26. Calvez and Perrin describe such substitution as an "accidental mode of subsidiarity" (op. cit., 336). It may be, however, that to speak of nationalization, for example, as an exercise of a subsidiary function is to stretch its meaning too far. For, if Messner is right that the concepts of subsidiarity and the common good are each other's

mirror images, then it is hard to see how the two could conflict. But there does seem to be such a conflict in this case. When the state nationalizes an industry, it is not performing a subsidiary function towards that industry as such, but rather towards society as a whole. The "aid" being given here cannot really be regarded as being given to the industry, since the industry's independent existence comes to an end.

27. Ibid., 332.

28. Compare this line of argument with J. D. Dengerink's analysis of subsidiarity in "De staat in de plurale samenleving," *Philosophia Reformata*, 56e jrg, 1991, no. 2: 132-57, from which I have profited in preparing this article. This is an extended review of a recent restatement of Christian Democratic political theory produced by the research institute of the Dutch Christian Democrats, for which see Wetenschappelijk Instituut voor het CDA, *Publiek gerechtigheid: een christen-democratische visie op de rol van de overheid in de samenleving*, (Houten: Bohn Stafleu Van Loghum, 1990). Dengerink proposes a somewhat different reformulation of the principle of subsidiarity. He suggests that it is valid as a principle calling for the decentralization of decision-making within any particular community, but is unhelpful as a way of distinguishing between different kinds of authority possessed by different kinds of community (154).

29. Dooyeweerd's classification of "social relationships" (including a wide range of communities and others kinds of relationships) is a remarkably fruitful, if partially flawed, attempt to map their rich complexity. For a brief statement of this classification, see Herman Dooyeweerd, *A Christian Theory of Social Institutions*, trans. M. Verbrugge, ed. J. Witte, Jr., (La Jolla, CA.: Herman Dooyeweerd Foundation, 1986).

30. Dengerink suggests that one of the problems with the concept of subsidiarity is that it implies that the decision as to whether as a matter of fact a lower community is fulfilling its function adequately ultimately falls to the state, thus rendering the rights of the lower communities dependent on the state (Dengerink, op. cit., 141-42). I am not sure that this need be regarded as a criticism. It is, inescapably, the duty of the state to determine the circumstances in which its interventions are necessary. We cannot hold the state responsible for ensuring public justice (or the common good) but deny it the right finally to decide when an issue of public justice is at stake. So long as the rights of other communities are securely established in law and so long as the government upholds the principle of the rule of law (and this principle is really enforceable by the courts), the independence of other communities need not be threatened. The main threat to this independence arises from the lack of sufficient legal protection for the rights of communities, not from the fact that the state must decide finally when such legal rights are in fact infringed.

31. Contrary to Dooyeweerd, I do not think that what he terms "public justice" alone can suffice to define the distinctive nature of the state. Something like the idea of the "common good" is also necessary (and, I suggest, is operative in his own thought, though there is no space to develop that view here). This point is briefly developed in my contribution to the volume cited in the note immediately following this essay.

Arendt on Polis, Nation-State and Federation

David T. Koyzis

In recent years, considerable attention has been paid to the thought of Hannah Arendt, the late political theorist whose explorations of the life of action and the life of the mind have earned her a place of respect among contemporary intellectual figures.[1] Her unconventional thought is difficult to classify in traditional categories such as left and right or progressive and conservative. At least one observer has placed her on the left, whereas others might be inclined to see her as a conservative of some sort.[2] Her concern with popular participation in public affairs would seem to put her in league with the Rousseauan tradition of the revolutionary left, whereas her (political) unconcern with poverty and her insistence that the "social question" is not a proper matter for the public realm seem to ally her with the right.

More accurately she might be described (along with the likes of Bernard Crick and Sheldon S. Wolin[3]) as a partisan of politics as a distinctive enterprise, given her lifelong preoccupation with differentiating the life of action from both work and labor, and the *vita activa* as a whole from the *vita contemplativa*. With roots in both European existentialism and in the Aristotelian tradition, her thought can be understood as an attempt to restore the dignity which she believes the public realm has lost in the centuries since its zenith in classical antiquity. Accordingly she is concerned to protect the genuine public realm from the inroads of economics, on the one hand, and of the ideologies, on the other.

In this essay I wish to explore Arendt's reflections on the western European nation-state and how her unique concept of politics interacts with this theme. Specifically, I shall briefly explain her notion of politics as founded on the polis, how politics is diminished in the nation-state, and how she works out her vision for a federal realization of the polis in the modern age as an alternative to the nation-state. In so doing, I wish to argue that, whatever deficiencies may exist in her concept of politics (which are beyond the scope of this essay), her preference for federal over unitary polities is basically sound.

The Polis as the Standard for Politics

For Arendt the ancient polis is the standard by which all other political phenomena must be measured. So attached is she to this somewhat idealized conception that her thought has been labelled an exercise in "Hellenic nostalgia."[4] The polis represents the most perfect realization of the public realm, precisely because it is a small-scale enterprise able to accommodate both community and individuality. Within the polis, men[5] meet as equals, free from the rhythmic and repetitive processes of natural life. Here there exists neither ruling nor being ruled. By contrast, the vast numbers of people encompassed in the empires of old, as well as in the modern bureaucratic state, render equality meaningless. In such contexts individuality is submerged within a mass of people who are capable only of being ruled and are stripped of their innate ability to act. Within the polis, however, there is no room for the coercion characteristic of the bureaucratic state. The cooperation needed for common action is secured instead by means of speech and persuasion, which are the only methods appropriate in a community of equals.

Action is one of the fundamental concepts of Arendt's political theory, and it is what genuine politics is all about. It is the most human of activities, which transcends the productive activities of work as well as the reproductive activities of *labor*. As Leah Bradshaw puts it, "action is history. It is men acting in the plural, creating and destroying communities and performing other sorts of changes in the world that subsequently are recorded by historians and story-tellers."[6] It presupposes the public space created by work but is not bound by its limitations. Arendt is rather cryptic concerning the proper object of action. We know that the social question is excluded, since the amelioration of poverty is a matter of technique or "the administration of things." But its positive contents seem to be filled by any matter over which genuinely free choice is possible.[7] Action and freedom are therefore closely identified. The polis is the arena in which this freedom finds a permanent home in the world.

The trend since antiquity away from the polis and towards various types of centralized rule means nothing less than the gradual erosion of the political and its replacement by what she refers to as the "social." As we shall see below, the "social," or "society," is for Arendt something along the lines of a false politics, which tends over time to replace the genuine article in much the same fashion as weeds choke out a lawn. There have historically been several stages in the advance of the social at the expense of the political, one of which corresponds to the rise of the nation-state.

In Arendt's classic work, *The Origins of Totalitarianism*,[8] which is devoted mainly to accounting for the rise of the totalitarian ideologies of this century, a secondary theme is woven through the fabric of her argument, namely, the role of the nation-state. She continues her treatment of this theme in *The Human Condition*. It is against the backdrop of the rise and decline of the nation-state that the ideologies played out their roles climaxing in the horrors of the two world wars. Without an understanding of the place of the nation-state in the history of Europe, Arendt believes that it is impossible to account for the rise of the "tribal" ideologies of racism, antisemitism, imperialism and the "pan-" movements (e.g., pan-

Slavism and pan-Germanism). In *The Origins* Arendt largely defends the nation-state against the totalitarians. In *The Human Condition* she is more negative in her evaluation, since she sees it as a far from adequate setting for the action and speech which make up genuine politics.

The Nation-State: Definition and Development

Arendt's conception of the nation-state is closely related to that of society, a specialized term she uses to describe a modern perversion of the public realm in which concerns formerly (and quite properly) limited to the private realm are exposed to the light of day and take on public significance.[9] Matters once related only to the management of the household, which was subject to the strictest inequality, have now become the business of the public realm. It is characteristic of the modern age that the word "economy"—originally referring only to the management of the *oikia*, or household—has been expanded to mean a "nation-wide administration of housekeeping."[10] Whereas the public realm is characterized by an equality in which all participants are equally free to *act*, the social realm is characterized simultaneously by that inequality once restricted to the private realm and by a false levelling equality in which all persons are equally compelled to *behave* according to the conformity inherent in society.[11]

To rule over others, that is, to compel them to conform to economic or ideological necessity, is not in accordance with the genuinely political, as Arendt understands it. A society of men can come together for the purpose of administering a household or an entire city. Aristotle took care to distinguish the rule of the household from life in the polis—a distinction which Arendt wholeheartedly endorses. Society, by contrast, knows no such distinction: the state is nothing other than an enlarged household, and to rule the former is essentially no different from ruling the latter.

Society, where necessity has triumphed over freedom, is organized politically (or rather pseudo-politically) in the form of the nation-state.[12] Again the private realm is the realm of the household, economic concerns, the family and its property. Similarly, the modern nation, though greatly enlarged in scope, is conceived to be an immense household, a macro-economy, an extended family with its own national territory. The difference between the household and the nation-state lies not in any qualitative characteristics but in the size of the operation. It is significant that this nation-wide family is not content to exist alongside the private family, as was the public realm of antiquity. It is actually a substitute family, a surrogate household which tends to replace the private family. The social realm, unlike the public realm, does not respect the sanctity of the private realm and tries to erase the boundary between the two.[13]

There are two important preconditions for the existence of the nation-state, namely, "homogeneity of population and its rootedness in the soil of a given territory."[14] Homogeneity can be understood in two senses. Ethnic or cultural homogeneity is possibly the more obvious. Supposed kinship and blood ties lend further credence to this conception of the nation-state as a family which is thus to be administered and ruled as such.[15] But homogeneity can also be understood in the wider sense of a unified will of the nation which may or may not claim an ethnic base. This unified will is expressed by means of national institutions and through the centralized state apparatus. It may come about spontaneously as a result of a common national interest or a self-conscious internal solidarity. It is expressed in the "active consent" of the people to the government which they recognize as the legitimate representative of their interest.[16] But this consent can also be cultivated in or enforced upon those who, for any number of reasons (again not necessarily ethnic), remain outside or on the fringes of the nation. Arendt uses "homogeneity" in both the narrower and wider senses.

This homogeneous population must be rooted in the soil of a given territory. This requires, first of all, the existence of an emancipated peasant class in a settled agricultural economy, and secondly, a limited national territory which is relatively compact.[17] If the nation-state is conceived in terms of a large family, its territory is analogous to the family's property.[18] Like this property, the territory of the nation-state has definite geographical limits. However, whereas property is privately owned by the family, the national territory is *collectively* owned by society as a whole.

The rise of the nation-state occurred in western Europe where the presence of these two preconditions made such a development possible. Although it did not come into its own before the nineteenth century, the origins of the nation-state go back to the end of the medieval era and the breakdown of the feudal order. During the ensuing era of absolutism, the king alone could claim to be the visible representative of his subjects' interests. But with the demise of the monarchy, the last bond between "a centralized state and an atomized society" disappeared,[19] and the common nationality of the citizenry seemed to be the sole remaining bond. This common nationality made itself felt in terms of homogeneity, either of culture or of will, and expressed itself by means of nationalism.

In recounting the history of the nation-state Arendt makes much of the tension between law and popular will which is seemingly inherent in this institution. Whereas law is stable and dependable and is rooted in the conviction that all people, including minorities, should be treated equally under its provisions, the popular will is fleeting and changeable and easily becomes oppressive of minorities. The twin concepts of nation and state, representing popular will and law, respectively, were joined at the time of the French Revolution, and in this symbiotic union they came to dominate the politics of the following century. Although both ideas were defended by the same persons on the basis of a single ideology, the inevitable tension between the two eventually led to the collapse of the European nation-state system.

By nation Arendt means one of a number of peoples which have become conscious of themselves . . .

> as cultural and historical entities, and of their territory as a permanent home, where history [has] left its visible traces, whose cultivation was the product of the common labor of their ancestors and whose future . . . depend[s] upon the course of a common civilization.[20]

Although in its original and ideal form nation and state were co-extensive, there was always the potential for the nation to operate apart from political organization and to conceive of itself as the source of all law and thus above the law. This new notion of national consciousness expressed itself in the demand for national sovereignty, a revolutionary slogan which echoed time and again throughout the nineteenth century.

The state, on the other hand, was inherited from the earlier monarchies and, even in the form of the nation-state, continued to function as the supreme legal institution, whose task it was to protect all the inhabitants of a territory.[21] With the coming of the French Revolution, this came to mean the protection of the Rights of Man, which were declared to be the inalienable heritage of all persons.[22] These rights were seen to be the basis of law rather than based upon law. The law (and the body politic in general) came to be seen as dependent for its validity upon something outside the public realm, which for Arendt can only result in the diminution of the latter's status. Rights existed prior to and apart from the body politic, and the possibility remained that the Rights of Man could be separated from the state. For Arendt, however, the state, insofar as it remains a state and carries out its appointed task, is a law-state (*Rechtsstaat*) and is characterized by the rule of law. Such a state militates against all attempts to locate an absolute outside of the law itself whether in the person of an absolute monarch or in the will of an absolute nation.[23] This lawful character was the saving feature of the nation-state.

When the demand for national sovereignty and the declaration of the Rights of Man were joined in a single ideology, this created two polarities which eventually proved to be mutually incompatible. Since the nation is sovereign or supreme, it cannot ultimately be subject to law. On the other hand, the declaration of the Rights of Man proclaimed a universal law to which all men could appeal irrespective of national origin. This contradiction was not immediately manifest, and it became the task of the nation-state to maintain a careful, often precarious, balance between nation and state, national sovereignty and the Rights of Man, the will of the people and the rule of law.[24]

Such a balance was indeed preserved until the end of the nineteenth century when the system of nation-states began to break down. At that point the tension between nation and state could no longer be held in suspension and the former finally conquered the latter.[25] National sovereignty finally won out over the Rights of Man as the nation increasingly refused to be bound by laws and justified its own arbitrariness in terms of the will of the nation or a mystical national soul. This development was especially acute in eastern Europe which had neither of the preconditions for the growth of the nation-state. The attempt to transplant this western European institution into this "belt of mixed populations"[26] to which it was ill-suited met with dire results and contributed to the growth of totalitarian ideologies.[27] The relationship between national sovereignty and the rights of minorities is crucial to Arendt's thinking, as we shall see shortly.

Political and Unpolitical Elements in the Nation-State

In *The Origins*, Arendt takes a largely positive attitude towards the nation-state for at least four reasons. First of all, it was in principle not tied to any specific class, and could therefore make a plausible claim to embody the national interest as a whole.[28] Second, the structure of the nation-state demanded equality of all citizens within the body politic.[29] This characteristic the nation-state shared with the ancient polis, whose form of government could be labelled isonomy, implying that it embodied "equality within the range of the law."[30] Third, along with this equality followed the conviction that the legitimacy of government rests upon the consent of the governed. This served as a potential check on the activities of the government and kept it from becoming tyrannical.[31] Fourth, the nation-state was territorially limited. According to Arendt, freedom has thrived only where it is spatially limited,[32] because it is only within the intimacy of a small community that individuals are able to distinguish themselves through speech and action. Even if the nation-state was too large to be a proper setting for speech and action, it was still contained within limits.

In short, Arendt believes that to a small extent the nation-state still offered a *political* form of organization. But of course, this typical product of modernity is not the polis of antiquity. To the extent that history has moved away from the small-scale Greek city-state, where genuine action was possible, and towards the large-scale homogeneous nation-state, which by its very size demands conformity to cement its internal unity, the "political" has been submerged within the "social," and another step has been taken in the process of alienation from the world.

Above all, Arendt is critical of the nation-state's claim to possess sovereignty. She sees sovereignty as the attempt to be complete master of one's own destiny, even at the expense of others. Sovereignty ignores what she calls the human condition of plurality, that is, that "not one man, but men inhabit the earth."[33] It represents an effort to free oneself from the intrinsic "weakness" of plurality, from the presence of others who may limit one's ability to act freely. But since plurality is part of the human condition, sovereignty is a dangerous illusion, particularly when imported into the public realm.[34] Indeed, for Arendt genuine political action requires plurality, in the same way perhaps that a theatrical actor requires both fellow actors and an audience in order, not only to give his own performance meaning, but also to realize the play as a whole.

We noted above that at first glance Arendt's political vision seems to be close to Rousseau's. Both reject large centralized government in favor of the small-scale city-state. And neither is friendly towards the idea that citizens should give up their capacity for political action to a representative assembly. But it is on the issue of sovereignty that Arendt parts decisively with Rousseau. She rejects the absolutism inherent in the *volonté général*, since its majoritarian character is likely to lead to arbitrariness and oppression, particularly of minorities.[35] The modern nation-state has inherited this absolutist character. If sovereignty entails the elimination of the human condition of plurality, then the subject of that sovereignty is ultimately unable to tolerate those who do not conform to the homogeneous character of its population. The nation-state is not easily able to accommodate unassimilable minorities.

In *The Origins* Arendt discusses at some length the Minority Treaties which were framed after the first world war.[36] It will be recalled that after the war the victorious western allies carved up the old multi-ethnic empires of central and eastern Europe and set up in their place western style nation-states which would presumably reflect the ethnic make-up of the continent with greater accuracy. But given the fact that the various ethnic groups within this "belt of mixed populations" were not easily separable into compact, contiguous geographic units, millions of ethnic minorities were left on the wrong side of the new political boundaries. Consequently Minority Treaties were drafted which gave the new League of Nations responsibility for protecting their rights. Of course, the League was unable to extend such protection because it lacked any effective power.

Why is this so significant for Arendt and why does she spend so much time on the plight of "stateless" people? The fact that she was herself twice a refugee is without doubt the principal reason. When Hitler came to power in 1933 she left Germany for France. After France fell to the Nazis she left that country in 1941 and went to the United States. From the time she fled Germany to the time she acquired American citizenship eighteen years later, Arendt was stateless and without political rights.[36] It might also be pointed out that her native city of Königsberg, in what was then East Prussia (also the home of Immanuel Kant), is now called Kaliningrad and is part of the Russian Soviet Federated Socialist Republic of the Soviet Union. It takes little imagination to understand why someone so affected by the turmoil of the present century should worry so much about "worldlessness" and care about people finding a place in the world.

Despite the fact that Arendt and Rousseau both champion the small communitarian republic and abhor the large centralized state, it is not accidental that one of the more centralized nation-states, namely the French Republic, looks back to Rousseau as one of its spiritual progenitors. Arendt's protestations against sovereignty and political absolutism are in an important respect closer to Alexis de Tocqueville's analysis of democracy as a potentially levelling phenomenon stifling individuality and leading to majoritarian tyranny. The nation-state, which claims sovereignty and regards itself as the expression of a single unified national community, not only stifles genuine politics but is also unable to accommodate the political aspirations of minorities who are very often the victims of such tyranny.

A Federal Realization of the Polis in the Modern Age

What then is her alternative to the modern nation-state and other forms of political absolutism? How is it possible to bring back the ancient polis whose very existence was, after all, predicated on an elitist male-dominated agrarian society of slaveholders? Of course, it is not possible to resurrect political forms of the distant past, and there is a certain pessimism running through her analysis of polis-like communities which have risen and fallen in the ensuing years. Yet we know something of what she favored from her treatment of such phenomena as the town meetings of New England, the revolutionary societies of the French Revolution, the soviets of the Russian Revolution, and the workers councils of the failed Hungarian Revolution of 1958. And although she believed that the American Revolution fell short of her ideal of true politics, she nevertheless expressed admiration for American federalism which divides sovereignty between two levels of government and even within each level. According to Arendt there is an "intimate connection between the spirit of revolution and the principle of federation."[38]

In *On Revolution* Arendt sets forth what is probably the clearest statement as to what a *politically* organized community (that is, one that embodies the polis and thus facilitates speech and action) might look like in the modern age. This occurs initially in the context of her discussion of Thomas Jefferson's proposed "ward system," which she sees as a way to institutionalize and give a permanent home to the fleeting popularly-based local councils which have come into being spontaneously in the initial stages of the revolutions.[39] The ward system, conceived in Jefferson's later years, would have multiplied the spaces for freedom by creating "elementary republics" where public-spirited citizens could come together to speak and act. The tragedy of the American Revolution, as Arendt sees it, is that, while it was so laden with possibilities for accommodating a free citizenry's capacity for action, it never fully realized this potential and the federal principle stopped at the state level.[40]

Arendt's ideal republic carries the federal principle much farther.[41] Beginning with the elementary republics and councils at the local level, there is an ascending hierarchy of republics with numerous levels between the lowest and highest bodies. The members of the elementary councils elect a representative to sit in the council at the next level, and so on up the ladder. The members of the highest council are not therefore directly elected by the citizens, but by the members of the several councils at the second-highest level. The country as a whole (if we are even justified in speaking in such terms) could thus be characterized as a federation of federations or a republic of republics. Authority does not flow from the top downwards as in authoritarian systems. Rather, "in this case authority [is] generated neither at the top nor at the bottom, but on each of the pyramid's layers."[42] Although the elementary councils are open to the participation of all, only those who are public-spirited actually take the opportunity to enter the public realm to speak and act. The system thus turns out to be somewhat elitist, but only in the sense that those who do choose to participate are very likely to remain a small minority of the community as a whole. No one is forced into the public realm, but no one is kept out either.

Despite the fact that the polis and the revolutionary workers' councils she celebrates were such short-lived phenomena, Arendt nevertheless speaks of such councils as glorious attempts to find a *permanent* home in the world for action and speech. And although there is some incongruity between her desire for permanence and her use of such transitory examples, she is possibly on firmer ground in extolling the New England town meetings and the Swiss cantonal meetings, which have endured for centuries and are quite unrelated to the modern revolutions.

Not only does she see her federal approach to rehabilitating the public realm as practicable, she even offered it as an option to the Jewish settlers in Palestine in the 1940s in an intriguing proposal which brought together her love for the polis and her concern for the plight of stateless minorities.[43] Although Arendt considered herself a nonideological Zionist and admired the achievements of the Jewish settlers of Palestine in the 1940s, she was nevertheless critical of their attempt to construct a monolithic Jewish nation-state based on conventional western European notions of homogeneity and sovereignty. She appealed to a non-nationalist tradition of Zionism which she saw as a more realistic and more political alternative to the dominant Herzlian version.[44] Jewish residents of

Palestine, she believed, should concentrate on building up such humane institutions as the *kibbutzim* and the Hebrew University, which embodied, not the exclusivistic ideas of nationalism, but a more universal hope for all mankind. These would be the proud achievements of a Jewish homeland, but not necessarily of a Jewish nation-state.[45]

When Arendt first began writing on Zionism in the early 1940s, it was far from certain what the future would hold for a Jewish homeland in Palestine. The fact that a Jewish state seemed unfeasible at the time undoubtedly colored her analysis to some extent. She feared that attempts at founding a Jewish state could endanger the existence of a Jewish homeland, particularly because the former would meet with the hostility of the surrounding Arab population and would have to depend for its very existence on an outside imperial power. For the sake of peace it was better to drop the demands of exclusive sovereignty which, after all, could not be reconciled with identical Arab demands. A homogeneous Jewish state, created along the lines of "German-inspired nationalism"[46] would end up creating "a new category of homeless people, the Arab refugees," who would become "a dangerous potential irredenta"[47] Needless to say, her fears have been proven correct over the last forty years.

But even apart from these fears, her lifelong attachment to the polis and federal constitutions prompted her to propose a "bi-national" federal Palestine built on Arab-Jewish cooperation, which could turn the country into "a thriving peaceful Switzerland" in the Middle East.[48] Such an arrangement would have created multiple public spaces for any citizen, Jewish or Arab, to act and speak. "Local self-government and mixed Jewish-Arab municipal and rural councils, on a small scale and as numerous as possible, are the only realistic political measures that can eventually lead to the political emancipation of Palestine."[49]

Concluding Comments

In retrospect, it appears that Arendt underestimated the staying power of the nation-state, though contemporary developments are once again demonstrating both its present limitations and its cloudy future. Less than a decade after she wrote *The Origins* and *The Human Condition*, this seemingly moribund institution was again transplanted into another "belt of mixed populations," which encompassed nearly the entire continents of Africa and Asia. Local leaders on these continents were largely educated in European or North American universities and brought back with them typical western (either liberal or marxist) ideas of politics. Most of these new countries, freshly liberated from western colonial control, sought to create western style unitary nation-states which could claim to embody the democratic will of their citizens.

But with few exceptions such efforts have not been successful. In most of the countries of Africa, in particular, western-style parliamentary democracy has broken down in the absence, not only of long-standing parliamentary traditions, but also of a unified sense of national community among the citizenry. This suggests that the homogenizing nation-state, which is still the received model in much of the world, is rapidly losing its relevance amid such contemporary trends as ethnic and regional secessionist movements, on the one hand, and current efforts at supranational integration, on the other. Hannah Arendt's expressed preference for federal polities, whatever their precise characteristics, seems to this writer to be sound, given the proven inability of traditional nation-states to accommodate diverse populations within a single territory.

At this point we might note that there seems to be an historical connection between Calvinism and federalism which can be observed in the polities of several countries. These include Switzerland, the Netherlands (prior to 1795), and the United States. And although Britain has never had a federal system, at least two Commonwealth countries of largely British settlement are federal in structure, namely Canada and Australia. An intellectual link may perhaps be found in the political theory of Johannes Althusius, the early seventeenth-century Calvinist whose writings are supportive of such an arrangement.

But even apart from the historical connection, I would further argue that a normative Christian approach to politics is compatible with federalism for at least two reasons. In the first place, the division of powers implied in this form of government is not easily reconciled with absolute sovereignty resting in a mere earthly personage. No political authority is likely to esteem itself a "mortal god," in the words of Thomas Hobbes, if it is hemmed in on several sides by other authorities possessing their own constitutional power bases.

Secondly, a normative view of justice would tend to predispose the Christian towards a non-majoritarian polity in which the status of minority communities would be acknowledged and protected. Admittedly, territorial federalism does not necessarily embody or even facilitate what might be called confessional or cultural pluralism (discussed in several other contributions to this volume). But the concurrent majority principle, championed by John C. Calhoun in the context of the early American federation, can be applied in this direction, as many have observed in the consociational polities of some of the smaller nations of Europe and elsewhere.

How close is Arendt's vision of federalism to a Christian vision of pluralism? Certainly her distrust of sovereignty is commendable, and she insightfully sees through the pretensions of would-be totalitarian rulers who attempt to negate what she refers to as the "human condition of plurality" and what the Christian would see as the created structures of human life. Her desire to accommodate minorities within the body politic is also in accordance with a normative principle of justice, although justice itself is curiously absent as a fundamental concept in her political theory.

This absence points to what may be the chief limitation of Arendt's thought, namely, that she generally avoids normative language and attempts to anchor her political theory as a whole in the sum total of empirical factors that condition human existence. But, fortunately, her attempt to ground her theory in what she calls "the human condition" does not (and perhaps cannot) prevent Hannah Arendt as a person from judging that totalitarianism means the death of politics and that political systems are best structured when they allow for the participation of the citizens and accommodate the aspirations of minorities.

Notes

1. The substance of Arendt's philosophy is contained primarily within two books: *The Human Condition*, (Chicago: University of Chicago Press, 1958) and *The Life of the Mind*, (New York: Harcourt Brace Jovanovich, 1978), the latter of which was published posthumously in its incomplete form. *In The Human Condition* she explores the three human activities within the *vita activa*, viz., labor, work and action. *The Life of the Mind*, published in two volumes, explores two faculties within the *vita contemplativa*, viz., thinking and willing. A third faculty, judging, remains only partially treated due to Arendt's death. See her posthumously published *Lectures on Kant's Political Philosophy*, edited by Ronald Beiner, (Chicago: University of Chicago Press, 1982). Recent books about Arendt's life and work include Elisabeth Young-Bruehl's biographical *Hannah Arendt: For Love of the World*, (New Haven: Yale University Press, 1982) and Leah Bradshaw, *Acting and Thinking: The Political Thought of Hannah Arendt*, (Toronto: University of Toronto Press, 1989).
2. In a letter to Arendt, Gershom Scholem identifies her with the "German Left," a label which she herself explicitly rejects in her response. This letter is published in Hannah Arendt, *The Jew as Pariah: Jewish Identity and Politics in the Modern Age*, Ron H. Feldman, ed., (New York: Grove Press, 1978), 240-51. Cf. Melvyn A. Hill, ed., *Hannah Arendt: The Recovery of the Public World*, (New York: St. Martin's, 1979), 333-34.
3. See Bernard Crick, *In Defence of Politics*, 2nd ed., (Harmondsworth, England: Penguin Books, 1982); and Sheldon S. Wolin, *Politics and Vision: Continuity and Innovation in Western Political Thought*, (Boston: Little, Brown and Company, 1960).
4. Noel O'Sullivan, "Hannah Arendt: Hellenic Nostalgia and Industrial Society," Anthony de Crespigny and Kenneth Minogue, eds., *Contemporary Political Philosophers*, (New York: Dodd, Mead and Co., 1975), 228-51.
5. With due respect to current conventions concerning inclusive language, I shall at several points in this essay use the term "men" to apply to those engaging in political action in the public realm. This is for two reasons: first, in the ancient polis itself, which Arendt treats at some length in *The Human Condition*, citizenship was limited to male heads of household; and second, Arendt herself uses it, even

when applied to modern bodies politic in which women possess full rights of citizenship.

6. Bradshaw, p. 10. The reference to "creating and destroying" seems somewhat out of place, since these seem to be the deeds, not of the actor (i.e., the one participating in action), but of the fabricator who engages in the activity of work. Nevertheless, this ambiguity concerning the identity of the heroic deeds recounted by story-tellers is present in Arendt herself. See, e.g., her discussion in *The Human Condition* (193 f.) of the deeds of Achilles, which, though performed in the context of the violence of the Trojan War and would thus seem to bear the characteristics of fabrication, she nevertheless sees as examples of action.

7. At a conference at York University in 1972, Arendt was asked pointedly what she conceived action and speech to be about. Her reply follows:

> Life changes constantly, and things are constantly there that want to be talked about. At all times people living together will have affairs that belong in the realm of the public—"are worthy to be talked about in public." What these matters are at any historical *moment* is probably *utterly* different. For instance, the great cathedrals were the public spaces of the Middle Ages. The town halls came later. And there perhaps they had to talk about a matter which is not without any interest either: the question of God. So what becomes public at every given period seems to me utterly different [Melvyn Hill, ed., *Hannah Arendt: The Recovery of the Public World*, (New York: St. Martin's, 1979), 316].

This is possibly the clearest statement Arendt made concerning the subject matter of action.

8. New York: Harcourt Brace Jovanovich, 1951.

9. *Human Condition*, 38f.

10. Ibid., 28.

11. Ibid., 41-42.

12. Ibid., 29.

13. Ibid., 59.

14. Ibid., 256.

15. *Origins*, 165f; *Human Condition*, 256.

16. *Origins*, 125.

17. Ibid., 228-29.

18. *Human Condition*, 256.

19. *Origins*, 231.

20. Ibid., 229.

21. Ibid., 230.

22. Ibid., 290f.

23. Arendt, *On Revolution* (New York: The Viking Press, 1963), 179f.

24. *Origins*, 229f.

25. Ibid., 275.

26. Ibid., 232, quoting C. A. Macartney.

27. Ibid., 269f.

28. Ibid., 17.

29. Ibid., 290.

30. *On Revolution*, 23.

31. *Origins*, 124f.

32. *On Revolution*, 279.

33. *Human Condition*, 234.

34. Arendt, *Between Past and Future,* (Harmondsworth, England: Penguin Books, 1977), 164-65.

35. Rousseau himself, of course, did not intend that the general will should lead to tyranny of the majority. He was careful to distinguish between the will of all, which is simply the sum of particular wills, and the general will, by which the sovereign assembly performs only those acts that are general in nature and in object (*Social Contract*, II.3). Nevertheless, the ambiguity in his concept of the general will, coupled with his aversion to particular communities that might fragment it, lend some weight to Arendt's charge that Rousseau has contributed to majoritarian politics.

36. *Origins*, 269f.

37. Young-Bruehl, 113f.

38. *On Revolution*, 270.

39. Ibid., 252-60.

40. Ibid., 241-42.

41. Ibid., 279-85.

42. Ibid., 282.

43. See Young-Bruehl, 222f, for an account of Arendt's associations with Judah Magnes, Hans Kohn, and other Jewish intellectuals who earlier suggested a federal solution for the Palestine question.

44. Arendt, "Peace or Armistice in the Near East," *Review of Politics*, vol. 12, no. 1, (January, 1950); reprinted in *The Jew as Pariah*, 209f.

45. Ibid., 212-15.

46. "Zionism Reconsidered," *Menorah Journal*, (October, 1944); reprinted in *Jew as Pariah*, 156.

47. "Peace or Armistice," ibid., 214.

48. Ibid., 212, quoting Dr. Judah L. Magnes, President of Hebrew University.

49. "To Save the Jewish Homeland: There is Still Time," ibid., 192.

David Mitrany's Functionalist World Order

Justin Cooper

Introduction

In the literature of international relations the functionalist approach to international order occupies a unique position. Although functionalism has never become a well-developed school of thought within the discipline, it nevertheless presents a distinctive rationale for international organizations which occupies the conceptual space between the realist idea of a system of independent states and the idealist notion of a world state. Rejecting the state as the principal political structure for maintaining international peace and justice, functionalism instead envisions a gradual transformation of the international system, under the impetus of science and technology, into a functional international order characterized by the predominance of interdependent capacities, international agencies and associative security.

In this essay we will analyze this functionalist conception of "a working peace system" as it has been presented in the thought of David Mitrany, the leading proponent of this position.[1] By summarizing its argument and clarifying its underlying assumptions, we will attempt to show that functionalism's conceptual framework is flawed by an overreliance on the transformative power of science and technology which distorts creationally-based aspects of political reality, and that, nevertheless, it raises important structural issues regarding the nature and task of international political authority.

The Background of Functionalism

Although its roots extend to the Enlightenment optimism of Kant and St.-Simon,[2] the functionalist perspective was developed at the turn of the century as scholars sought to explain the rise of international organizations and public unions which occurred in the latter half of the nineteenth and early twentieth century.[3] It had some influence in the establishment of the special committees of the League of Nations and reached its zenith in the 1940s, both conceptually in the thought of Mitrany and practically in the creation of the specialized agencies of the United Nations. Functionalism was also later modified in the 50s and 60s by the neofunctionalists, who sought to explain the phenomenon of integration in the European Economic Community.[4]

To be understood properly, functionalism in international relations must be distinguished from sociological functionalism, as pioneered by Parsons and Merton and which seeks to explain how equilibrium is maintained in a society. The assumption that "form follows function" is taken in international functionalism as the basis for a conception of gradual but significant social and political change leading to the emergence of new functions, novel international political institutions and a world society.

Finally, functionalists do not attempt to provide a well worked out theory or blueprint of future world order. Rather, consistent with their basic pragmatic orientation, functionalists prefer an open-ended and somewhat eclectic approach which focuses on what Mitrany calls "the relation of things," that is, the principal factors at work in this gradual process of change,[5] while leaving the specific details of its institutional results to the interplay between experiment and experience, social need and institutional response.

This has contributed to the fact that functionalism has never developed as a school of thought and also makes it necessary to reconstruct the functionalist argument in order to arrive at a coherent summary. However, as will become clear in the section which follows, the functionalist approach, despite its pragmatic and eclectic character, does provide a interpretative framework in terms of which to understand future world order.

A Summary of the Functionalist Argument

The functionalist argument is based on a thoroughly historical view of social and political institutions, which is understood in terms of a dynamic interaction between state and society. Given this fundamentally developmental perspective, functionalism focuses on the political changes which have occurred over the past century as science and technology have become increasingly dynamic factors in western society. According to functionalism, what we are witnessing is a process which will fundamentally alter the nation-state and its overriding predominance as a cultural and political entity.

The functionalist account of this process of political evolution is a complex one which involves all three levels of analysis: the attitudes and loyalties of persons are expected to be refocussed, the structure and capacities of states altered and the nature and *modus operandi* of the international system transformed. Central to this process is a decoupling of cultural identity from the state, allowing the emergence of ethnic, regional or religious communities as well as a world society, and a shift in the organization of political authority from a territorial to a functional basis and, at least in part, from a national to a supranational or international level, leading to the development of a non-hierarchical working peace system.

To provide a rationale for this vision, Mitrany's functionalist argument begins by emphasizing the novel social conditions which have been created by the rise of modern science and its technological application to daily life. Mitrany points to three areas of novelty in this century: the capacity of science and technology to create improved social conditions and material abundance, the increasing popular demand for such economic advancement and social welfare, and the tendency of the technological capabilities which are developed (such as air travel and radio communications) to shrink distances, transcend the boundaries of nation-states and generate problems which are beyond the capacity of these states to address individually.[6]

In these trends Mitrany sees a dynamism which is linked to a process of political institution-building with positive international consequences. The precise nature of this link can be clarified by focusing on the nature of a "function." In the development of such new functions, Mitrany sees a conjunction of technical imperatives and political organization with great potential for the emergence of a peaceful world order.

When functionalists refer to the development of new functions in the economic, social and technical areas, they mean practical tasks or services which utilize some technology in their performance, require some form of continuous supervision if they are to operate properly, and fulfill some general society-wide need. Since supervision is required for such functions to be carried out properly, this leads to the establishment of administrative or regulatory organizations which at the same time utilize the relevant technical skills associated with the task in question.

Furthermore, because the need is general, a new area of political responsibility is thereby created, with the result that the function is either performed or regulated by government. However, since the task is a specialized and technical one, the authority established to oversee it is usually a single-purpose agency which is organized separately from the main administrative apparatus of government.

Referring to "technical self-determination" as one of the "cardinal virtues of a functional approach," Mitrany maintains that a function itself can, often does and should serve as a factor in the institutionalizing process,[7] determining the scope of jurisdiction and the administrative organs most appropriate for effective operation. Depending on the function involved, this may mean an agency with regional, continental or global jurisdiction, with responsibilities ranging from general coordination to daily management of activities. For Mitrany, education is an example of a function to be dealt with on a regional basis within existing state boundaries, while rail travel in the European context is a continental affair and air travel a global concern. His point is that in each case the nature of the function should be paramount and not the political boundaries of nation-states.

However, since the operative scope of technologically based functions (or their ecological side-effects) is often wider than the territory defined by the boundaries of existing nation-states, functionalists expect many new functional agencies to be transnational or international in scope. This is also supported by the observation that in most functional areas the "common index of need" obtains, whereby a basic human need and the method for satisfying it are similar across different states.[8]

But why should such international functional agencies contribute to the development of a more peaceful world order? The answer to this question lies in Mitrany's understanding of the nature of functional institutions and their impact on national populations and on the structure of the state itself. Since functionalism is only a method or approach, no detailed account of the typical structure is provided. Nevertheless, certain key features can be discerned.

Functional agencies are independent of any state, having limited authority over a specific function which requires a transnational or international jurisdiction. Further, they are administered by experts with relevant technical knowledge, who are responsible to councils or "functional parliaments" made up of representatives allocated proportionally according to the relevant functional capacity of each member state and drawn from the respective public which is served.[9] Finally, they operate as much as possible on a consensual basis, using empirical evidence obtained by scientific method as the basis for decisions and, if necessary, employing only non-violent enforcement techniques, involving the threat of a withdrawal of service or membership rather than of physical force or violence as a means of ensuring compliance to rules.

Mitrany often contrasts the technical or functional with the political in order to indicate the novel and non-state character of functional agencies. Evident here is his contention that many international disputes which are in fact technical in character become distorted when inappropriately combined with ideological or nationalistic considerations by leaders of nation-states. Hence his conclusion that, if such areas are organizationally separate and thereby insulated from such considerations, they will be administered in a more efficient and conflict-free manner. In effect, then, despite Mitrany's distinction of the technical and the political, functional agencies represent a novel kind of political institution, spawned by the technological age, which is distinct from the state in its organization and mode of operation.

According to the functionalist thesis, the development of an increasing number of such functional institutions will have a significant effect on the nation-state, diminishing its present preponderance on the domestic as well as the international scene. With the establishment of each functional institution, Mitrany argues that "a slice of sovereignty" is being removed from the participating states and pooled in the international institution. Such piecemeal transfers of sovereignty are central to the contention that the functionalist approach represents a practical but substantive means of "sneaking up" on sovereignty, without resorting to the improbable vision of the wholesale surrender of the sovereignty of states to a world government.[10]

However, if the functionalist approach would in fact diminish sovereignty, why should the leaders of states be expected to allow such a development? Mitrany suggests several reasons. First, scientific discovery and technological innovation will continue to develop new devices which are of such a nature that they cannot be used without international cooperation to set common standards or coordinate activities. The reality of a shared environment which is affected by the side-effects of such technological advancement is a negative example of the same principle. Here the emphasis falls on unintended consequences and the tenor is deterministic as Mitrany speaks of governments being "forced" to adapt to new realities.11

Second, what might be called the demonstration effect is expected to operate, as successful functional experiments are copied in other fields. If functional agencies are more effective and efficient, the gain of advancement may seem worth the loss of formal control. Here the emphasis falls on the intentional choice of political decision-makers and their ability to apply lessons learned in one area to others.

Finally, Mitrany also points to pressure from the populace of modern, materialistic mass democracies as a factor which will facilitate the development of authoritative functional agencies. Demands for the greater welfare which such administration would bring are expected to encourage otherwise reluctant governments to place certain areas of jurisdiction under the functional aegis.12

In this type of pressure Mitrany sees not only potential for change in the administrative structure and capacity of states but also a point of entry into the citadel of nationalism which maintains a sense of political legitimacy and cultural identity as the exclusive preserve of the state. Specifically, three changes related to the identity and outlook of persons are included in Mitrany's conception of the movement toward a working peace system. First, as the efficacy of functional agencies is demonstrated, he asserts that a sense of loyalty and legitimacy will develop which will serve to break the state's monopoly and lead to a situation of multiple loyalties, paralleling the piecemeal transfer of sovereignty.

Second, working with the assumption that people have the potential for both conflictual and cooperative behavior, Mitrany argues that participation in and observation of the more consensual context of functional administration will enhance the development of a cooperative ethos which supports the legitimacy of a regime of functional agencies and the diminished role of national administration.[13] Finally, given the reality of a greater amount of international interaction and of the reduced claims of the state, Mitrany envisions both the devolution of corporate identity, allowing the flowering of other regional, cultural, ethnic and religious identities discouraged by the state's demand for uniformity, and the development of a sense of belonging to a world society, encouraged by a wider experience of other peoples made possible by modern technology and facilitated by its functional regulation.[14]

The outcome of the process of transformation outlined in the preceding pages is a new type of functional international order described by Mitrany as a working peace system. Consistent with his developmental framework, this is not seen as a final result but rather as a new stage which may continue to adapt and unfold. What distinguishes it from the present, more war-prone international system is the fact that the presence of states is supplemented by a multiplicity of functional bodies of varying and geographically over-lapping jurisdictions, thereby reducing the identification of political authority with a definite territory. Mitrany refers to such a network of institutions as "various strata of government" in order to em-phasize the overall non-hierarchical character of such a configura-tion of political institutions.[15]

Mitrany also speaks about "functional federalism," a new type of political formula for unifying diverse political elements which is more effective than the complete unification of a number of states. The stages through which such a federalizing process might proceed are envisioned by Mitrany as four-fold: greater coordination within functions, coordination between related functions, the development of an international planning agency, and the emergence of an overall international authority.[16]

Specific questions such as whether this authority would con-stitute what is usually taken to be a world government are of less concern to Mitrany. Any development would take place gradually, having a basis in political experience and in a world society. What is more important, in his view, are the qualitative improvements associated with a functional international order. These can be summarized in terms of a greater realization of the basic human values of freedom, justice and peace.

A functional order promises more freedom in the ability to join a variety of associations which are not necessarily limited to a national scope, to direct cultural or ethnic affairs on a regional basis, and to participate in the direction of functional agencies to ensure that services are provided in an appropriate manner. Greater social justice is conceived in terms of the provision of an increasing material abundance and better social conditions which are equally available to all.

Finally, the culmination of this conception is the enjoyment of greater peace and stability. Peace in functionalism is understood not simply as the absence of war. Rather its meaning is broadened beyond "the old static and strategic view" to "a social view of peace" which brings nations "actively together" in the pursuit of the goals of social security. Included in this definition, however, is also the decreased likelihood of war.[17]

It is Mitrany's contention that the attenuated capacities of states together with the multiplicity of loyalties and changed attitudes of people will make it more difficult for states to go to war. Further, he maintains that conflict will be less frequent and less extensive in functional institutions and will be settled by non-violent means when necessary. Thus a working peace system represents a desirable and feasible alternative to the present states-system.

This summary of the functionalist argument clearly illustrates the distinctiveness of its vision of future world order. We turn now to an evaluation of its assumptions.

An Assessment of Functionalism

Since functionalism presents an argument for political evolution which envisions the elimination of the state's primacy under the impetus of science and technology, our assessment will first of all focus on the relation of technology and politics which is assumed and then consider the adequacy of functionalism's alternative to the state. This will in turn lead to an examination of its view of human nature and, finally, to an investigation of the central role given to science and technology.

To begin, it must be acknowledged that the argument for international functional political institutions is based on some valid observations about the relation of technology and politics. Perhaps the most significant insight of the functionalist approach is its recognition that the dynamic relationship between technological change and the public order constitutes one of the important features of the modern "relation of things." The application of new technologies in communication, industry, transportation, health, etc., as well as the unforeseen side-effects of these applications, have created new demands for public choice and/or regulation. As a result, the scope of public responsibility has increased, and with it, the size of the administrative branches of modern governments.

Furthermore, one of the useful and distinguishing features of modern technology is its reduction of the significance of geographic location, thereby creating new linkages among national societies.

However, since its functional scope is wider than the territory of any given state, the concomitant extension of public responsibility will also exceed the territorially limited administrative capacities of individual sovereign states and require some form of international collaboration. In short, the implementation of new technologies may create new demands for public justice which cannot be satisfied by the nation-state because of its territorial basis.

Finally, the exercise of this political responsibility often requires the establishment of a new institution or organization to oversee the on-going use of the technology in question. In this sense, technology may necessitate the creation of new governmental institutions at the national or international level. The dramatic increase over the past century in the number of government agencies and regulatory bodies as well as international organizations is in part due to this type of development.[18] At the international level, some of these are merely advisory or consultative, but some also perform state-like political functions of coordination and regulation.

Here the question arises as to whether such institutions can in fact serve as a satisfactory alternative to the state. The functionalist contention is one of transformation, namely, the emergence of new and better forms of government which will constitute the basis of a superior world order. To assess this position, we will examine what happens to the various creational dimensions of the state in the new functional order. Briefly, in maintaining a legal order of public justice, the state displays four main characteristics: possession of a monopoly or preponderance of coercive capacity, organization as a territorially-based and general political authority, and a basis in a sense of political community or normative consensus, in the context of which conflicts occur in the processes of decision-making. What becomes of these in a functional order?

In the international setting in which there is no monopoly of military force, the emphasis in functionalism falls on the concept of nonviolent forms of enforcement as a means of guaranteeing compliance with rules set by international organizations. Located between the less direct methods of protest and international public opinion and the more effective use of violent force, this type of coercion can be effective and therefore appears to be plausible for public institutions at the international level which do not possess an independent military capability.

However, such a non-violent capacity on the part of any given functional agency would be insufficient to deal with a general threat to overall security by an aggressive state. In such a case, a general functional embargo, if it could be worked out among the various agencies, would present a stronger measure; however, as Mitrany acknowledges, the security function would need to be addressed directly. He therefore proposes the creation of security councils, organized along continental or regional lines and separate from the administration of any state.[19]

Whether such councils would come to exercise a preponderance of force is open to question, since states would resist the transfer of this function as long as possible. However, if the functionalist prescription were followed, it is clear that it would not eliminate war, so much as provide a number of intermediate steps before the legitimate resort to force would become necessary.

The next area we will examine is the expectation of a more cooperative style of politics in the context of functional agencies. This expectation is based on two assumptions. The first has to do with the scope of the conflict involved. Because functional agencies have a specific focus, it can be argued that conflict will be limited to a given area, without interfering in other spheres of cooperation. Further, to the extent that a functional sector is built on a physical or environmental linkage of interdependence, conflict in that sector will be bounded by the need to maintain the shared framework. Scholars have begun to speak of "games of interdependence," thereby acknowledging the reality of this notion.[20]

However, the functionalist argument goes further and includes a second assumption which is expressed in the idea that the separate structure (detached from nationalistic states) and specific focus (one specialized functional area) of such institutions will result in less frequency of conflict. Essential to this contention is the distinction in functionalism between the technical and non-controversial on the one hand, and the political and controversial on the other. In terms of this distinction, functional administration is seen as a mode of public policy-making in which rational problem-solving will take place among experts on the basis of a consensus about welfare goals and the scientific procedures for determining the best means of fulfilling them. In contrast, policy-making by those connected with the state is seen as inherently more prone to conflict.

Here distortion occurs in the functionalist thesis. Conflict is associated with the imposition of symbolic values of ideology and nationalism on matters which in themselves are seen as essentially neutral and objective. Functional agencies are organized so that this improper interference will be minimized. However, functionalism does not distinguish between the subjective imposition of extraneous values and an appropriate role for value judgements which are an integral part of policy-making. Instead, the application of scientific rationality is assumed to be necessarily beneficial and unambiguous in fulfilling welfare purposes, a claim which is clearly exaggerated. In short, the functionalist view of cooperative politics purchases consensus only at the price of distorting the realities of political choice.

Having considered the dimensions of coercive capacity and conflict in policy-making, we turn now turn to the question of a general political authority. Mitrany's "functional federalism" emphasizes a gradual process of integration, which will take place first within and then between functional sectors in the absence of a comprehensive political authority, whether regional or global. Structurally, the idea that political authority need not move immediately from the limited scope of the nation-state to a comprehensive global institution merits further consideration. It is conceivable that such authority could develop in stages and at different rates in different issue areas or functional sectors, such as aviation, satellite communications and the environment.

Such an increase in the number of political authorities at the international level might in fact diminish the sovereignty of nation-states as it is now understood, thereby confirming the functionalist contention that the sovereignty of the state is historically based and malleable over time. However, certain issues of feasibility and cogency must also be noted. Functionalism tends to underestimate the ability of states to manage interdependencies on an intergovernmental basis and to overestimate the ease with which new international functional alternatives will be developed. Further, as students of the specialized agencies of the Untied Nations have noted, international administration is no less susceptible to typical bureaucratic problems of organizational inertia and empire-building and perhaps is even more so given its autonomous character.[21] Therefore, resistance to integration could be expected not just from states but from functional agencies themselves.

However, if the feasibility of gradual integration is granted, a more basic question must be posed regarding the nature of the political issues it would raise and the type of political institution required to address them. Mitrany refers to the development of an international planning agency and, finally, of an overall political authority. But inadequate attention is paid to the substantive political issues which would be raised by the interactions among functional sectors, as well as between such institutions and states and the multiplicity of other non-political associations and communities.

Mitrany does allude to an assembly of nations which could make recommendations and, in its stronger suit, set general lines of policy. However, the functionalist preoccupation with the negative effects of comprehensive political authority and its bias toward administration over legislation and specialized expert over political generalist result in a failure to address the typical political function of public legal integration which its own conception of a federalizing process would require.

Instead, functionalism assumes a process of integration in which conflicts are less frequent and restricted to low-level disputes which do not involve substantive value-judgements. Implied is a view of integration which is akin to piecemeal social engineering, gradual system-building or growing systemness, in which each specialized piece of the working peace system naturally fits into a rationally ordered whole. The image in functionalism is not so much a pluralist conception of denigrated sovereignty in favor of the sufficiency of lesser associations,[22] as "technological politics," in which governing is reduced to the recognition of what is necessary and efficient for the functioning of a large-scale system.[23]

This same pattern of reduction is also evident in Mitrany's account of community and the process of community-building. This sense of community is to provide the socio-political consensus which will support the emerging functional order.

Given the ideological and cultural diversity in the international context, the absence of common experiences and the lack of a common external enemy, the development of international or world community is indeed a difficult prospect. The functionalist approach may be understood as an attempt to base such community on a developing cosmopolitan, instrumental culture which combines the objective reality of physical and biological links of interdependence with the subjective attitudes learned from and associated with cooperation to meet material needs, including a respect for the authority of science.

Inherent in this project is a characteristic ambivalence about the role of basic values in political community. On the one hand, the ascendency of science is associated with the decline of ideology, religion and other traditional, non-empirical values on which political community has been based. On the other hand, science itself, an as authoritative avenue to effective insight and progress, serves as a new source of allegiance which forms the basis of the new global community.

If it is granted that a world-wide consensus on the importance of welfare goals is developing and, further, that the preservation of common frameworks of interdependence can serve as a effective motivation for cooperative action (e.g., saving the ozone layer), the question arises as to whether this is a sufficient foundation on which to build a viable political community of common responsibility and obligation.

On closer analysis it is evident that the essential ingredient which determines legitimacy in the context of welfare goals is that of service, benefit or advantage. Such a notion of legitimacy is capable of sustaining a mode of justice, but it remains a narrow one, bounded by expectations of mutual advantage and reciprocity, and falls far short of the deeper sense of purposive or redistributive justice which is needed to sustain obligation in the face of the sacrifices required to build community in a global setting of vast inequality.[24]

It can be argued that functionalism attempts to escape the narrow confines of a community of interests (*Gesellschaft*) by appealing to a deeper unity based on a common allegiance to science, or at least to the good of humanity which it can promote. From this perspective, each functional experiment becomes a symbol of the efficacy of scientific rationality, which improves some common condition of humanity and also promotes cooperation in achieving it. Although this quiet pragmatic faith in scientific method lacks the explicit religious trappings of St.-Simon's "new Christianity," such an allegiance is associated in functionalism with the development of a "cooperative ethos."

On a deeper level, however, the community of science-based cooperation which functionalism envisions in fact threatens the very basis of morality. Because the best need satisfiers are at the same time international agencies which link states and discourage war, a linkage is established between the individual pursuit of greater welfare and world peace, which is analogous to Adam Smith's notion of the "hidden hand." In this case it is not laissez-faire but rather the underlying logic of the piecemeal application of scientific rationality. However, the consequence is the same. Functionalism in effect makes a virtue of selfishness; cooperation becomes simply a means to the greater end of self-gratification. In short, the strategy of functionalism encourages an individualistic and materialistic ethic.

An equally serious objection to functionalism is its treatment of the human personality, which undermines human freedom and responsibility as that is exercised in statesmanship and citizenship. The functionalist approach to future world order is a gradual and indirect one, relying on unforeseen side-effects and incremental change to accomplish its purposes. But whose purposes are these? Ultimately, it is science which assumes the role of artificer of organization and creator of community in functionalism. The approach of indirection and gradualism reverses the normal relation of subject and object. Science becomes the agent of change and human personality and institutions the objects which are shaped and transformed.

This tendency comes to expression clearly in Mitrany's attitude toward political leaders. According to him, the "force of events," which in effect means science-induced change, will overtake their commitment to outmoded dogmas of national sovereignty.[25] Such reliance on instrumental rationality to create situations which will compel decisions by political leaders removes their political responsibility to evaluate and respond. "Sneaking up" on sovereignty turns out to be a denial of the freedom of statesmanship.

However, this approach is not restricted to recalcitrant politicians. The same tendency is apparent in the notion of community-building through changes in the attitudes and loyalties of the general populace. In the functionalist idea of social learning, such change takes place not so much by rational persuasion as through insight gained in actual experience. However, the key to this positive experience is a functionally restructured and administered social and political order. Only in such an environment can the experience of the cooperative fulfillment of needs occur, thereby imparting new knowledge about its value and source. Thus organization, as shaped by the principles of instrumental rationality, is given primacy.

Such a process takes on the character of manipulative rehabilitation and reinforcement of behavior to achieve a desired result in a mass populace rather than an appeal to the conscious political choice associated with citizenship. Through reorganization and rehabilitation, science becomes the transformer of human subjectivity. In structuring the environment in order to pre-determine outcomes, the piecemeal social engineering of the functionalist approach to world order undermines human responsibility and choice which are the very basis of human dignity.

The conceptual problems which have been disclosed in our analysis of the functionalist argument are neither superficial nor random but rather stem from a common religious root. The elevation of science to the position of paradigm in the gradual transformation of the polity toward a functional alternative results in the reduction of political realities and the distortion of both science and politics. The place of normative issues in political decision-making, the task of political integration and the nature of political community are not properly recognized and therefore the creational task and dimensions of the state are not accounted for. In addition, the instrumental and specialized knowledge of science becomes an end in itself and thereby a misleading ideology.

At bottom, what is at issue is the status of a transcendental dimension of created reality and the human freedom it implies, which is the foundation of religion and morality as well as the polity. The functionalist project is intended to harness and utilize the transformative and unifying power of science in a pragmatically limited manner, so that it remains the servant of liberal, democratic and human values. The assumption of the harmony and mutually reinforcing character of science and human values is the ultimate basis of the analytical framework of functionalism.

However, by concentrating on the instrumental rationality of science as the means to the greater ends of human freedom, world unity and peace, these ends have in fact been reduced to results or byproducts of a deterministic process in which science becomes an end in itself. The consequence is not simply a distorted conception of political reality which misconstrues important dimensions of politics and the state but, ultimately, the elimination of purpose or transcendental meaning and with it the destruction of human freedom and morality.

Conclusion

On the basis of our assessment we must conclude that the functionalist approach rests on a presuppositional framework which is seriously flawed. The assumption of an unintended yet morally and politically beneficial process of increasing interdependence or systemness, prefigured in functionalism and found in much of the contemporary literature on interdependence, is seductive but misleading. Based on a misplaced faith in the nature and effects of modern science and technology, this perspective leads to an overly optimistic expectation of evolutionary political transformation which sets aside or distorts important dimensions and structures of political reality, grounded in its created character, as these have come to expression in the contemporary nation-state. Consequently, the functionalist approach cannot serve as a basis for reflection on future world order.

Nevertheless, our assessment of functionalism should not be entirely negative. In spite of its flawed perspective, the functionalist approach includes a number of insights which challenge the notion that the modern state is the only structural expression of political authority which is consistent with the creation order. We must consider the possibility of and need for significant forms of political authority above the level of the nation-state, which are able to respond to novel political issues engendered by the application of new technologies. Further, it is plausible that such institutions of international government may not be entirely state-like in their structure and operation, particularly their means of enforcement. Finally, the continued development of functionally based international authorities raises the prospect of less comprehensive forms of political authority as a conceptual alternative to the establishment of world or even regional government.

In this way, although it is misdirected, functionalism presents other approaches with a challenge to move beyond the traditional alternatives of state or world-state, and of absolute or obsolete sovereignty, in order to come to grips with the contemporary perplexities of complex interdependence and diminished sovereignty. Functionalism is relevant, therefore, to the extent that it raises the central issues of the nature of political authority and political community at the supranational level, which must be addressed by contemporary international relations theory.

Notes

An earlier version of this essay appeared as "Functionalism's Working Peace System,'" in *International Conflict and Conflict Management*, second edition, R. O. Matthews, A. G. Rubinoff and J. G. Stein, eds., (Toronto: Prentice-Hall, 1989), 547-62.

1. *A Working Peace System: An Argument for a Functional Approach to International Organization*, (London, 1943) was the central work in which Mitrany elaborated the functionalist position. This work was reissued, together with some other articles, in 1966 by Quadrangle Books as *A Working Peace System*; this is the edition cited in this article. His other main works include: *The Progress of International Government*, (London: George Allen and Unwin, 1933); *The Road to Security*, (London: National Peace Council, 1944); and *The*

Functional Theory of Politics, (London: London School of Economics and Political Science/Martin Robertson, 1975).

2. For more on the roots of the functionalist approach, see F. Parkinson, *The Philosophy of International Relations*, (Beverly Hills/London: Sage Publications, 1977), ch. 6; also ch. 2 of my doctoral dissertation, *Functionalism Revisited: An Assessment of the Functionalist Approach to International Relations* (University of Toronto, Dept. of Political Science, 1986).

3. Other proponents of the functionalist argument prior to Mitrany include Paul Reinsch, *Public International Unions*, (Boston and London: World Peace Foundation/Ginn and Co., 1911); Leonard Woolf, *International Government*, (New York: Brentano's, 1916); Sir James Arthur Salter, *Allied Shipping Control*, (London: Oxford at the Clarendon Press, 1921); and H. R. G. Greaves, *The League Committees and World Order* (London: Oxford University Press/Humphrey Milford, 1931).

4. Same of the principal neofunctionalists include Ernst B. Haas, *The Uniting of Europe*, (London: Stevens and Co., 1958), and *Beyond the Nation-State*, (Stanford: Stanford University Press, 1964); Leon H. Lindberg, *The Political Dynamics of European Integration*, (Stanford: Stanford University Press, 1963); and Lindberg and Stuart A. Scheingold, *Europe's Would-Be Polity*, (Englewood Cliffs, N.J.: Prentice-Hall, 1970). For an excellent discussion of neofunctionalism, see Charles Pentland, *International Theory and European Integration*, (London: Faber and Faber, 1973).

5. This term, borrowed by Mitrany from his mentor, Leonard Hobhouse, is intended to indicate how functionalism moves beyond mere ideals and dogmas, penetrating to more fundamental and empirical realities. See Mitrany's "The Making of the Functional Theory" in his *The Functional Theory of Politics*, 16-18.

6. The novelty of the present historical period is discussed by Mitrany in *A Working Peace System*, 18-19 (hereafter abbreviated as *WPS*), and in "The Functional Approach in Historical Perspective," *International Affairs*, vol. 47, no. 3 (July 1971): 532-33.

7. This concept is discussed by Mitrany in *WPS*, 72-73 and 162-63.

8. See *WPS*, 159.

9. See "An Advance in Democratic Representation," in *WPS*, 121-30.

10. For Mitrany's criticism of the constitutional approach and world federalism see *WPS*, 43-54. For his discussion of sovereignty and its piecemeal transfer, see *WPS*, 30-31 and 143.

11. This tendency comes through most clearly in *The Progress of International Government*, 37-45 and 92-94.

12. The universality of the new philosophy of social welfare is referred to in *WPS*, *17-19*; "*The Functional Approach to World Organization, International Affairs*, vol. 24, no. 3 (July 1948), 358-59; and "The Functional Approach in Historical Perspective," 539-40.

13. The case for the development of a cooperative ethos is made most clearly in Mitrany, "Address to the Conference," in *Proceedings of the International Congress on Mental Health, vol. IV: Proceedings of the International Conference on Mental Hygiene*, (London: H. K. Lewis/New York: Columbia University Press, 1948), 71-85.

14. Mitrany repeatedly affirms the principle of cultural diversity. See *WPS*, 26-27, 68; and "Nationality and Nationalism," in *The Functional Theory of Politics*, 138-45, and especially 144.

15. *WPS*, 85.

16. For his discussion of this topic see "Functional Federalism," in *WPS*, 167-73.

17. *WPS*, 92.

18. From the 1860s to the mid-1970s, the number of intergovernmental international organizations increased from five to over three hundred; most of this growth has occurred since World War II. For more on this, see Harold K. Jacobson, *Networks of Interdependence*, (New York: Alfred A. Knopf, 1979), ch.3; and Michael D. Wallace and J. David Singer, "Intergovernmental Organization in the Global System, 1815-1964: A Quantitative Description," *International Organization*, vol. 24, no. 3 (Summer 1970): 239-87.

19. For Mitrany's treatment of the security function, see *WPS*, 31, 38, 63, 81 and 86-77; and The Road to Security, especially 18-19.

20. This concept is borrowed from Stanley Hoffmann, "Notes on the Elusiveness of Modern Power," *International Journal*, vol. XXX, no. 2 (Spring 1975): 191-92.

21. For an example of this discussion, see Leland M. Goodrich, *The United Nations in a Changing World,* (New York: Columbia University Press, 1974), ch. 10, especially 216-19.

22. The association of functionalism with the pluralist position is made by James Patrick Sewell, *Functionalism and World Politics,* (Princeton: Princeton University Press, 1966), 328-29. Mitrany himself makes reference to the pluralist school's attack on sovereignty in *The Progress of International Government,* 67-68. For a further discussion of the pluralist school see Bernard L. Zylstra, *From Pluralism to Collectivism: The Political Thought of Harold Laski,* (Assen, The Netherlands: Van Gorkum, 1970).

For other analyses of functionalism, see Inis L. Claude, Jr., *Swords Into Plowshares,* 4th ed., (New York: Random House, 1971), ch.17; A. J. R. Groom and Paul Taylor, eds., *Functionalism: Theory and Practice in International Relations,* (London: University of London Press, 1975); Kenneth W. Thompson, *Ethics, Functionalism and Power in International Politics,* (Baton Rouge, LA: Louisiana State University Press, 1979); Robert E. Riggs and I. Jostein Mykletun, *Beyond Functionalism,* (Oslo and Minneapolis, 1979); and John Eastby, *Functionalism and Interdependence,* (Lanham, MD.: University Press of America, 1985).

23. This concept is taken from Langdon Winner, *Autonomous Technology,* (Cambridge, Mass.: MIT Press, 1977), ch. 5, especially 173f.

24. This line of criticism is derived from Sewell, *Functionalism and World Politics,* 319-23.

25. See Mitrany, *The Progress of International Government,* 92; see also 37 and 43.

Liberalism, Pluralism
and Christianity

Paul Marshall

There are two major current Christian approaches to the phenomenon of social pluralism. One is to strive for an accommodation along liberal lines, the other is to try to achieve a Christian society. I believe that both of these responses are inadequate and so would like to suggest what a proper response should be.

As a means to this I will discuss the nature and problems of *liberalism*, because the relation between liberalism and pluralism lies close to the heart of many contemporary problems with pluralism. Currently liberalism is asserted as a form of pluralism; indeed liberals often assume that theirs is the *only* genuine form of pluralism. Many Christians have, in turn, accepted this assertion of a close association between liberalism and pluralism as accurate and so have either rejected pluralism because they feel they must reject liberalism, or else have embraced liberalism because they believe they must embrace pluralism. Contrary to this, I will argue that liberalism is *not* an adequate form of pluralism but instead leads to a large measure of the homogenization in society. Consequently, if Christians reject liberalism, as I believe we should, this does not imply a rejection of pluralism. Instead it means that we need to investigate the possibility of a more authentically Christian form of pluralism. However before proceeding further, I need to clarify what I mean by liberalism and pluralism.

It is not an easy thing to say what they are. This is because both are *historical* things—they change through time and, in particular, change due to the formative activity of human beings. Consequently their shape is convoluted and variable, and they have a contingent character which probably includes a future in which new things will appear. If a definition is intended in a brief set of words to say what a thing is and is not, then it is very difficult, if not impossible, to define something that appears in history. Whereas an abstract thing, such as a concept, may have sharp boundaries (a clear "definition," as in photography), historical things do not. Given this situation, I will not define either pluralism or liberalism. Instead I will try in general terms to depict what I mean when I use these words. The depictions are not tight, for their subjects are not tight and we do need to portray reality.[1]

The meanings ascribed to pluralism vary within disciplines, and also between disciplines such as sociology, philosophy, political science or history. Within political science there are four chief claimants to the term. These are (a) federalism, which concerns the division and distribution of political power according to geographical areas within a state; (b) separation of powers, which concerns the allocation of particular political functions to discrete institutions within a state structure; (c) diverse centers of power within a society—that is, that the power to initiate and shape social change is distributed amongst different types of institutions—political, economic, confessional and educational; (d) the co-existence within one political jurisdiction of people with publicly important different beliefs and ways of life.

The meaning with which we are most concerned at present is the last of these, which is also the meaning most similar to that common among sociologists. This meaning also dovetails with ideas current among philosophers. The current philosophical sense of pluralism is that there exist different philosophical views which cannot be reconciled with one another. Some refer in this context to "incommensurate ideological communities," a typification that can serve us politically and sociologically as well. These senses taken together suggest that a situation of social pluralism is one in which there is the co-existence of peoples having importantly different beliefs and ways of life whose differences are for practical purposes incommensurate.

As I am concerned with politics, I will not address the question of whether on epistemological or other grounds the current differences can in principle be overcome or resolved. I will focus on situations where such differences do exist, where no ready resolution is in sight and state policies must somehow deal with the actual historical fact of differences. In this respect we need to distinguish between the *fact* of pluralism and *policies* of pluralism. Different people may agree that our societies are pluralistic but may react to that fact quite differently. By political means we may try either to restrict, to accommodate or to promote plurality. I will proceed on the basis that in most Western societies we have the factual circumstances of pluralism, and focus on how we and others have responded and should respond to this circumstance.

Liberalism has elements of a political theory and the patterns of a political movement. These two features do not cohere well and so we need to mention both if we are to get some sense of what liberalism is. Occasionally liberalism is defined very broadly. One collection of supposedly liberal writings has as its first two exponents Socrates and Peter Abelard.[2] This is probably stretching the point. More commonly, and accurately, the roots of liberalism are traced to certain developments in the early modern era, notably (a) the appearance of independent men (or families) due to urbanization, the growth of a market economy, and industrialization, with the consequent growth of individualism and theories of autonomy and freedom; (b) the attempt to found the state on a "non-religious" basis due to the problem of the sixteenth and seventeenth century religious wars, which led to a stress on separating "religion" and politics; (c) the growth of rationalism and enlightenment philosophies leading to an anti-dogmatism and a belief in the autonomy of and progress through reason. These impulses took a specific organized form in responses to the French Revolution. In the decade 1810-1820 there arose (alongside the new "revolutionary" or "radical" mode of political thought) the ideas of *restoration*, *conservatism*, and *liberalism*. The first example of an explicitly self-conscious liberal party seems to have been the *Liberales* in the Spanish *Cortes* in 1812. This was a liberal constitutional party which formed a front against attempts at restoration.[3]

Since then liberalism, and liberal parties, have had a convoluted history. Liberalism is a set of political opinions and attitudes whose character has been shaped in powerful ways by the forces with which it has contended. Originally it was a European and American movement which did not wish to be conservative in that it wanted to move ahead, though not as fast as the radicals. Depending on the power of these competing movements, liberalism has appeared in different guises. In Europe, liberal means a conservative individualist, one who resists more revolutionary socialist or social democratic pressures. Raymond Aron and Friedrich von Hayek are examples of such liberals, that is, exponents of a free market. In America the *word* liberal means "progressive," vaguely "pink," as there is no socialism against which it can be arrayed and defined. Liberalism, in its nineteenth century heyday, was anti-clerical, but in modern Europe it fuses with Christian Democracy. In the United States nearly all politics and parties are in some sense liberal. Even though the *word* liberal means "progressive," liberalism as a political orientation covers nearly the whole political spectrum; politics is a conflict of left, right and center liberals.

The political creed of liberalism has also varied over time. However, one peculiar feature of modern liberalism is that it often claims that it has no, or is no, creed. This feature is certainly not universal. It was certainly not readily apparent, in Latin American Liberal-Conservative wars. Indeed where liberalism has a strong opponent, then its position as *position* becomes much clearer. But in the latter twentieth century where liberalism is ascendent or dominant, then its claim to be no claim comes to the fore. This claim is made because, according to most political theorists, the principal theoretical feature of liberalism is something like "a set of beliefs which proceed from the central assumption that man's essence is his freedom and therefore that what chiefly concerns us in this life is to shape the world as we want it."[4] This stress on freedom leads liberals such as Rawls, Ackerman, Nozick and Dworkin to emphasize that they do not wish to impose their way of life on anyone else, but that their desire is rather that all should be free to live out their own ways of life with the least hindrance. Hence liberalism claims to be a *neutral* philosophy. So for Ronald Dworkin, the liberal state "must be neutral on . . . the question of the good life . . .; political decisions must be, so far as possible, independent of any particular conception of the good life, or of what gives values to life."[5] Bruce Ackerman advanced the "Neutrality Principle." "No reason (that purports to justify a social arrangement) is a good reason if it requires the power holder to assert (a) that his conception of the good is better than that asserted by any of his fellows, or (b) that, regardless of his conception of the good, he is intrinsically superior to one or more of his fellow citizens."[6] Similar sentiments may be gathered from Rawls or Nozick. This view also manifests itself in the common liberal piety that "you can't impose your beliefs on others."

Taken together these various facets of liberalism reveal a variable political attitude that stresses individuality, freedom, autonomy, rights, the separation of religion and politics, reason, tolerance, the non-imposition of belief, and decent progressiveness. As Voegelin says, this is not a tight picture. Indeed it is doubtful that much of a coherent view can be welded from these disparate elements. But a movement does not have to be coherent, it only has to move, and this is how the movement currently appears.

The fact of pluralism—especially pluralism of religion—poses many challenges to Christianity. It is probably fair to say that the Christian churches still do not know politically how to respond to it. One common response has been to try to limit plurality by political means—perhaps by imposing some variety of *pax Christianum* or, to be more North-American about it, *pax Judaeo-Christianum*. Such a view is present among American fundamentalists, among certain Catholics, and among adherents of a more organic, traditional view of society. It was a response of C. S. Lewis as well as Jerry Falwell. I will not try to explore this view but merely point out that it has

left-wing as well as right-wing variants. If traditional Catholics are
not too open to diversity, neither are liberation theologians.
Another Christian response has been to accept a type of pluralism
via an accommodation with liberalism. This approach is taken on
the right by Michael Novak, and perhaps, Richard Neuhaus.[7] It also
has left-wing variants among some more "progressive" evangelicals.
While I believe that neither of these responses is a good one I will
focus in this paper only on the second one—the accommodation
with liberalism. The problems of this response stem from treating
liberalism as the only pluralist option and so I will try to show that
liberalism can be damaging to many important features of a just
pluralism.

Given liberalism's stress on neutrality and openness, liberals see
themselves as exponents of pluralism *par excellence.*[8] They wish to
provide the setting in which each individual can pursue his or her
own freely chosen life, in which each tolerates the other, each view
is held in equal respect, where no view is imposed upon another, and
where the state is neutral between all competing particular value
claims. However, such a view can lead not to an open society but to
the imposition of individualism upon all, replacing a plural society
with a homogeneous liberal one. In order to illustrate how this can
happen, I will consider some examples taken from liberal theory in
order to show its inner logic and then I will try to illustrate the
movement's actual effects through some examples.

To illustrate the closure of society induced by liberalism it is
useful to consider Robert Nozick's *Anarchy State and Utopia.* This
book is the most libertarian of contemporary liberal works in political theory and has been credited with single-handedly making liber-
tarianism intellectually respectable. What other liberal theorists like
Rawls or Dworkin might forbid, Nozick allows. Consequently if we
can show that even Nozick's ideas lead to closure in society, then
our criticism is likely to apply *a fortiori* to other liberal writers. Nozick
emphasizes the wide diversity of people in the world. He provides a
partial list: "Wittgenstein, Elizabeth Taylor, Bertrand Russell,
Thomas Merton, Yogi Berra, Allen Ginsberg, Harry Wolfson,
Thoreau, Casey Stengel, the Lubavitcher Rebbe, Picasso, Moses,
Einstein, Hugh Heffner, Socrates, Henry Ford . . . Peter Kropotkin,

you and your parents. Is there really one kind of life which is best for each of these people?"[9] Given this rich diversity he exhorts us to develop a society whose hallmark is not what is supposedly best for everyone but rather one which respects the right of each person to live in their own way. Nozick's utopia is primarily one which allows each person to pursue their own utopia. Unlike many liberals Nozick is aware that a way of life is a communal thing and that a healthy society is composed of communities, not individuals. So he wants, and thinks he has, the framework for a society that allows for the growth of many diverse communities. This society does not try to be a community itself but seeks only to be a framework in which many utopias, many communities can exist and co-exist. These communities can themselves be quite illiberal. They can exclude, they can discriminate, they can be authoritarian. They can be anything their members choose. But the key is the matter of *choice*. Each member chooses to be in a particular community, and must be able to choose to leave. They can join another community or just hang out for a while. The illiberality of certain communities is not an affront to liberalism because the only people in them are ones who have *chosen* to be so, who want to follow a particular way of life, and who are under no compulsion to stay. The overall society has a liberal character because it is composed of voluntary communities.

However this central stress on voluntariness is not as benign as it might appear. This is because, for Nozick, in order for free will to be real, it must be an *informed* will. Each person must be continually aware of their right to leave. Since each person is in a community, then each community must respect the liberal priority of individual choice by reminding and advising its members that they can go at any time. Clifford Orwin refers to this as a kind of "Miranda rule for enthusiasts."[10] In the end the right to choose overrides the right of any community to claim (and, hence, honestly believe) that it holds to the truth. The priority of choice undercuts the ability of a community to shape its members and succeeding generations so that they will uphold the truth at all costs. Consider, for example, an Amish community where each member is advised (and educated and informed enough so that the advice means something) that they are and should be free to leave at any time, that the community respects this right and will not insist that communal solidarity comes before individual will. Whatever such a community will become, it is no longer an Amish community in its heart, and it will soon cease to be an Amish community in its practices. The Amish themselves realized this fact and fought diligently and so far successfully to limit the education of their children. A similar strain affects any community that believes that what it holds to is true. If it must inform its members that they can quit at any time, then it must inform them that its beliefs are not the most fundamental thing of all. Communities thus become half-minded and thus half-hearted. As Orwin points out, they become communities founded on prior respect for individual choice and thus become mirror images of the larger liberal society. In this liberal society, communities are not left free, but are constrained to become liberal associations.

The situation is comparable to some current practices in state schools. In many of these schools the ideal is pedagogically to replicate the liberal society. This is done, in theory, by exposing each child in a full, fair and balanced way to the options that exist, exhorting them to give serious consideration to these options, and then perhaps to make a serious commitment to one of them. This approach is applied only in certain parts of the curriculum; it is not done in physics or math, or in matters of creation and evolution. But it is applied in politics, ethics and religion. What a child learns from this approach is not that one religion supposedly set before her is true, but that no religion has a compelling claim to be treated as true. Hence the child learns implicitly that each religion has a claim as good as any other so that what is paramount is the priority of her own individual choice. In so far as this education works, the pupil becomes trained in the dogmatics of liberalism.

Nozick is laudably genuine in his desire that people should be legally free to live in different ways. He wants a society in which different commitments can live alongside one another. But this is only done by pushing each community towards "half measures for the half-hearted, dilettantism on a grand scale."[11] The result is similar to George Grant's depiction of liberal society: "As for pluralism, differences . . . are able to exist only in private activities: how we eat, how we mate, how we practice ceremonies. Some like pizza, some like steaks; some like girls, some like boys; some like the synagogue, some like the mass. But we all do it in churches, motels, restaurants indistinguishable from the Atlantic to the Pacific."[12]

Alasdair MacIntyre has highlighted a similar phenomenon in the development of the modern university.[13] He points out that the

> foundation of the liberal university was the abolition of religious tests for university teachers. What the enforcement of religious tests had ensured was a certain degree of uniformity of belief in the way in which the curriculum was organized, presented, and developed through enquiry. Each such preliberal university was therefore to some degree an institution embodying either one particular tradition of rational enquiry or a limited set of such traditions. The Scottish universities articulated one kind of Protestant tradition of enquiry. . . . The University of Paris in the thirteenth century was the milieu for conflict between contend-ing Aristotelian and Augustinian thinkers.[14]

Later either religious tests were gradually abolished or else universities were founded that did not have such tests. The result was not, however, that universities became places where alternative points of view were elaborated and debated. Instead, questions about points of view and their influence in shaping the university tended to be ignored or even excluded:

> In the appointment of university teachers considerations of belief and allegiance were excluded from view altogether. A conception of scholarly competence, independent of standpoint, was enforced in the making of appointments. . . . Appointed teachers present what they taught as if there were indeed shared standards of rationality, accepted by all teachers and accessible to all students. Universities became institutions committed to upholding a fictitious objectivity."[15]

Consequently the student usually meets "an apparent incon-clusiveness in all argument outside the natural sciences, an incon-clusiveness which seems to abandon him or her to his or her pre-rational preferences. So the student characteristically emerges from a liberal education with a set of skills, a set of preferences, and little else. . . . "[16] MacIntyre notes that in such settings education is "abstracted from and deprived of the particularities of our histories" though he also adds: "Happily, of course, not all education in our culture is in this sense liberal." But, insofar as liberalism does shape the pattern of commitment in the modern university, the result is not contending views of rationality but the assertion of neutral rationality in some areas (notably the natural sciences) combined with a pastiche in the humanities which trivializes choice, and, more particularly, the object of that choice.

Canada is a country that has proudly, if somewhat hypocritically, contrasted the United States "melting pot" with its own ideal of co-existing communities.[17] Canadians are inclined to think of the country as founded by "peoples" rather than "the people." While it is overstated, there is truth in this self-image. Canadian conservatism has seen its task less as developing a social ideal than allowing the relatively just co-existence of the communities that happen to be within its boundaries. I am not suggesting that Canada has been a superlatively just country—for there are many other forms of injustice, and worse forms of injustice, than the liberal one. But Canada has often allowed for genuine pluralism and communal diversity.[18] This is shown in constitutional documents. Although the Constitution was modified considerably in 1982 by the incorporation of a series of rights since interpreted largely along liberal lines, it still retains distinct group rights and status. These include the rights of dissentient schools, which are given in Section 93 of the *British North America Act*. There are also language rights (Sections 16-23 of the Charter of Rights and Freedoms) and the rights of aboriginal peoples (Sections 25, 35, 37), both of which have been recently reaffirmed. Other pluralist provisions have been newly introduced, such as the provision for interpretations consistent with "multiculturalism" (Section 27) and the "affirmative action" provisions of section 15(2) on equality rights. Finally, depending upon modes of interpretation, the "reasonable . . . limits . . . demonstrably justified in a free and democratic society" mentioned in Section I and the "Fundamental Freedoms" of religion, thought, assembly and association contained in Section 2 may also enhance pluralism.[19] Failed attempts to amend the constitution in 1990 and 1992 both incorporated extensive group rights.

However, despite this stress on more than individual rights, a liberal constitutional interpretation has become dominant. The sections of the Charter of Rights and Freedoms that have received most publicity and litigation, that have attracted (and been the occasion of creating) special interest groups, and that are rapidly reshaping Canadian political culture are those which are individualist in character. The multiple stresses on *individual* freedoms, *individual* rights, and the equality of *individuals*, together with the proscription of discrimination between individuals, generate the most concern, and even devotion. These individualist dynamics have the momentum to reshape jurisprudence and, with that, the country. Society is treated as an association of individuals wherein the chief political problem is securing one individual's right against all other individuals.

This stress undercuts certain distinctive features of Canada. For example, many language rights should properly be understood as group rights. Guaranteeing persons the right to speak their language is one thing, a good thing, but it will not maintain a language. Languages require someone else to hear, and someone else to talk back; they require a culture, a community. As the Canadian Royal Commission on Bilingualism and Biculturalism pointed out years ago:

> " . . . although an Anglophone isolated among French-speaking Canadians may possess all the theoretical rights imaginable, each is able to exercise these rights to a very limited extent. A milieu is not transformed for one individual, a university is not built for a single family."[20]

The matter of language and individual rights has become a matter of grave concern, particularly in the province of Quebec. Successive governments in Quebec have believed that since it is a relatively small, predominantly French-speaking province amid a North American ocean of English speakers, then the French language needed and needs special protection. With the flood of

English language television, radio magazines, newspapers, books and packagings, French may persistently be eroded and marginalized. Many have believed that this erosion of French is well underway. One response to this situation was the introduction of the "Charter of the French Language," popularly known as Bill 101. This complex Bill restricted the use of English by, for example, requiring that all signs, posters, and commercial advertising be exclusively in French. The Bill prompted a storm of protest, not only from English speakers in Quebec who were personally affected but also from liberals religiously threatened by an assault on their deepest commitment, individual choice and freedom. Hence Bill 101 was denounced as a violation of fundamental human rights, and challenged on the ground that it violated the Canadian Charter of Rights and Freedoms.[21] In this instance, as in all real political situations, there are many complicating factors. There is dispute whether French *is* in danger and whether Bills 101 and 178 could help it. However, if the facts asserted by the Bill's proponents are correct, the case for these Bills is at least plausible. Hence a challenge to this legislation in the name of individual rights may undercut a culture and way of life, thus illustrating the very real tension between plural ways of life and the liberal stress on individual rights.[22]

Similar dynamics are present in the view of religion manifested in discussions of items such as Sunday observance. Perhaps the clearest illustration was the report of the Sub-Committee on "Equality Rights" of the Canadian Parliament. This Committee examined Canadian laws to determine what changes needed to be made in order to bring the laws into conformity with Section 15 of the 1982 Constitution. Section 15 demands equal treatment for each and all before and under the law.[23] The Committee's report, *Equality For All*, depicts Canada largely as a collection of individuals with only incidental ties.[24] Such individuals have their own particular characteristics—some are Jewish, some not; some are homosexual, some not; some are men, some not; some are over sixty-five, some not; some are handicapped, some not. These characteristics were portrayed merely as personal idiosyncrasies, private matters which should be left at home when people enter the social, political and economic world. The writers of the report see them as irrelevant to social interaction.

But this is not an accurate image of Canada (nor of anywhere else). Several of these characteristics *are* of public importance. They are major factors shaping social interaction. Countries are comprised of cultures, commitments, groups, associations and institutions. Over two-thirds of Canadians are members of voluntary associations. There are tens of thousands of such associations, and churches, political parties, trade unions, cultural groups, cooperatives, academic associations and public interest organizations. There is cultural and ethnic diversity, a plurality brought about by French, English and many other languages, varied subcultures, many native bands and nations, diverse schools and educational systems, a wide spectrum of religious belief systems and church denominations, and several competing political parties and ideologies. None of these is purely an individual matter, and many are of the utmost public significance.

The report's lack of attention to communities and institutions in the treatment of religion is striking. The only two recommendations in *Equality for All* that directly concerned religion are recommendations 39 and 40 that deal with providing people a choice about holidays and days of rest. These are good provisions, but they are the *only* provisions concerning religion. The report regards religion as a matter only of holding certain religious ceremonies. The religious "observances and practices" singled out are "religious days of rest, other days of religious observance, prayer breaks and dress requirements."[25] The religious matters over which an employer may have to make accommodation are, observing a Sabbath or religious holidays, taking prayer breaks during the workday, adhering to certain dietary rules, refraining from work during a mourning period for a deceased relative, declining to undergo medical examinations, and following certain dress requirements and grooming habits. Apart from these, the report asserted quite openly that religion is irrelevant to the affairs of social and public life. Religion is not "relevant to a person's fitness to compete for a given job or reside in particular accommodations. . . ."[26] When the Committee noted some group *contexts* of section 15 it recognized "the separate protection afforded to aboriginal rights (section 25)" and "the general extension of the rights and freedoms to both male and female persons . . . (section 28)."[27] But, curiously, section 29, safeguarding the rights of religiously oriented schools, was not cited as an example of separate protection. Indeed, religious practice was traced to an "ethnic" heritage.[28] These sections of *Equality for All* seem to deny that peoples' religious beliefs have shaped and do shape their life patterns—social as well as individual, communal as well as personal, public as well as private. They ignore the fact that not only must employers make provision for their employees' beliefs, but that many employers and institutions are, as *collective bodies, themselves religiously oriented*—and themselves employ hundreds of thousands of people. Apart from churches, synagogues, mosques and temples there are relief organizations, missionary associations, group homes, schools, children's aid societies, colleges, family services, hospitals, publishers, universities, magazines, public interest groups, newspapers, TV and radio producers, political organizations, counselling services, seminaries, senior citizen's homes, cooperatives and artistic groups all seeking to live and work in the context of specific religious commitment. The teaching of religious beliefs is not only a matter of church, but of school as well: there are hundreds of thousands of children who attend religiously oriented schools. Religious teaching touches on every aspect of life. Religious guidance and instruction is given not just for an individual portion of life called "religious" but for the whole of life, public as well as private. Religion is not a private matter, but is of the utmost relevance to all of human life and so needs protection in corporate as well as individual expression.

The effects of liberal individualism can also be traced through the history of Canadian native peoples and in the history of confessional schools.[29] In each case particular communities have found themselves under attack by those who assert the priority of individual freedoms. Similar patterns exist throughout the world and affect minorities, national groups, language groups and aboriginal peoples.[30] The picture that emerges is that liberalism is not neutral with respect to different ways of life. Rather, it undermines distinctive and traditional communities and replaces them with a uniform regime of individual choices. Liberalism results in the preservation of liberals, discrimination against non-liberals, and the erection of a liberal social order. It also uses the coercive power of the state to achieve these ends. Under the sincerely held belief in diversity through individual freedom liberals recreate a society in their own image. The great liberal philosopher, John Rawls, takes a relatively sanguine view of the ways of life that may be destroyed in this process: "a well-ordered society [i.e., a society that follows Rawls— P.M.] defines a fair background within which ways of life have a reasonable opportunity to establish themselves. If a conception of the good is unable to endure and gain adherents under conditions of equal freedom and mutual toleration, one must question whether it is a viable conception of the good and whether its passing is to be regretted."[31] The dynamic is described by MacIntyre:

> Liberalism thus provides a distinctive conception of a just order which is closely integrated with the terms set by a liberal polity. The principles are not neutral with respect to rival conflicting theories of the human good. Where they are in force they impose a particular conception of the good life, of practical reasoning, and of justice upon those who willingly or unwillingly accept the liberal procedures and the liberal terms of debate. The overriding good of liberalism is no more and no less than the continued sustenance of the liberal social and political order.[32]

This brief survey of the relation between liberalism and diversity leads me to suggest that many Christians' fears of pluralism may really be fears of liberalism. We may have sensed that liberalism does not give much freedom for communal diversity, especially religious diversity, and so may have rejected the whole package. If this is the case then we may ask whether there are approaches to pluralism which are more amenable to Christian, and other, concerns. Candidates could be found in instances such as the development of Dutch Calvinism from Althusius to the present, contemporary European Christian democracy, the English pluralist tradition associated with names such as J. N. Figgis and F. W. Maitland, or the French pluralist tradition associated with Lamennais.[33] Even

Burkean conservatism has a tendency to preserving different ways of life as in, for example, the Canadian co-existence of French Catholicism and English Anglicanism.[34] These positions accept the *fact* of plurality while not necessarily rejoicing in that fact. But they forswear the use of state compulsion to eradicate differences. Similarly I suspect that many Christians do not want policies that *promote* religious plurality, but want to deal with existing plurality in a just way. Even so, a Christian pluralism that demands the political acceptance of different ways of life, may receive wide support from those who are not Christians. Insofar as Christians promote an *institutional and communal diversity*, they can provide room for others and, since communities are politically efficacious while individuals are not, they will provide for a stronger political pluralism. They could provide more room for liberals and Christians than liberalism would for Christians and liberals.

However, it is questionable whether liberals would see things quite this way. They are liable to respond that the limitations on individual choice that this approach implies are a violation of liberal tenets, and they would be correct in doing so. Liberalism offers others individual choices within homogenous institutions. Christians could offer others communal diversity with relative limits on individuals. Each wants to provide freedom for the other, but each sees the other's proposed freedom as a partial violation of themselves. Between these two frameworks there can be no simple reconciliation, for each is a claim about what just reconciliation actually is. They are not claims for particular freedoms but are frameworks *for judging* particular claims to freedom. Both positions call for diversity and freedom, but they cannot both at the same time be the paradigm of society. One or the other must win out: one version of freedom will succeed. Each allows a type of freedom to different ways of life, but the freedoms cannot co-exist with one another. We might hope that pluralism is possible in society, but the state itself cannot be plural. Alternatively, we might say that pluralism is certainly possible, but one cannot have a plurality of pluralisms.

Notes

This is a revised version of "Liberalism, Pluralism and Christianity: A Reconceptualization," published in *Fides et Historia*, vol. XXI:3, Oct. 1989, 4-17.

1. These depictions also suffer from defects due to my incompetence, but my point is that, even were I less incompetent, fundamental problems would still remain. An excellent discussion of pluralism which gives tighter definitions than those sought here is *Pluralism and Horizons: An Essay in Christian Public Philosophy*, by Richard Mouw and Sander Griffioen, (Grand Rapids: Eerdmans, 1993). See especially ch. 1.

2. J. S. Schapiro, ed., *Liberalism: Its Meaning and History*, (New York: Van Nostrand, 1958). See also A. Arblaster, *The Rise and Decline of Western Liberalism*, (Oxford: Blackwell, 1984), 12.

3. Cf. the discussion by Eric Voegelin, "Liberalism and Its History," *Review of Politics*, vol. 37 (1974): 504-20 esp. 506.

4. George Grant, *Technology and Empire*, (Toronto: Anansi, 1969), 114.

5. Ronald Dworkin, "Liberalism" in Stuart Hampshire, ed., *Private and Public Morality*, (New York: Cambridge University Press, 1978), 127.

6. Bruce Ackerman, *Social Justice in the Liberal State*, (Yale University Press, 1980), 11. In the 1980s liberals sought to replace or supplement theories of formal neutrality with commendations of the beneficial results of a substantive political neutrality.

7. Though Neuhaus himself criticizes liberalism on this point, see P. L. Berger and R. J. Neuhaus, *To Empower People: The Role of Mediating Structures in Public Policy*, (Washington, D.C.,: American Enterprise Institute, 1977); R. J. Neuhaus, *The Naked Public Square*, (Grand Rapids: Eerdmans, 1986).

8. Cf. R. M. Seltzer, "Judaism and Liberal Causes: A Severed Covenant," 21-33 of N. Biggar, J. S. Scott, and W. Schweiker, eds., *Cities of Gods*, (Westport: Greenwood Press, 1986), 21.

9. Robert Nozick, *Anarchy, State and Utopia*, (New York: Basic Books, 1974), 312. See the discussion by Clifford Orwin, "Robert

Nozick's Liberal Utopia," paper presented to the Annual Meeting of the Canadian Political Science Association, Guelph, Ontario, 1984.

10. Orwin, op. cit., 8. I am indebted to Orwin's insightful discussion of Nozick's "utopias."

11. Orwin, op. cit., 7. It may also be noted that certain individual choices are foreclosed. For example, if an Amish community is not possible, then no one can make a real choice to be Amish.

12. Grant, op. cit., 26.

13. Alasdair MacIntyre, *Whose Justice? Which Rationality?* (South Bend, IN: University of Notre Dame Press, 1988).

14. Op. cit., 399.

15. Loc. cit.

16. Op. cit., 400.

17. Indeed Joe Clark, the former Prime Minister, then Minister of External Affairs, referred to Canada as a "community of communities." I am not sure whether he, or his speechwriter, was aware that this is a quotation from Althusius (*communitas communitorum*).

18. See my "Anglo-Canadian Perspectives on the United States Constitution," 87-110 of R. Wells and T. Askew, eds., *Law and Liberty*, (Grand Rapids: Eerdmans, 1987).

19. See my "Individualism, Groups and the Charter," paper presented at the Conference on the "Charter of Rights and Freedoms," sponsored by Canada-U.S. Law Institute, University of Western Ontario, London, Ontario, 1987.

20. Quoted in C. Michael MacMillan, "The Character of Language Rights: Individual, Group or Collective Rights?" paper presented at the annual meeting of the Canadian Political Science Association, Winnipeg, Manitoba, 1986, 5.

21. The Canadian Supreme Court ruled on December 15, 1988, that Bill 101 was unconstitutional. The government of Quebec responded by passing Bill 178 which allowed the use of English (as well as French) on signs *inside* stores, but otherwise follows Bill 101.

22. On this see MacMillan, op. cit.

23. See my "Individualism, Groups and the Charter," and the briefs of Citizens for Public Justice, "Submission on Equality Rights and

Employment Equity in a Pluralistic Society," to the Parliamentary Committee on Equality Rights, June 28, 1985; "Submission on the Canadian Human Rights Act" to the Minister of Justice and Attorney General of Canada, June 27, 1986.

24. *Equality for All: Report of the Parliamentary Committee on Equality Rights,* (Ottawa: Supply and Services Canada, 1985).

25. Op. cit., 70.

26. Op. cit., 29.

27. Op. cit., 5, 6.

28. Op. cit., 70.

29. See my "Religion, State and Education in Canada," paper presented to Christian Legal Society, Washington, D.C., 1983; Sally Weaver, "Federal Difficulties with Aboriginal Rights Demands," 139-47 of M. Boldt and D. Long, eds., *The Quest for Justice: Aboriginal Peoples and Aboriginal Rights,* (Toronto: University of Toronto Press, 1985); Michael Asch, *Home and Native Land: Aboriginal Rights and the Canadian Constitution,* (Toronto: Methuen, 1984), esp. 74-88; Tim Schouls, *Liberal Democracy and Canada's Aboriginal Peoples: Negotiating Basic Group Rights within the Framework of Political Individualism, 1969-1988,* M. Phil. F. thesis, Institute for Christian Studies, Toronto (1989).

30. See note 34.

31. John Rawls, "Fairness to Goodness," 536-54 of *Philosophical Review*, vol. 84 (1975), 549.

32. MacIntyre, op. cit., 344-45.

33. See J. W. Skillen and R. M. McCarthy, eds., *Political Order and the Plural Structure of Society,* (Emory University Studies in Law and Religion) (Alpharetta, GA: Scholars Press, 1992); R. M. McCarthy, "Liberal Democracy and the Rights of Institutions," *Pro Rege*, vol. 8, No. 4 (1980): 4-11; Kenneth Macrae, "The Plural Society and the Western Political Tradition," *Canadian Journal of Political Science*, vol. 12, (1979): 675-88.

34. See my "Individualism, Groups and the Charter," op. cit., and V. VanDyke, "Justice as Fairness: for Groups?" 607-14 of *American Political Science Review*, vol. 69, (1975), 611f. On the notion of group rights see also Michael McDonald, "Collective Rights and Tyranny," *University of Ottawa Review*, vol. 56 (1986): 115-23; V. Van Dyke,

"Collective Entities and Moral Rights: Problems in Liberal Democratic Thought," *Journal of Politics*, vol. 44 (1982): 21-40.

Public Philosophy and Religious Pluralism

Sander Griffioen

Introduction

This essay is concerned with the relationship between "public philosophy" and "religious pluralism." The term "religious pluralism" is used in different senses depending on the context. I shall use it in this essay to refer to the co-existence within a single society of a diversity of religions and religious forms. My aim is to explore whether the varying conceptions of what "public philosophy" is can deal adequately with the phenomenon of religious pluralism. The first section provides an initial orientation, taking as its point of departure the relationship between revelation and publicness. The second and third sections present a brief survey of the most prominent forms of "public philosophy," illustrating the difficulties each form has in finding public room for religious pluralism. The final section concludes with a proposal for conceiving of public philosophy in a way which seeks to avoid these difficulties.

The term "public" means the *forum* or *arena* in which matters of general interest can be decided. As such "public" has a broader meaning than "politics." I shall use "public" throughout this essay in this broader sense, to refer to everything pertaining to the common good. The authors to be discussed have in common a concern, contrary to the individualistic and privatizing tendencies of our times, for the rehabilitation of public life. My interest in discussing them is with their varying answers to the question: what does "public philosophy" do with the phenomenon of religious pluralism? Will these authors' conception of public philosophy allow fundamental differences of a religious nature to come up for discussion in the public arena? I am not only or even primarily thinking of differences between religions such as Christianity and Islam, but more generally of differences between fundamental views of the meaning and purpose of life.[1]

This question arises out of a dissatisfaction with the current way in which religious pluralism is regarded. Typically, the pertinent question is taken to be how the common good can be saved. But the commonness sought for seems to amount to a communality which stands apart from the clash of fundamental convictions. This searching for what is left of commonness *in spite* of religious pluralism leads to a compartmentalizing of the private and the public. It limits the public to that which people still have in common, while anxiously trying to keep controversial matters outside the public domain. But, however large are the issues which religious pluralism places before modern society, such a compartmentalization does nothing to resolve them. For, if fundamental convictions are demoted to the level of private opinions, then the common good, stripped of everything controversial, must lose all its flavor.

Orientation

The primary meaning of "public" is "accessible to all." A relationship between "public" and "revelation" is thus already implied. The Greek term for "public" meant "disclosure." Since the era of the Enlightenment the predominant meaning of "public" has derived from the Latin *publicus*, meaning that which belongs to the *res publica*, the common interest.[2] But from the very beginning "public" meant "revealed," "not secret."[3] And "revelation" is obviously linked to "not secret." One dictionary defines "revelation" as "the making public . . . of something which is not yet known." More importantly, the Bible itself makes this connection—Jesus says to Annas, "I said nothing in secret." The gospel, by its very nature, is directed to public life. It does not announce itself as a secret teaching nor only as a message for private life, but is to be proclaimed in the open as good news for *all* of life. Its "witnesses speak *publicly*, in the *wide* street of the *great* city."[4] There are texts which point in the opposite direction, such as Matthew 6:1-18, on the giving of alms, praying and fasting *in secret*. But no contradiction arises unless public and private are viewed as compartmentalized. The difficulty disappears when the secret life and public behavior are regarded as different aspects of a single movement. Johan van der Hoeven speaks in this connection of a rhythm, a "rhythm of going out and coming in," referring to the "going" and "coming" of Psalm 121.[5]

I have been speaking of public in the sense of *accessible to all*. What is the relationship between the Christian faith and public in the sense of the *res publica*? It is precisely this connection which is controversial. There have always been attempts at compartmentalizing the two. The philosophers of the Enlightenment carried out this division systematically. They attributed the first and last word to reason in the public domain and consigned the appeal to revelation to the realm of private opinion. While orthodoxy protested violently against deism and atheism, it otherwise resigned itself to the privatization of religion.[6] Rediscovering and demonstrating again the validity of the Gospel's public significance demanded a long, hard struggle. In the Netherlands this struggle was carried on principally by the *Reveil* and by neo-Calvinism. The results of these movements of religious renewal were of course mixed and can never be regarded as definitive of how revelation ought to receive public expression. Nonetheless, the Netherlands even today is distinguished by the degree to which the Christian religion has achieved recognition in public life. Witness the inclusion in the social polity of Christian schools and universities, confessional parties and trade unions, and so on. (It was this aspect of Dutch history which was a particular source of inspiration to my friend Bernard Zylstra whom we are commemorating with this volume.)

Of late, however, tension has once again been increasing. The problem is not primarily renewed attacks from the camp of reason— which, as is well-known, is itself having a very rough time[7]—but rather controversies arising from religious pluralism. More than ever we are being confronted with the fact that no single religion any longer determines the nation's vision. The Christian religion seems everywhere to have been reduced to one option alongside others. The consequences of this pluralism are reminiscent of those occasioned by the strife between reason and revelation. What is common to the conflicts between them is that appeals to revelation are yet again being relegated to the private realm. The major difference lies in the way in which privatization is defended. In the past it was a self-assured reason which called for the exclusion of everything which could not defend itself before her tribunal. In contrast, contemporary attempts to neutralize religious pluralism reveal a defensive attitude: the common good must be made safe, even at the cost of an attenuation of public debate.

The assumption on which this essay stands or falls is that "privatization" is not an irresistible, necessary process. Some will not share this assumption. F. R. Ankersmit has recently argued that this process can no longer be halted. With the acceptance of the principle of toleration the decisive step, in his opinion, had already been taken:

> It was the idea of toleration which privatized this public terrain of religious opinions and only from that time on could anyone reasonably say that he was in possession of a certain religious view just as he was in possession of a house or a cow. And with this privatization religious opinion has lost a great deal, if not all, public meaning and significance.[8]

Ankersmit feels that in the meantime we have gone so far down this road that the idea of a public domain as the center of the political and social order has lost all value. Certainly it must be acknowledged that privatization has to some extent occurred. The Christian religion has generally lost its public status, and to deny this is to fly in the face of the facts. But for a proper assessment of this situation, we need to discern, behind these factual processes, quite deliberate and systematic attempts to keep the two domains apart.

We need not only a proper assessment of the situation but also *new* answers. To illustrate this need, we may allude to the characteristic neo-Calvinistic critique of the classical ideal of reason, namely, the argument that theoretical thinking is not self-sufficient, that reason cannot undergird itself, and that at the deepest level reason itself is religiously laden. As Van Peursen wrote on the retirement of Herman Dooyeweerd, this argument has indeed been effective against the ideal of reason. When Dooyeweerd's *Wijsbegeerte der Wetsidee (The Philosophy of the Law Idea)* appeared in the 1930s, the ideal of an unprejudiced practice of philosophy and science was still being generally upheld, but by the time of his retirement in 1965 the situation had drastically changed. "One can even say," Van Peursen wrote, "that the development of recent philosophy shows Dooyeweerd to be right."[9]

This argument, however, is significantly less effective as a weapon against pluralistic relativism. It is indeed still important to demonstrate that trust in reason cannot itself be rationally grounded.[10] But can more be expected within the present climate than that the ideal of reason, too, will be set aside in the pantheon of private convictions? It is precisely at this point that a rethinking of the meaning of public life is urgently needed.

Basic Forms of "Public Philosophy"
Using the term "public philosophy" may suggest a greater degree of unanimity than actually exists. It is more correct to speak of "public philosoph*ies*." The diversity, however, is not so boundless that no patterns can be discerned. Two major positions stand out, which I shall term, respectively, "consensus" and "plurality."

Consensus
No work is so characteristic of the "consensus"-type as Walter Lippmann's *The Public Philosophy*,[11] one of the classic works in this area. Lippmann began writing the book in 1938, deeply conscious of the impotence of Western democracies in the face of fascism and national socialism, but he did not complete it until fifteen years later.

Lippmann's concern is that in the free world politics is in danger of becoming the plaything of the fickleness of public opinion. He illustrates this in the changing attitudes of the United States towards Nazi Germany. At first the general public did not want war, then during the war it could be satisfied with nothing less than unconditional surrender, while after the war interest in the observance of the peace accords quickly ebbed away (25-27). This is just one symptom of a wider and deeper problem: the lack of a compass. At one time the "public philosophy" had pointed the way and it was from this the western democracies had derived their vitality.

Lippmann deliberately uses the singular "public philosophy," for this philosophy rests in his opinion on universal and unchanging principles whose nature is that of natural law (see 79-85). Recognizing that these principles come to the fore in changing historical circumstances, he does not deny the significance of history: the one "public philosophy" lies embedded in the multiplicity of "traditions of civility." It is characteristic of these traditions that all of them in some way couple an unconditional love of truth with a recognition of the relativity of concrete reality (115-19). When, however, all adherence to firm principles falls away, the balance of ideal and real gets disturbed and one of two things can happen: either a fatal breakthrough towards totalitarianism occurs, in which the real is subjected violently to the ideal, or some form of privatization appears. The latter occurs when the ideal is pushed out of public life. The free society can then only find unity around a minimal level of mutual accord. With strong convictions consigned to the private realm, nothing is left but a meagre pseudo-consensus, lacking inner conviction, without a compass, with little or no capacity to resist totalitarian ideologies. This is the malaise in which the western democracies find themselves. In one important passage Lippmann describes the downward movement towards a pseudo-consensus, revealing a penetrating insight into the causes of privatization. The kernel of what Neuhaus was later to call the *"naked* public square," is already here in embryonic form. Of interest also is the appreciative reference to John Courtney Murray, who, as we shall see, pioneered reflection on this question within the Catholic Church.

Within the Western nations, as Father Murray has put it, there is a "plurality of incompatible faiths;" there is also a multitude of secularized and agnostic people. Since there is so little prospect of agreement, and such certainty of dissension, on the content of the public philosophy, it seems expedient not to raise the issues by talking about them. It is easier to follow the rule that each person's beliefs are private and that only overt conduct is a public matter.[12]

Lippmann's analysis of privatization is a profound one. His remedy is a return to the one "public philosophy." The Christian religion, however, has public status as but one of the *traditions of civility*. Diversity has a place, but unity has the last word. And in the last analysis it makes little difference for Lippmann whether the ideal is a Platonic kingdom of ideas or the Kingdom of God.

Plurality

When Lippmann published *The Public Philosophy*, Hannah Arendt was also working intensely on the theme of public and private. In rudimentary form this theme is already present in *The Origins of Totalitarianism* (1951), though it is fully developed only in *The Human Condition* (Chicago, 1958). Behind both Arendt's and Lippmann's conception of "public" lies the republican ideal of the "polis," the community in which free citizens collectively manage the *res publica*. The difference, however, is that the former puts *plurality* and not consensus first. The polis is the place where individuals can meet each other as equals; it is not consensus but debate which constitutes the essence of politics. Indeed it is the very tradition of unity which is suspect. This feeling is eloquently put in a letter Arendt wrote to Karl Jaspers (4 March 1951): "This western philosophy has never had nor could have had a pure concept of politics, because it necessarily spoke of *man as such* and treats the fact of plurality as incidental."[13]

Arendt's concern turns on the concept of "space," an arena within which events can take place; and "public" is connected to "space." Her interest is not in some imaginary point where all things converge, but in a space in which distinctions are maintained, in which individuals, while preserving their own individuality, communicate. Put more strongly, it is only in this space that true individuality can blossom, because only there do continuity and distinction, communality and separation go together.[14]

For Arendt this space is a free creation, and therefore *not* a natural given. Public life is like a surrounding wall[15] that shuts out everything that is natural. This includes private life: caught up as it is in the blind cycle of needs and labor, it falls under the regime of necessity. Freedom comes into existence where people leave routine cares behind them (*The Human Condition*, 30, 37, 65). Arendt's distinction was expressed poetically by W. H. Auden in 1940. In his *New Year Letter* he explained:

> There are two atlases: the one
> The public space where acts are done,
> In theory common to us all,
> Where we are needed and feel small,
> The agora of work and news
> Where each one has the right to choose
> His trade, his corner and his way,
> . . .
> The place where we prefer to live;
> The other is the inner space
> Of private ownership, the place
> That each of us is forced to own,
> Like his own life from which it's grown,
> The landscape of his will and need
> Where he is sovereign indeed. . . .[16]

What is significant about Arendt's thought is that she breaks with the current tendency to connect "public" with "consensus," and "private" with "diversity." This was not possible in Lippmann's thinking because, amid the diversity of "civil traditions" he is still looking for the gold-vein of the one law of nature. Nevertheless Arendt's contribution to the theme "public and plurality" is limited. For her, thinking has an even more republican tendency than

Lippmann's. Lippmann classifies Christianity with the great civil traditions, while Arendt bases her thinking exclusively on the Greco-Roman traditions. The Christian religion in her opinion is non-political and non-public. Jesus did not look for publicity; his kingdom is one of brotherhood, without room for debate (35, 53, 60, 74). Hence for Arendt it appears that *religious* pluralism does not enter the picture.

Indeed she does not view plurality as a multiplicity of views which are ultimately irreconcilable. It is significant that "space" is her preferred metaphor for the public domain. Plurality appears here as spatial diversity. Within the one space of the public domain individuals take different positions and from there develop a variety of perspectives on the matter to be discussed (57). So plurality is merely one of differing points of view. It must immediately be added that she escapes the consequences of the relativistic perspectivism which is lying in wait by introducing the idea of "representative thinking." When operating in normal circumstances, the political debate brings each participant to a consideration of the points of view of the others. Her hope is that, by means of a mode of thinking which is able to "represent" others' points of view, an integrated vision will come into being.[17]

Survey

Having outlined the two basic types of public philosophy, "consensus" and "plurality," I shall now attempt briefly to locate a range of further writers against the background of these two types.

Murray

In North American Roman Catholic circles it was John Courtney Murray (1904-1967) who initiated reflection on the theme of public philosophy. Initially he met with strong resistance. In 1955 the Jesuit order placed him under a writing interdict on the subject of church and state, a measure which was retained for ten years. In 1962, nevertheless, he accompanied Cardinal Spellman to Vatican II, at which he commanded considerable authority on the issue of freedom of religion.

Murray derives the term "public philosophy" from Walter Lippmann.[18] He shares Lippmann's strong emphasis on "consensus," so much so that this concept in effect coincides with that of "public philosophy." In *We Hold These Truths* (1960), for example, he expresses the hope that a "new American experiment" will lead to the discovery of a new public philosophy, "the public philosophy, the consensus we need."[19] The correspondence between Murray and Lippmann goes still further. Murray, too, bases his ideas on natural law. Indeed, the influence of faith in matters within the natural realm is marginalized to such an extent that Charles Curran feels it necessary, in an otherwise sympathetic study, to point out that Murray does not have Catholic doctrine on his side here.[20]

The essence of Murray's theory can be summarized as follows. Within a framework sharing a great deal with Lippmann's (and little with Arendt's), he proposes a new vision of the relationship between state and church. The old model, that of the "confessional state," is urgently in need of replacement. It presupposes, wrongly, that the state cannot function without religious legitimation, and that only the Catholic church is in a position to provide that legitimation (see Curran, 205-11). For Murray, constitutional democracy can manage perfectly well without such a legitimation. However, defending the *autonomy* of the state—and this is his aim—is something entirely different to defending *neutrality*. In the so-called "atheistic state" he sees nothing less than a capitulation to the forces which are privatizing religion. This explains why he shrinks from a *separation* of church and state (217). What he envisages is a distinction, not a separation. The church ought to be able to maintain a public presence alongside the state, distinct from the state, but not separated from it. What he has in mind here is the exercise of political influence by Catholic lay people.[21]

Neuhaus

Richard John Neuhaus's best-known work is *The Naked Public Square*.[22] Once a supporter of Martin Luther King and active in the civil rights movement, he has increasingly taken a critical stand towards progressive movements within the American churches. His primary point of criticism is that the progressives lack a Christian view of public life and that, intentionally or unintentionally, they are playing into the hands of the "radical relativists" for whom in effect any public appeal to normativity conflicts with the pluralistic character of society.[23] In *The Naked Public Square* he argues that the constitutional separation of church and state is increasingly being seized upon as a justification for the *separation of politics and faith* (a justification never intended by the "Founding Fathers").

It is instructive to compare Neuhaus with Lippmann. Negatively, both have the greatest possible objections to debarring strong convictions and normative judgments from the public realm. What we described as Lippmann's "downward movement," appears in Neuhaus as a striving for public neutrality. Both regard this development as crippling. Positively, both share a striking emphasis on consensus. Moreover, both feel that the consensus is embedded in a multiplicity of traditions. For Lippmann they are the "traditions of civility," for Neuhaus they are any communities which keep alive and pass on the "Judeo-Christian" tradition.

The differences between them are, however, significant. Neuhaus, far more than Lippmann, exposes the religious dynamics of the process in question. His whole diagnosis is *religious* in character. He regards the idea of neutrality as an idol, and denies that the "nakedness" of public life can be sustained indefinitely. Rather, the neutrality idea will reveal itself as a quasi-religious power, a "jealous god" which will tolerate nothing else beside it (148). Accordingly, there is a further difference in the way the consensus-idea is worked out. Whereas this idea is supported in Lippmann (and Murray) by natural law, Neuhaus proceeds emphatically from a religious foundation. His "public philosophy" is irrevocably religious; "cannot but be religiously attuned;" "cannot be discussed apart from the religious reality of the American people."[24]

Although Neuhaus's diagnosis is particularly significant for our subject, his own viewpoint encounters serious difficulties. His sympathetic references to Kuyper and North American Kuyperians (51, 175, 267, 271), in whose thought the reality of fundamental religious diversity is fully acknowledged, might suggest that he has jettisoned the consensus idea.[25] But it becomes clear that this is not the case. His problem is that to cling to this idea while also rejecting

Lippmann's and Murray's approach leaves him with only one alternative, namely, to relativize the reality of religious pluralism. He does this in different ways. One is by means of a demographic argument, an appeal to the basic conviction of "the overwhelming majority of Americans."[26] Or, as he puts it elsewhere, "Again, the democratic reality, even, if you will, the raw demographic reality, is that most Americans derive their values and visions from the biblical tradition" (139). Sometimes he takes another route by relativizing the political-cultural significance of that which falls outside the Judeo-Christian tradition. This recent statement is a good illustration:

> Much is made, for instance, of the large presence of Muslims and adherents of Eastern religions in America. There is no evidence to date, however, that these groups are, when it comes to the public order, doing anything other than accommodating their traditions to the cultural and constitutional arrangements that are, in largest part, derived from biblical religion.[27]

My objection to these arguments is that they contain no clear vision of the relationship between "public and plurality." As a result, the public meaning of the Christian religion appears to be left dependent on special circumstances, for example, on the fact that according to the polls a majority of the population "still" regards the Bible as the norm for public life. This shortcoming weighs more heavily than any objections which one might have to Neuhaus's "belief in America" (*The Naked Public Square,* chapter 4), a position which could not but attract vehement criticism.[28] (It should be borne in mind that Neuhaus advocates a *critical* patriotism: one nation *under God* means for him emphatically a nation *under judgment,* and thus one on which there is a mortgage (76, 90, 122-24).

Bellah and Colleagues
In *Habits of the Heart* (1985)[29] by Robert Bellah and others, a new approach to the question of public philosophy is developed which appears to avoid the dilemmas of the "consensus" position. The main theme is the individualism of American society, people's

dissatisfaction with it, but also their inability to escape it, caught as they are in the utilitarian language of individualism ("what's in it for me?") (e.g., 237). According to Bellah and colleagues, to escape it would require nothing less than a reappropriation of public traditions (e.g., 292).

In *Habits of the Heart* we find another retreat from the ideal of unity which dominates so much of the reflection on the concept of "public." It does this by emphatically connecting "public" with "discourse" and "debate." The goal and subject-matter of this debate must be the common good, "our common future," for the only way to triumph over individualism is to recognize the priority of the communal (252-71, 283-87). No unified position, however, is taken in the book. The authors expect nothing from looking for a consensus in the downward direction (cf. our discussion of Lippmann) and do not believe in a higher unity. In their eyes a minimal or "thin" political consensus would lack integrating power and thus offer no relief for the problem of individualism (287). As for the higher unity they cherish no illusions. On the contrary they assume a lasting diversity of irreconcilable, mutually contradictory starting points and convictions (246, 301). Unanimity is not necessary either, for argumentation and debate are the marrow of every tradition.[30]

We seem to be coming closer to Hannah Arendt (though she is not mentioned) than to Lippmann, Murray and Neuhaus. Just as with Arendt, however, the conclusions regarding *religious* pluralism are disappointing, albeit for different reasons. Arendt, we found, thinks of pluralism spatially, as a multiplicity of points of view, needing no deeper foundation for this diversity. Bellah and his associates are, on the contrary, very much aware of philosophically- and religiously-rooted conflicts. But, strangely, these never get "really serious." Religious pluralism is relativized here in two ways. Not only does the book not choose between the two most important public traditions which it distinguishes, the Christian and the republican, but furthermore, it also tries to judge, and so relativize, the public debate from a meta-position.

Regarding the first point, repeatedly the authors mention both main streams in one breath (e.g. 118, 282, 285), without attempting to clarify what divides or unites them. On the one hand, some of them dissent from the idea of a civic covenant, an idea with an unmistakable *biblical* background, while on the other hand, the republican notion of civic virtues appears equally to have left its mark.[31] The second kind of relativization is revealed where, alongside such terms as "contestation" and "conflict," a word like "conversation" suddenly pops up:

> We do not see public social science as unitary or monolithic. We have argued that any living tradition is a conversation, an argument in the best sense, about the meaning and value of our common life. (303)

But would anyone who was actually *involved* in a dispute be able, *at the same time*, to regard it as a "conversation"? Such a characterization can only come from an outsider, from someone who believes that from his lookout post he can see the limitations of all the convictions at stake, and then ironically observing that no one has a monopoly on the truth. It is not surprising that "conversation" in such contexts is often accompanied by irony.[32]

Bellah addresses the question again in a recent article[33] in which he appeals to a passage from Reinhold Niebuhr's *The Children of Light and the Children of Darkness*. Niebuhr's point is that every expression of a strong faith conviction should be accompanied by a humble recognition that all expressions of faith are historically contingent and relative.[34] But Niebuhr demands the impossible. One cannot *at the same time* give expression to a faith conviction *and* admit its historical contingency. Why not? Because the expression presupposes a point of view within the dispute, while the admission presupposes one outside it. What Bellah refers to as the "Niebuhrian dialectic of affirmation and humble recognition of one's finiteness"[35] is simply unattainable.

Conclusion

How is it that the consensus-idea continues to recur? In conclusion I want to suggest that it does so because every public order indeed presupposes a *certain kind* of communality. There is an element of truth in the consensus-idea. If communality is totally absent, public life will shrivel up and nothing will be left but a form of politics characterized by MacIntyre as "a continuation of civil war with other means."[36] Those who defend *plurality* consistently must face the question in what way a public order characterized by plurality alone would differ from disintegrating societies such as Northern Ireland, Lebanon or some of the newly independent Balkan republics. If we want to avoid Bellah's problem—the telescoping of the viewpoints of participants and onlookers—then it will have to be shown that a form of communality can be found which does not exclude really deep differences. To use Martin Marty's terms, it is a question of showing that "conviction" and "civility" do not need to be mutually exclusive.[37]

At this point, I suggest, the approach rooted in what has come to be known as "reformational" political philosophy can assist us. What is striking in the most important publications associated with this approach is that equal emphasis is placed on the struggle between conflicting *religious-ideological persuasions*, and on the need to establish *structurally specific norms* in the political arena, centrally that of "public justice."[38] The norms belong to the *structure* of the political realm: they are what actually constitute phenomena as *political* phenomena.

Put differently, *such normativity is constitutive of political life.* What this conception points to is the possibility of a definite, structure-specific communality among diverging persuasions. The "civility" of the "convictions" is given with the structure within which the persuasions can articulate their beliefs. It is the normative structure of the political realm itself, rather than any substantive consensus among the different religious-ideological persuasions, which provides the basis for the communality. The norms in question, such as "public justice," arise from the very nature of the political community. For the political community to remain viable at all, these norms must be operative. This communality remains intact as long as movements do not seek to exploit the political structure for the pursuit of non-political ends. Examples of this would include Islamic fundamentalist movements like those in Iran, or ethnic-religious extremists like those in Northern Ireland, or combinations of the two such as in Lebanon. Only at that point would MacIntyre be shown to be right: "Modern politics is civil war carried on by other means." Maybe Auden was right when he said:

> . . . true democracy begins
> With free confession of our sins.
> In this alone are all the same,
> All are so weak that none dare claim
> "I have the right to govern," or
> "Behold in me the Moral Law,"
> And all real unity commences
> In consciousness of differences. . . .

Notes

This text was translated by Judy Peterson. A shorter Dutch version of this article appeared in H. M. Vroom, ed., *Cultuur als partner van de theologie* (Kampen: J. H. Kok, 1990), a Festschrift dedicated to G. E. Meuleman on his retirement as Professor of the philosophy of religion at the Vrije Universiteit, Amsterdam. My thanks to are due the publisher and the editor for permission to translate the text.

I could not have written this article without the help of Richard J. Mouw, with whom I have recently written a book on pluralism, *Pluralisms and Horizons* (Grand Rapids: Eerdmans, 1993). It was he who, at an early stage of our project, fathomed the meaning of "public philosophy" and introduced me to the work of Murray and Bellah. While working on the section on Hannah Arendt, I profited greatly from discussions with Bart Prins of the Vrije Universiteit.

1. By "religions" I mean not only established religions, but also worldviews such as humanism.
2. See the entry "Öffentlich/privat" in *Historisches Worterbuch der Philosophie*, vol. 6, J. von Ritter and K. Grunder, eds., (Darmstadt: 1984), 1131-34.
3. According to Sennett "public," meaning "the common good," emerged as early as the fifteenth century, appearing around 1470 as "publyke wele." The second sense, meaning, for example, "open to

the scrutiny of everyone," emerged at the end of the seventeenth century, (*The Fall of Public Man*, New York: Knopf, 1977), 16. In most cases no distinction was drawn between the two meanings.
4. K. Schilder, referring to Revelation 11:8, in *De Openbaring van Johannes en het sociale leven*, 3rd impression, (Delft: Meinema, 1951), 260.
5. See the final passages of his "On the Public-Private Distinction in the Light of 'Encounter'," in K. Otto-Apel, et al., in S. Griffioen, ed., *What Right Does Ethics Have? Public Philosophy in a Pluralistic Culture*, (Amsterdam: Vrije Universiteit Press, 1991), 123.
6. Hegel, not unfairly, interpreted Enlightenment and orthodoxy as each other's mirror images (see *Die Phänomenologie des Geistes*, especially the section entitled "Der Kampf der Aufklarung mit dem Aberglauben," 1807).
7. See my contribution on Paul Ricoeur's "decentralization of reason" in *Vrede met de rede?* J. Klapwijk, S. Griffioen and G. Groenewoud, eds., (Assen: Van Gorcum, 1976), 37-62.
8. F. R. Ankersmit, "De staat: huisvader werd buurman," in *NRC-Handelsblad*, 13 March 1990.
9. C. A. van Peursen, *Trouw*, 14 October 1965.
10. In my *Veranderingen in het denkklimaat*, (Leiden: Leidse Universitaire Pers, 1981), I suggest that the Dutch humanist J. P. van Praag comes to the point of conceding this (cf. 17). M. F. Fresco challenges my interpretation in *De mens als feit, als moqelijkheid en als norm*, (Utrecht: *Humanistisch Verbond*, 1981), 3-4.
11. New York: New American Library, Mentor Book, 1956.
12. Lippman is referring in *The Public Philosophy* to John Courtney Murray's "The Problem of Pluralism in America," *Thought*, (Fordham University, Summer, 1954).
13. *Briefwechsel, herausgegeben von Lotte Kohler & Hans Saner*, (Piper Verlag: München, 1985) 201-203. This letter was inspired by the appearance of *The Origins of Totalitarianism*. Jaspers had asked "whether Jahweh has not disappeared altogether?" (letter, 15 February 1951). Arendt's answer was that the Christian and Jewish religions as religions are passé because they have no answer to the modern form of evil, namely that of an impersonal complex which can no longer be characterized in terms of sin. But, she continues,

the philosophical tradition suffers from another kind of one-sidedness. Then follow the words quoted.

14. Cf. *The Human Condition*, 52-53. Both separation and relatedness receive a new, non-natural quality here. Bernstein has understood this well: "By plurality, Arendt does not mean sheer otherness, but the distinctive individuality of human beings that is revealed and *appears* in the public realm;" R. J. Bernstein, *Beyond Objectivism and Relativism*, (Oxford: Blackwell, 1983) 208.

15. According to Arendt *polis* originally connoted something like a "ring-wall" (*The Human Condition*, 64, note 64).

16. From W. H. Auden's "New Year Letter, To Elizabeth Mayer," (January 1, 1940), *The Collected Poetry of W. H. Auden*, (New York: Random House, 1945), 296.

17. "Truth and Politics," in Hannah Arendt, *Between Past and Future*, (New York: Penguin, 1977), 241.

18. According to David Hollenbach in *Justice, Peace, and Human Rights: American Catholic Social Ethics in a Pluralistic Context*, (New York: Crossroad 1988), 77.

19. Quoted in David Hollenbach, op. cit.

20. "Murray," as Curran remarks, "never appeals to scripture in his theological considerations of political ethics." "Murray is not unaware of the Catholic teaching that one cannot observe the substance of the natural law for a long time without grace or a change of heart . . . but such a teaching does not enter into the heart of Murray's understanding." Charles E. Curran, *American Catholic Social Ethics*, (Notre Dame, IN: University Press, 1982), 180-81, cf. 218, 219. For a more expanded commentary see J. Leon Hooper, S. J., *The Ethics of Discourse: The Social Philosophy of John Courtney Murray*, (Washington: Georgetown University Press, 1986), especially the section entitled: "The impact of consensus theory on natural law theory," 93-99.

21. "The effort of the church, through the action of laity conscious of its Christian and civic responsibilities, is to effect that Christianization of society in all its dimensions which enable and oblige the state, as the instrument of society, to function in a Christian sense" (Curran, 206). What makes this passage interesting is its correspondence with the Kuyperian view of Christian influence in politics.

22. Grand Rapids: Eerdmans, 1984. Unless otherwise indicated, all page references in this section are to this book.

23. *Unsecular America*, R. J. Neuhaus, ed., (Grand Rapids: Eerdmans, 1986). The "radical relativists" (59) are, according to Neuhaus, out to banish "all cultural and historical referents from our common life" (61); what motivates them is a "hostility to normative culture" (66).

24. Cf. Richard J. Neuhaus, "From Civil Religion to Public Philosophy," in *Civil Religion and Political Theology*, Boston University Studies in Philosophy and Religion, vol. 8, Leroy S. Rouner, ed., (Notre Dame, IN: University Press, 1986), 106.

25. On the Kuyperian conception of religious pluralism, see for example J. W. Skillen and R. M. McCarthy, eds., *Political Order and the Plural Structure of Society*, Emory University Studies in Law and Religion, (Alpharetta, GA.: Scholars Press, 1992), Part III. For its reception and articulation in America, see G. S. Smith, *Seeds of Secularization: Calvinism, Culture and Pluralism in America 1870-1915*, (Grand Rapids: Christian University Press, 1985); and R. M. McCarthy, et al., *Society, State and Schools: A Case for Structural and Confessional Pluralism*, (Grand Rapids: Eerdmans, 1981).

26. *Unsecular America*, 63.

27. *This World*, vol. 24 (1989): 83.

28. Robert Bellah says: "It is as though Neuhaus has suddenly forgotten about sin" (*Civil Religion and Political Theology*), 89. Ronald Wells calls the "belief in America" a "major flaw" of *The Naked Public Square*: "As a Christian I am a member of a transnational and transhistorical community of belief and my loyalty to a given nation-state cannot be the starting point for my engagement of the political process," "Under the Sacred Canopy," *The Reformed Journal*, vol. 34, Nov. 1984: 19-20.

29. Robert N. Bellah, Richard Madsen, William M. Sullivan, Ann Swidler, Steven M. Tipton, *Habits of the Heart, Individualism and Commitment in American Life*, (Berkeley and Los Angeles: University of California Press, 1985). References are to the Harper and Row reprint, New York, 1986.

30. P. 303; see also the appreciative reference to MacIntyre's concept of tradition as a continuing debate (309, note 1 to chapter 2, in
A. MacIntyre, *After Virtue*).
31. On the notion of a covenant, see *Reconstructing Public
Philosophy* by William Sullivan, (Berkeley: University of California
Press), the philosopher among the authors of *Habits of the Heart*,
Sullivan opposes "covenant" to "contract." The heart of the "civil
tradition" in his opinion is "the moral imperative to live according
to the principles of justice and mutual support grounded in civil
covenant" (180). He appeals here to Bellah's *The Broken Covenant*,
(New York: Seabury, 1975). Sullivan says, "Unlike the liberal idea
of a contract, which emphasizes mutual obligations within clearly
defined limits, a civic covenant is a bond of fundamental trust
founded upon common commitment to a moral understanding"
(160-61).
32. The combination of "conversation" and "irony" is typical of
philosopher Richard Rorty.
33. See Robert N. Bellah, "Public Philosophy and Public Theology
in America Today," in *Civil Religion and Political Theology*, 87.
34. New York: Scribners, 1944, 944, 134.
35. Bellah, op. cit., 89. Interestingly enough, Bellah is speaking here
about Neuhaus's *The Naked Public Square*. He feels that Neuhaus
is at one with Niebuhr, except, however, on his patriotism. Here
Bellah misses "the Niebuhrian dialectic."
36. *After Virtue*, (London: Duckworth, 1981), 236.
37. See the discussion between Bernard Zylstra and Hendrik Hart
on whether the existence of incompatible ultimate visions of life
renders a society unsustainable. Hart claimed that it did, while
Zylstra, rightly in my view, insisted that it was precisely the genius
of "pluriform democracy" to make a harmonious coexistence of
different visions possible. Cf. *The Guide* (Toronto: Christian Labour
Association of Canada), January-February 1982, and *Anakainosis*
(Toronto: Institute for Christian Studies), vol. 4, no. 3, March 1982.
38. For further background to this tradition, see Bernard Zylstra's
"Introduction" to L. Kalsbeek, *Contours of a Christian Philosophy:
An Introduction to Herman Dooyeweerd's Thought*, (Toronto:
Wedge, 1975). Zylstra's bibliography in this same work contains

numerous references to political theorists who have developed the notions of religious pluralism, public justice and related ideas. See especially the references to H. Dooyeweerd, J. P. A. Mekkes, H. van Riessen, J. D. Dengerink and B. Goudzwaard.

Trudeau and the French Canadians

John L. Hiemstra

Introduction

Political scientists recognize that federalism is crucial for a proper understanding of provincial and national politics in Canada. Recognizing the centrality of federalism, however, does not mean that political scientists and politicians agree on what federalism is, what it can do, and where it will lead. In this paper I will analyze Pierre Elliott Trudeau's political philosophy, how it shapes and give content to his idea of federalism, and how he sees federalism as a means of gradually dissolving and assimilating minorities into a larger common society.

Just prior to his election as Prime Minister in 1967, Trudeau dedicated a collection of essays on political philosophy and federalism to "the progress of the French Canadians."[1] A helpful perspective on this puzzling dedication is given by Bernard Zylstra in his perceptive assessment of Canada's new Constitution. The key to Trudeau's ideas on federalism, Zylstra argues, is rooted in his rejection of the political stance of classic Roman Catholicism—still a force within French Canada of the fifties—and a commitment to liberalism so complete that he became "the most perfect embodiment of the ideology of liberalism in Canada."[2] Furthermore, Zylstra argues, liberalism tends to denigrate, trivialize, or dissolve the religious, cultural, and social-structural plurality that are important to "French Canadian" society.[3] It is in the context of this ideology that Trudeau uses the concept of federalism.

The significance and impact of Trudeau's liberalism was greatly multiplied because he became Prime Minister at the same time that liberalism became the accepted public ideology in Canada. Therefore, even though Trudeau was a political theorist in his own right, his political ideas became important, not so much for any originality or academic influence, but because they were significant in creating a number of public policies in Canada. During the sixteen years of his prime ministership, Trudeau played a crucial role in creating the institution of "First Minister's Conferences"; designing the policies of "Bilingualism" and "Multiculturalism"; patriating and amending the Canadian Constitution, and drafting the new "Charter of Rights and Freedoms"; fighting against "sovereignty association" in the 1980 Quebec referendum campaign; and more recently, helping oppose the proposed Meech Lake Accord amendments to the Canadian Constitution. All of these policies were closely related to his vision of federalism.

This essay will present a systematic overview of Trudeau's basic assumptions and political philosophy. It will then show how these ideas led to a particular conception of how diverse religions, cultures, and social structures ought to be accommodated within a single public order. These fundamental components of his thought are crucial for understanding both his analysis of (French Canadian) nationalism and his conviction that federalism can be a solution for nationalism. The paper concludes that Trudeau's conception of federalism, as directed by his political philosophy, was ultimately hostile to genuine freedom for various religions, cultures, and societal structures in Canada. Despite his deep commitment to individual freedom, Trudeau's conception of federalism has the unintended consequence of gradually undermining the very individual freedom he intended to expand, when he dedicated his book to "the progress of the French Canadians."

The Role of Political Philosophy

In order to understand Trudeau's political philosophy, it is necessary first to outline his distinctive conception of the role of all political philosophies. The one inherent danger that looms over all political philosophies, he argues, is that they might crystallize into dangerous ideologies and become the "true enemies of freedom."[4] Ideologies develop when political ideas become too universally accepted among the political elites who then claim "exclusive possession of the truth."[5]

Trudeau begins his own political philosophy with an attempted categorical rejection of all ideologies, and with the pragmatic assertion that he has no fixed political ideas other than a few basic principles such as "liberty, a democratic form of government, a parliamentary system, respect of the individual, [and] balance between federal and provincial governments...."[6] As a pragmatist, he starts from "the given facts" and proceeds to "seek and define the conditions of progress in advanced societies."[7] Since Trudeau understands progress as "the slow journey towards personal freedom"[8] he states that political philosophy's role is simply to guarantee an order which encourages the greatest measure of individual liberty. The political philosopher carries out this task by discerning the direction of elite opinion and ideology, and then developing the appropriate counterweights.[9] The judicious use of these counterweights, or checks and balances, by practical politicians will help create and maintain an equilibrium in society that in turn yields greater individual liberty and thus progress.

Trudeau's political career is marked by choices made in this manner, as for example, his reactions to certain "ideological" developments in Canadian federalism:

In the 1950s [Trudeau] was a staunch supporter of Duplessis' policy of provincial autonomy and a severe critic of the post-war centralization in Ottawa, even to the point of taking the unpopular stand of opposing federal aid to universities. In 1965 when the extension of provincial autonomy threatened to destroy legitimate federal [national] power, he entered federal politics as a defender of constitutionalism and Canadian federalism.[10]

Basic Assumptions

Trudeau's idea of the role of political philosophy implies a reactionary and conservative type of political action. However, his basic assumptions concerning individual freedom, equality, rationality, ethical competition, and historical progress give his political ideas a truly dynamic and optimistic thrust.[11]

At the centre of Trudeau's assumptions is the over-riding idea of the "infinite value" of the individual.[12] An individual should never be identified with a particular mass of humanity, since the individual precedes and supersedes the claims of all external or collective entities, including "capital, the nation, tradition, the church and even the state."[13] Progress within history is moving away from such collective constraints towards greater individual freedom.

The central characterizing feature of the individual, he further assumes, is freedom. "Liberty is a free gift—a birthright, which distinguishes man from the beast."[14] The ultimate purpose of this freedom is individual self-fulfilment, understood as "the right of every individual to do his own thing."[15] This freedom and right implies the power to reshape human and non-human nature.

> The first visible effect of freedom is change. A free man exercises his freedom by altering himself and—inevitably—his surroundings. It follows that no liberal can be other than receptive to change and highly positive and active in response to it, for change is the very expression of freedom.[16]

His third assumption is equality, the logical correlate of his idea that the essence of our humanity is our liberty. Individuals are unequal in many ways, but they are equal in regards to their inherent right to liberty. This individualistic idea of equality is often expressed by Trudeau in terms of "equality of opportunity."[17] Equality requires the provision of some "means"—economic, social, or cultural support—for genuine "equality of opportunity" to exist.[18]

Trudeau's personal motto "Reason over Passion" signals his fourth assumption of rationality. An individual can be free and equal because he is capable of rationally directing his passions. In politics, the inversion of reason and passions leads to distortions such as nationalism, defined by Trudeau as an emotional attachment to the state. History, he is convinced, testifies to the war, revolution, and carnage left in the wake of nationalism.[19] The positive concept of rationality that Trudeau works with most frequently is calculative self-interest.[20]

The ethical ideas of Trudeau form a fifth set of assumptions. The essence of ethics is full freedom of action based on individually calculated preferences. No outside authority of any kind is required because these choices stand solely within the private authority of the individual.

> I believe that in the last analysis, a human being in the privacy of his own mind has the exclusive authority to choose his own scale of values and to decide which forces will take precedence over others. A good constitution is one that does not prejudice any of those questions, but leaves citizens free to orient their human destinies as they see fit.[21]

As Trudeau suggests, such ethical freedom can be practised most successfully within the context of a "constitution" that recognizes and ensures such choice. Such a constitution entrenches several of the most fundamental values beyond the reach of governments. But what type of values should be entrenched? Trudeau answers this question with his (implicit) distinction between particular and universal values. Certain values are, or become, so self-evidently important in setting the conditions for achieving the central goal of individual freedom that they move up from the status of particular and private values towards being more universal and public values.[22]

Particular values, in Trudeau's writing, are local and private and are identified with particular cultures, languages, racial groups, ethnic groups,[23] or regional qualities. Universal values, on the other hand, are those values that transcend the boundaries of particular values, and are identified as liberty, democracy, truth, life,[24] equality of opportunity, and certain technological and economic values such as efficiency and competition.[25] While particular values are recognized as transitional and only useful in our own age,[26] universal values have lasting utility, and are international and common to all men, although ultimately they always fall short of being absolute and eternal.

This distinction between types of values is also important for his sixth assumption of historical progress. History is being created by individuals who struggle to realize themselves through the competitive discovery and practice of new and superior values. A dynamic interaction occurs within history, between various particular values and between particular and universal values, that yield greater individual freedom—that is, progress.[27]

The evolution of values within history is influenced by the two factors of competition and protection. The dynamic force behind such change is competition, because it is the means through which individuals entertain and test new values.

> I just feel that the challenge of the age is to live together with people who don't have all the same values as yourself. I believe that the way to progress is the free challenge of ideas and confrontation of values . . . the challenge is to have all these values challenge each other in terms of excellence, and it is this challenge which permits a society to develop on the basis of excellence.[28]

Although at one point, Trudeau suggests that the particular values found in French Canadian institutions "do not deserve to survive at all unless they can successfully survive external competition,"[29] he softens this conclusion with the second factor of protection. A degree of protection limits the harder effects of competition and allows all values an equal opportunity to compete.[30] Without the proper balance of competing values, unbridled competition would cruelly and unfairly decimate particular values that certain groups of individuals still require to survive. However, over-protection can also lead to negative results such as cultural isolation, inadequate cross-fertilization of values, and ultimately the creation of a "hot house" culture.[31] The attractiveness of a "middling" position between competition and protection is that it yields gradual and controlled change, and therefore will be more likely to lead rational individuals to the recognition that their particular values are irrational, and thus prepare them wilfully and successfully to accept "more" universal values.[32]

In the historical process competing particular values have the ultimate fate either of fading away as their utility is diminished and other values dominate, or of flourishing in the competition and gradually ascending to a higher and wider range of acceptance constitutive of the (more) universal values. Trudeau illustrates this dynamic in terms of nationalism:

> And just like clannishness, tribalism and even feudalism, nationalism will probably fade away by itself at whatever time in history the nation has outworn its utility: that is to say, when the particular values protected by the idea of nation are no longer counted as important, or when those values no longer need to be embodied in a nation to survive.[33]

The Individual and the State

Trudeau's basic assumptions provide both the logical foundation for, and the dynamic thrust behind, his social and political philosophy. To begin, he understands society to be a human functional creation meant to serve the free individual in his self-fulfillment. "The point of human society is that men living together, by mutual help, co-operation, and the division of labour, can fulfil themselves better than if they lived apart."[34] Social structures have the limited authority to restrict certain individual freedoms, according to Trudeau, only because individuals chose to delegate such authority.

Based on the idea of society as voluntary and cooperative action by autonomous individuals, he then argues that the state ". . . is by definition the instrument whereby human society collectively organizes and expresses itself." His doctrine of the "servant state" suggests that the state exists solely to serve individual self-fulfillment through the provision of collective goods such as hospitals and

schools. The authority of the state is not derived from a higher
"intrinsic duty" or "Divine calling to enforce justice," since that
would imply that its authority is independent of, and greater than,
the individual's freedom. On the contrary, state authority originates
in the individual, who delegates it to the state through active consent.[35] Thus all social and political collectivities are created by
individuals, to serve individuals, and continue to do so by the
ongoing consent of individuals.[36]

The task of the state, according to Trudeau, cannot be understood in terms of a substantive value of "justice" because that would
seriously infringe on the individual's freedom to determine his or
her own values. The role of the state to procure justice must be
understood in a strictly "procedural" manner[37]—that is, the state
must function only to maintain those services necessary for the
individual to be free to choose his or her own path to self-fulfilment.
Thus the content of justice is simply a function of individual values
and interests and has no substantive meaning itself.

In the same way, a government ought to determine the "common
good" by calculating the common denominator of all the competing
private "goods" and interests. It does so through the active democratic participation of all of the citizens. In this way "the laws, in a
sense, reflect the wishes of the citizens and thus turn to account the
special wisdom of each one; social order to some extent embodies
all the wealth of human experience that the citizens possess."[38] The
majority mechanism is the means by which the "special wisdom" of
all is instrumentally realized.

> For if all men are equal, each one the possessor of a special
> dignity, it follows inevitably that the happiness of fifty-one is
> more important than that of forty-nine. It is normal, then that .
> . . the decisions preferred by fifty-one should prevail.[39]

Although Trudeau is quick to concede that the majority
mechanism is a weak instrument[40] and not an infallible guide to the
truth—since "one person may be right and ninety-nine wrong"[41]—
still the weight of his ideas force him in this direction. He has faith[42]
that participatory democracy channelled through the majority

mechanism is the best available means for ensuring the triumph of the public good over the private goods. He defends this idea by arguing that a dissenting individual still has the procedural right, within a liberal democratic constitution that includes freedom of speech, to attempt to convince the other ninety-nine of his opinion.

However at the close of his series of articles on this topic, Trudeau abruptly backs off from direct participatory democracy and falls back on representative democracy. He justifies this reversal with the argument that average citizens don't know enough about the details of specific policies, and consequently, they are only required to vote on "a set of ideas and tendencies, and on the men who hold them and give effect to them."[43] This is not to suggest that Trudeau thinks lightly about participation within a procedurally defined order, for as Prime Minister during the upheaval in Quebec in the October Crisis (1970) he justified the use of state force against certain individual freedoms in order to maintain such a procedural order.

This is the beauty of the democratic process: it permits that subjective view of justice—which everyone holds—permits that subjective view of justice to express itself peacefully through discussion, through reason, and through the voting process. . . . I think that as the guardian of justice elected by the people it is our duty to use whatever forms of force—police, army—to make sure that at least the freedom of choice is preserved.[44]

Trudeau's advocacy of a constitutionally entrenched Bill of Rights for Canada also comports well with this procedural view of the state and justice. As early as 1958, Trudeau argued for a Bill of Rights that would entrench certain rights and values against infringement by other individuals and beyond the grasp of the state.[45] These rights and values would guarantee a (procedural justice) framework within society, that would recognize the liberty of every individual to select subjectively his or her own values.[46]

This procedural view of justice further illuminates the earlier discussion of Trudeau's equilibrium view of the role of political philosophy. In a procedural justice state, political philosophy can not function in its classical role of discerning the truth for a society or of guiding citizens towards greater virtue. Instead, political philosophy is simply a means of assessing the disequilibrium of a society and designing the counterweights required to maintain a procedural order guaranteeing individual liberty.

Religion, Culture, and Social Structures

Trudeau's assumptions and political ideas give a distinct color to his account of how a diversity of religions, languages, cultures, and social structures ought to be accommodated within a single political jurisdiction. These will be dealt with in terms of three questions.

First, what is the place of religious convictions[47] within the public realm and within institutions required by, or impacted by, public law? In concise terms, Trudeau understands religion to be an individual and private question on which the public realm should be neutral. A public place and role for religious values would immediately threaten the individual's freedom to determine his or her own ultimate values. Thus Trudeau's commitment to the goal of increased individual freedom requires a privatized and limited idea of religion.

Second, how can several distinct cultures co-exist and develop within the territorial jurisdiction of a single state? To begin with, culture for Trudeau is strictly an individual quality based on preference and choice.[48] The suggestion that a particular culture has an intrinsic or substantive value would again diminish and undermine the primacy of free individual choice. This became obvious, for example, when the Trudeau government proposed the elimination of "special status" for Canada's aboriginal peoples. The rationale he defended was that his policy would make native people "equal" with other Canadians and thus free to compete with other cultural values within the Canadian state. He argued this even though the native peoples of Canada loudly rejected his assumption that culture is an individual and non-substantive value.[49]

For Trudeau, culture and language achieve public recognition solely on the basis of aggregate individual power. "In terms of *realpolitik*, French and English are equal in Canada because each of these linguistic groups has the power to break the country. And this power cannot yet be claimed by the Iroquois, the Eskimo, or the Ukrainians."[50]

Although in many societies language is viewed as an essential component of culture, for Trudeau language is only important if it functions to carry other more universal values and not because of its own intrinsic value.

> French [as a language] will only have value to the extent that it is spoken by a progressive people. What makes for vitality and excellence in language is the collective quality of the people speaking it. In short, the defence of the French language cannot be successful without accomplishments that make the defence worthwhile.[51]

Third, what is the place of social structures and associations within society, and how should they relate to the state? Trudeau wants to create greater religious and cultural freedom for individuals by arguing that the private sphere should be as large as possible and the public realm should be neutral. But the logic of this idea yields an ironic conclusion. As a starting point, he argues that individuals must be free to choose their own values without interference from social institutions or other collectivities. Empirically, however, individuals live out their cultural and religious values within social structures and, furthermore, these social structures can only function successfully if they have the authority to impose on individuals the values that are necessary to achieve the task that is distinctive of this social structure. In Trudeau's scheme, such "collective" impositions on individuals are prevented by having the political majority create a procedural order for the operation of these social structures that entrench the supremacy of individual freedom, for example, through the Charter of Rights and Freedoms and Education Acts.

The irony is this: the procedural order forces the religious and cultural minorities that live and act within and through social structures to accept that their values are always secondary and subservient to the majority's imposed procedural value of guaranteeing individual freedom. For example, the meaning of a Roman Catholic

school requirement that their teachers must live according to
Catholic morality because it reflects the absolute "law of God," is
completely relativized when interpreted within an over-arching procedural order that says the individual is absolutely free to choose his
or her own moral values. The procedural order is intended to
advance individual freedom, but when a group of individuals form
an institution, such as a school, to carry out the implications of their
free religious or linguistic choices, the procedural order effectively
denies them the freedom to practice this freedom in the schooling
they choose for their children.[52] While a liberal procedural order
allows individuals the freedom to dissent and to fight for its reform,
it does not leave them the public room to practice religious and
cultural values that conflict with majoritarian ways.[53]

Before moving to Trudeau's analysis of and solution for
nationalism, it is necessary to return briefly to Trudeau's characterization of the role of political philosophy discussed above. Although he strongly asserts that his ideas are non-ideological and are
designed to prevent ideology, in fact the opposite is true.[54] Trudeau
tends to make his assumptions of individual freedom into an "absolute truth in politics."[55] While this goal of increasing individual
freedom is not substantive in character—in that it does not dictate
a particular substantive truth as the goal for society and the state,
as do the ideologies he attacks—it does function as a procedural
goal. All other issues are conceptualized, justified, and judged
according to whether or not they can function within boundaries
and criteria required for individual freedom. In this way, the goal of
individual freedom inspires an ideology to which all other goals and
means must be made to conform.[56] Thus Trudeau's description of
the role of political philosophy in political action is inadequate for
understanding the actual role of his own ideas in his use of federalism.

The Heresy of Nationalism
Trudeau's political analysis and action was historically aimed at
French Canadian nationalism,[57] the "offending" ideology of his own
time and place. These nationalists argued that any group that shares
a common culture, language, religion and social heritage, and lives

in a compact geographic area, constitutes a nation and provides a sufficient reason for creating a new state to preserve these characteristics.[58] This foundational idea of the nationalists is problematic for Trudeau because it undermines his basic assumptions and political ideas, and consequently would severely hinder the "progress" of the French Canadians.

A closer examination of Trudeau's critique of nationalism shows that in fact he sees it as an inversion of his basic assumptions. The nationalists place the national collectivity above the freedom of the individual. They stress the equality of nations rather than the equality of individuals. They emphasize passions as the "glue" of society rather than reason. They see the path to progress as achieved through nations rather than individuals.[59] These distortions, Trudeau concludes, lead to all manner of dangers such as chauvinism, racism, jingoism, crusades, and wars.[60]

Politically, the nationalists err in their designation of the state as the servant of the nation rather than of the individual. Justice is not defined as a procedure which maximizes individual freedom, but rather as a specific substantive idea of the nation's self-interest in maintaining a particular culture, religion, and/or social structure. The common good is understood to be a function of the nation's good, not the aggregate of individual goods.

> In attaching such importance to the idea of nation, they are surely led to a designation of the common good as a function of an ethnic group, rather than of all the people, regardless of characteristics. . . . A truly democratic government cannot be "nationalistic" because it must pursue the good of all its citizens, without prejudice to ethnic origin.[61]

Once the common good has been made a function of the nation, the individual is no longer free to help determine the common good but is reduced to being a passive recipient of a predetermined common good. For this reason he argues that "a nationalistic government is by nature intolerant, discriminatory, and, when all is said and done, totalitarian."[62]

Perhaps the greatest problem with nationalism, for Trudeau, is that it undermines the means of social, intellectual, and cultural progress. Genuine value progress is impossible within a nationalist state because individual value competition is subverted to the values of the nation. This leads to anaemic culture,[63] social introversion, and intellectual sterility. Thus he characterizes everything held by the nationalist as temporary and inferior:

> The nation is, in fact, the guardian of very positive qualities: a cultural heritage, common traditions, a community awareness, historical continuity, a set of mores; all of which, at this juncture in history, go to make a man what he is. Certainly, these qualities are more private than public, more introverted than extroverted, more instinctive and primitive than intelligent and civilized, more self-centred and impulsive than generous and reasonable. They belong to a transitional period in history. But they are a reality of our time, probably useful, and in any event considered indispensable by all national communities.[64]

It was characteristic of the nationalists, Trudeau argues, that when the progress, universality, and potential of liberalism was too much for their particular concerns, they "took refuge in the bosom of its mother, the Holy Nation."[65]

The Federal Solution to Nationalism

Trudeau turns to the political instrument of federalism as the most suitable solution to "poly-ethnic pluralism"[66] and for the particular "distortions" of nationalism. He begins with a classical form of federalism which, he suggests, would have consisted of a state that "divided the totality of its sovereign powers between regional and central governments with such sharpness and adequacy that those governments would have been able to carry on their affairs in complete independence of one another."[67] He doubts whether this form of federalism ever existed and argues that even if it had, it would be in conflict with the facts of the modern world. Therefore, he makes a significant amendment to this classical definition by adding the provision that there must be frequent "cooperation and interchange between the two levels."[68]

At first glance it appears that Trudeau's appreciation for federalism is based solely on its compatibility with his basic assumptions. Federalism respects the individual freedom of each citizen, for example, in that it places no further collective constraints on the individual. The power of the state is simply divided into two levels without adding more government. This division of powers is based on the common agreement of individual citizens, with the points of consensus forming the national level, and potentially divisive issues being delegated to the regional level.[69]

Federalism also respects his assumption of the rationality of individuals. Emotional and particular values, such as those that constitute nationalism, can be secured on the local level, while the points of rational agreement are put on the national level. Furthermore, federalism respects the rational participation of the citizens by allowing them to calculate whether it is in their interest to remain within the federal system or not.[70] In this way reason and freedom are balanced within federalism.

> The French revolution attempted to delineate national territories according to the will of the people, without reference to rationality; the Congress of Vienna claimed to draw state boundaries according to reason, without the reference to the will of the people; and federalism arose as an empirical effort to base a country's frontiers on both reason and the will of the People.[71]

Trudeau also understands federalism to be compatible with his political ideas, especially the idea of justice as procedure. The federal mechanism is not biased toward substantial concerns and thus it can be pragmatically adjusted to create an equilibrium that best fits the place and circumstance.[72] The division of powers between national and regional levels is also a question of means and not ends.[73] National unity is maintained within diversity, by fine-tuning the equilibrium between divisive regionalized loyalties and the centralizing effect of national integration.[74]

In functioning this way, federalism complements the operation of the "procedural justice" state. Just as the procedural state establishes a consensus in the public realm and relegates individual differences to the private realm, so the federal mechanism delegates areas of broad consensus to the national realm and individual and collective particularities to the federal sub-divisions.[75]

However, federalism as a geographically based division of powers between levels of government, really concerns the management of regional centrifugal forces that may well be independent of the diversity of religions, cultures, and social structures that exist within it.[76] Trudeau's discussion of federalism tends to merge the geographically based problem with the other three discussed above. When federalism is empirically applied as a solution for these other types of diversity, it is evident that it does not solve them, but instead duplicates them![77] For example, within the national federal jurisdiction of Canada there is a diversity in cultures, languages and social structures, dominated by English Canadians, while the provincial subdivision of Quebec has the same diversity but instead is dominated by French Canadians. Members of the both French and English majorities are minorities in the opposite federal jurisdiction. Furthermore, other minorities such as the native peoples are politically no freer to practice their culture or religion within Quebec than they are in Canada.

While this observation may seem like a truism, it misses the central thrust of Trudeau's ideologically charged idea of federalism, namely, that it will solve "the worldwide problems of ethnic pluralism"[78] and lead to the "progress of the French Canadians." It is the character of this solution that shows how important the motivating ideas are behind political instruments like federalism.

Federalism and Progress
According to Trudeau, federalism is a superbly suited instrument for enabling the competition of values and thus historical progress. He recognizes that the great diversity of individual values within the Canadian state[79] would be threatened in, and destroyed by, an excessively competitive environment. Federalism solves this problem by setting up the right balance between value competition and

protection. Values entrenched at the national level are commonly accepted, while those values delegated to the lower jurisdictions can be protected by local governments while at the same time undergoing competition between federal units.

> Canadian federalism is ideal. While requiring French Canadians, in the federal sector, to submit their way of doing things (and especially their political forms) to the test of competition, the federal system allows us at the same time to provide for ourselves in Quebec the form of government and educational institutions that best suit our needs.[80]

As a result of the limited value competition within the protection of the federal system, some values would emerge as more universal in character and live on in the national federal consensus and other values, such as those implied in nationalism, would be rejected as too particular. For this reason, Trudeau praises the political tool of federalism as a "brilliant prototype for the moulding of tomorrow's civilization."[81]

If we turn to the direct implications of federalism for the "progress of French Canadians," it is clear that federalism is not intended to preserve and enhance the growth of the "French Canadian nation." Indeed, a few of their particular values may achieve a more universal status,[82] but other new values will have to be adopted, and many of their values will simply vanish, or fade away into the irrelevance of the private realm. Ultimately, it means the necessary disappearance of what is today known as Quebecois society. Thus the tool of federalism, within the context of Trudeau's political philosophy and assumptions, ultimately helps answer the question concerning the place of religious, cultural, and social structural diversity within the public realm, by dissolving diversity and making the question irrelevant.[83]

Trudeau's conclusion that the eventual success of the federal instrument also means its demise, should not be surprising given his view of political philosophy as a means of developing temporary checks and balances for specific political problems. Federalism is simply one of many temporary tools that are useful for dislodging "ideological" answers to the complex of issues tied up with diversity in religion, culture, and social structure.

The implications of Trudeau's views do not stop with the disappearance of French Canadian society. Ultimately Canada will itself fade away for "neither Canada's present constitution nor the country itself represents an unchangeable reality."[84] Beyond that it is impossible to predict the end result, since there is no permanent outcome to the pursuit of the goal of individual freedom. The only permanency possible is movement toward an increasingly universal state containing individuals with increasingly homogeneous values. In Trudeau's own words,

> To seek to create the just society must be amongst the highest of those human purposes. Because we are mortal and imperfect, it is a task we will never finish; no government or society ever will. But from our honest and ceaseless effort, we will draw strength and inspiration, we will discover new and better values, we will achieve an unprecedented level of human consciousness. On the never-ending road to perfect justice we will, in other words, succeed in creating the most humane and compassionate society possible.[85]

While Trudeau is optimistic that this "movement" will be beneficial, he offers us only the criteria of "increased individual freedom" to judge whether it is good or bad.[86] This raises at least one final question: if the "movement" towards greater individual freedom implies a "truly open culture"[87] where the French Canadians' linguistic, cultural, social and religious values have disappeared, then doesn't progress also imply the impossibility of a group of individuals continuing to choose freely to be Quebecois—except in all but the most frivolous private practices—once the majority has progressed toward the "civilization of tomorrow"? And if the choice to be French Canadian is impossible in public and irrelevant in private, is it still meaningful to speak of increased individual freedom?

Conclusion

Trudeau's liberal philosophy defined federalism—what it is, what it can do, and where it will lead—in such a way that federalism was assumed to be a solution to many problems for which it was not a suitable answer. When Trudeau directed the instrument of federalism towards the problems associated with diverse religious, cultural, and institutional groups within Canada, it failed as a solution and even threatened to reduce individual freedom. But if a liberal definition of federalism can lead to problems, where can we turn for other viewpoints? This brings me back to Bernard Zylstra's assessment of the Canadian constitution at the outset of this paper. He argued that Canada needs a "spiritual vision" other than "political liberalism" to serve as "an architectonic alternative framework for constitution building."[88] Zylstra wanted to return to the Christian tradition for such a vision. However, he turned away from the solution of the mainline churches in Canada because they

> did not address themselves prophetically to the ideology of liberalism during the constitutional debate. . . . Their contributions were piecemeal, ad hoc, and issue-oriented. They did not offer a spiritual vision necessary for [developing] an alternative to political liberalism."[89]

Instead, Zylstra turned to the Dutch tradition of Christian democracy as a source of principles for revising Canadian theory and practice. These Christian democratic principles, he argued, avoid the liberal and socialist assumption "that religion is a matter of individuals, not institutions." On the basis of these principles, Zylstra wanted to avoid the form of government known as "Christian" democracy in favor of "pluriform democracy" where ideologically differing institutions are granted equality before the law in Canada.[90] Perhaps if Canadians want to develop fresh policy solutions to the problems related to plurality within Canada—that have resisted solutions based on the architectonic frameworks of liberalism, nationalism, and socialism—it may be fruitful to examine the idea of "pluriform democracy" developed by the Dutch Christian democrats.[91]

Notes

This paper was first presented at the Annual General Meeting of the Canadian Political Science Association, Victoria, British Columbia, May 27-29, 1990.

1. *Federalism and the French Canadians*, (Toronto: Macmillan, 1967), xxvi. This work will be referred to by the initials *FFC* from here on. In this paper, I will use the term "French Canadian" when working with Trudeau's ideas, and "Quebecois" in all other contexts.
2. *Liberalism or Liberty: An Assessment of Canada's New Constitution*, (Toronto: Christian Labour Association of Canada, 1983), 6.
3. Zylstra stresses that liberalism has made several important political contributions, he also notes that this is far less true in its response to diversity. See Ibid., 1-7.
4. *FFC*, xxii.
5. *FFC*, 205.
6. Pierre Elliott Trudeau, *Conversation with Canadians* (Toronto: University of Toronto Press, 1972), 11. This work will be referred to as *CWC* from here on. Also see *FFC*, 53.
7. *FFC*, xxii, xxiii.
8. *FFC*, 209.
9. *FFC*, xxiii. Trudeau affirms this position in "The Values of a Just Society" in *Towards a Just Society: The Trudeau Years*, Thomas Axworthy and P. E. Trudeau, eds., (Markham, Ont.: Viking, 1990), 361. It is noteworthy that the political philosopher and the practising politician were one and the same in Trudeau's case.
10. John T. Saywell in the "Introduction" to *FFC*, xii. Although such dramatic swings in Trudeau's practical political positions are more common, there is remarkable consistency in his basic liberal framework from his early articles in the 1950s to his March 1988 submission to the Senate Hearings on the First Ministers' Accord, achieved at Meech Lake.
11. By and large, these assumptions are simply asserted and are neither discussed nor argued for in any detail. As such, these assumptions have more of the character of a "worldview" than a political philosophy. On the distinction and relationship between

worldviews and political science, see *Stained Glass: Worldviews and Social Science*, Paul Marshall, Sander Griffioen, and Richard Mouw, editors, (Lanham, Md.: University Press of America, 1989).
12. Pierre Elliott Trudeau, *Approaches to Politics*, (Toronto: Oxford University Press, 1970), 27. This work will be referred to as *ATP* from here on.
13. *FFC* 205. Also see a similar discussion about nation, state, and church, *FFC*, 159.
14. *ATP*, 31.
15. *CWC*, 4.
16. *CWC*, 86.
17. See references to equality in *ATP*, 80, 88; *FFC*, 114; and *CWC*, 205. For a related discussion see Pierre Elliott Trudeau, "Economic Rights," *McGill Law Journal*, vol. 8, No. 2, 1961: 121-25.
18. Trudeau, "The Values of a Just Society," (note 9 above), 358.
19. *FFC*, 57.
20. Again, while this is not a phrase that he uses, it conceptually describes his meaning well. Reginald Whitaker and Leah Bradshaw point out that in an individualistic society founded on liberty and equality the only form of reason that can be assumed to be common to all is calculative self-interest. See Whitaker, "Reason, Passion and Interest: Pierre Trudeau's Eternal Liberal Triangle," *Canadian Journal of Political and Social Theory*, vol. 4, no. 1, Winter, 1980: 18 and Bradshaw, "Trudeau's Liberal Society," unpublished paper presented at the conference on "The Political Thought and Practice of Pierre Elliott Trudeau," University of Calgary, Oct. 19, 1979.
21. *FFC*, 11. In this viewpoint, Trudeau stands in the mainstream of liberal ethics where each individual is free to choose and rank his or her own values. This is in fundamental contrast to the classical (Greek) notion of natural law, understood as "a standard of right and wrong independent of positive right and higher than positive right: a standard with reference to which we are able to judge of positive right." Leo Strauss, *Natural Right and History*, (Chicago: University of Chicago Press, 1953), 2. It also stands apart from Christian ethics as the guide for all human action, based on divine revelation.

22. While Trudeau uses the term universal values, it is still a relative concept in his writing since a society can never achieve absolute values, only move towards them.

23. For references to these values, see respectively, *FFC*, 46 and 188; 46-47, 188, and 159; and 34-35 and 188.

24. For references to these values see respectively, *FFC*, 6 and 157; 6 and 150; 146 and 157.

25. *FFC*, 22-23 and 206.

26. *FFC*, 172.

27. *CWC*, 16.

28. *CWC*, 195.

29. *FFC*, 33-35.

30. *FFC*, 47.

31. *FFC*, 29 and 33.

32. *FFC*, 29-35. In this way, Trudeau reflects the liberal tradition of mediating change through a carefully constructed equilibrium of competing forces.

33. *FFC*, 189.

34. *ATP*, 34, 43 and 84. The discussions on the majority mechanism and the common good are primarily found in the collection of essays, *Approaches to Politics*, referred to above.

35. *ATP*, 50; also see 31 and 35, and *FFC*, 184.

36. *ATP*, 31 and *FFC*, 209.

37. Trudeau does not use the term procedural, but it is conceptually the best term to describe what he means by justice. See Reginald Whitaker for a discussion of a general liberal view of the procedural justice state, ibid., 10.

38. *ATP*, 78.

39. *ATP*, 88.

40. Ibid.

41. *ATP*, 88-89.

42. Trudeau uses religious terminology such as "believe," "democratic faith," and "gospel" to discuss democracy. See *FFC* 122-23, and the entire chapter, "Some Obstacles to Democracy in Quebec," 103-23. Bernard Zylstra understands liberalism to be a mild variety of humanism, which is a secular version of Christianity in the modern age. Ibid., 1.

43. *ATP*, 89.

44. *CWC*, 69. Denis Smith asks how Trudeau can reconcile his use of state force against an individual's freedom, in order to maintain individual freedom of choice. However, this action is more understandable in view of Trudeau's assertion that freedom can only exist within a procedural order. See *Bleeding Hearts . . . Bleeding Country: Canada and the Quebec Crisis,* (Edmonton: M. G. Hurtig Ltd., 1971).

45. Trudeau argues that the Constitution Act 1982 "enshrined the values" he, as Prime Minister, had defined in 1968. "Values and the Just Society," (note 9 above), 362.

46. Pierre Elliott Trudeau, *The Constitution and the People of Canada*, (Ottawa: Queen's Printer, 1969), 14. Trudeau confirms that his intent was to entrench procedural values when he states that the purpose of the Charter was not to "instill in [governments] any particular ideology." See "The Values of a Just Society," 271. For further discussion see my *Trudeau's Political Philosophy: Its Implications for Liberty and Progress,* (Toronto: Institute for Christian Studies, 1983), 72-3, 76.

47. By religion I mean both the human capacity to respond to God, or a substitute, and the resulting way of life that reflects this ultimate commitment. In this sense all people are religious both in capacity and in response. See, for example, James H. Olthuis, "On Worldviews," in *Stained Glass: Worldviews and Social Science*, Paul A. Marshall, Sander Griffioen, and Richard J. Mouw, eds., (Lanham, Md.: University Press of America, 1989), 30-32.

48. *FFC*, 150. This particular idea of culture underlies his observation that Canada has ". . . the federal data that some like to live by the sea, some in the plains, and that some prefer to speak French." The terminology of "like" and "prefer" suggest choices in circumstances that frequently have little or no opportunities for choice, e.g., birth into a French or English speaking family.

49. See Sally M. Weaver, *Making Canadian Indian Policy*, (Toronto: University of Toronto Press, 1981), especially 53-65.

50. *FFC*, 35. Also see *CWC*, 34-36.

51. *FFC*, 30. Also see 46, and *CWC* 39. Many Quebecois, including René Levesque, have "rejected Trudeau's notion that French Canadian survival could be reduced to a matter of individual excellence and language rights." See J. Laxer and R. Laxer, *The Liberal Idea of Canada: Pierre Trudeau and the Question of Canada's Survival*, (Toronto: James Lorimer, 1977), 179. Canada's Bilingual and Bicultural Policy, implemented by the Trudeau government, is also influenced by this ideological view of culture and language. Also see Trudeau's testimony to the Senate Hearings on the Meech Lake Constitutional Accord, *Senate Debates*, March 30, 1988, esp. 2993 and 2984.

52. This is a dilemma in much liberal thought. Trudeau recognizes it in his discussion of the inclusion of the "collective rights of minorities" in the Charter. However, he clearly sees it as an exception. "It is clear, then, that the spirit and substance of the Charter is to protect the individual against tyranny—not only that of the state but also any other to which the individual may be subjected by virtue of his belonging to a minority group." "The Values of a Just Society," (note 9 above), 365. If genuine religious freedom is to be guaranteed within institutions a distinction needs to be made between "tyranny" and the maintenance of the religious identity of an institution.

53. This is also true for non-liberal majorities. For example, if the Moral Majority in the United States were to become the political majority, their imposition of Christian moral values through public law would be a violation of liberal values. At the heart of this problem is Trudeau's mistaken assumption that the values entrenched in a procedural order are "common to all." "The Values of a Just Society," (note 9 above), 363, 368.

54. See Daniel Bell, *The End of Ideology*, (Glencoe, Ill.: Free Press, 1960), for an example of this type of thought. In this paper, ideology will be understood as a system of ideas that together are intended to justify and achieve a certain over-riding goal, by prescribing a set of political and other types of actions. This goal is considered more important than, and thus the measure for, all other goals and means.

55. *FFC*, xxi and xxxii.

56. Bob Goudzwaard's distinction between partial and "full-fledged" ideologies is helpful to clarify that in Trudeau's case, we are dealing with a partial ideology. See his *Idols of our Time*, (Downers Grove, Ill.: InterVarsity Press, 1984), 24-25.

57. At other times, he states, the ideological problems have been rooted in "clannishness," "tribalism" and "feudalism."

58. Trudeau's counter-argument that a "nation" is constituted by a state—that all citizens of a state constitute the nation—is an inherently stronger position than nationalism, although in arguing so he fails to recognize the valid justice claims of "nation-like" groups.

59. *FFC*, 168.

60. See *FFC*, 157-58 and 175.

61. *FFC*, 169. While Trudeau correctly criticizes the nationalists for instrumentalizing the common good to a "part" of the national citizenry, he also instrumentalizes the common good to a "part" of the nation, namely the majority.

62. *FFC*, 169.

63. *FFC*, 170.

64. *FFC*, 177.

65. *FFC*, 206. It is noted above that Trudeau also takes refuge in the "bosom" of the majority when genuine participatory democracy seems impossible!

66. Federalism is conceptualized in one of two general ways, (1) as a way to unite people already linked by a common nationality, by allowing political power to be dispersed among the constituent units, or (2) as a means of unifying diverse peoples without disrupting their primary ties to local polities that become constituent units of the federation.

67. *FFC*, 134.

68. Ibid. This amendment is significant because by adding the requirement to "cooperate and interchange" to the classical definition, he is setting up federalism as an instrument for competition.

69. See *FFC*, 192. Practically, dividing powers based on the common agreement of individual citizens is very difficult, as witnessed in the 53 year struggle to repatriate the Canadian constitution, and the problems the Quebecois had in winning a "yes" vote in the "sovereignty association" referendum.

70. Although, as noted, this is extremely difficult in practice, Trudeau's theoretical statement of the possibility is practically supported by both his personal willingness to allow Quebec to pull out of the Canadian federation and his tenacious fight to persuade Quebecois to stay in.

71. *FFC*, 195.

72. *FCC* 35.

73. *FFC*, 148.

74. In his arguments against the Meech Lake Constitutional Accord, Trudeau argues that "With Meech Lake there is no national will left." *Senate Hearings*, March 30, 1988, 2989.

75. For Trudeau, the new Canadian Charter of Rights and Freedoms serves not only as the ground rules for competition within a procedural justice state, but also as ground rules for the operation of federalism. See Pierre Elliott Trudeau, *The Prime Minister's Address to the House of Commons in the Constitutional Debate,* (Ottawa, March 23, 1981) (Published separately in edited version), 22.

76. This geo-political problem is based on the historical experiences that citizens have of the remoteness or nearness of their government.

77. This is so, except in those rare circumstances when a religious or cultural group's regional presence precisely and exclusively corresponds to a federal sub-jurisdiction. This has never been the case in Canada.

78. *FFC*, 154

79. *FFC*, 6.

80. Pierre Elliott Trudeau, "In Defence of Federalism" in Paul Fox, editor, *Politics: Canada*, second edition, (Toronto: McGraw-Hill Ryerson, 1966), 110.

81. *FFC*, 179. He understands that empirical studies on federal states, such as the Soviet Union, Canada, Nigeria, India, United States, Malaysia and Switzerland indicate that countries have had vastly different experiences with federalism, with wide variations in resulting political cultures, ideologies, economic and technological developments, and social, cultural and linguistic composition. This is the most likely reason he emphasizes Canadian federalism as the "prototype."

82. *FFC*, 180.

83. Trudeau dislikes the American "melting pot" method of dealing with pluralism which has the same end effect, simply because it is too harsh a tool to handle Canada's diverse makeup.
84. *FFC*, 37.
85. *CWC*, 42.
86. In the discussion above, it was indicated that Trudeau thought the French Canadians had achieved equal language rights simply by power. George Grant observes of this typical liberal suggestion that "If history is the final court of appeal, force is the final argument." This raises yet another range of questions which are beyond the scope of this paper. *Lament for a Nation: the Defeat of Canadian Nationalism,* (Toronto: McClelland and Stewart, 1965), 89.
87. *FFC* 29.
88. Zylstra, (note 2 above), 6.
89. Ibid.
90. Ibid., 5 and 6. In relation to political science, Zylstra was a proponent of the "inner reformation" of political philosophy and science. For a discussion of this concept, see Hendrik Hart, "The Idea of an Inner Reformation of the Sciences," in *Social Science in Christian Perspective*, Paul A. Marshall and Robert E. Vander-Vennen, eds., (Lanham, Md.: University Press of America, 1988), 13-31.
91. For an overview of the pluriform social and political system in the Netherlands see Arend Lijphart, *The Politics of Accommodation: Pluralism and Democracy in the Netherlands*, (Los Angeles: University of California Press, 1975). For a discussion of several Dutch Christian democratic theories on pluriform democracy see James A. Skillen, "The Development of Calvinist Political Theory in the Netherlands, with special reference to the thought of Herman Dooyeweerd," unpublished Ph.D. dissertation, Duke University, 1974.

Two Critiques of Legal Ideology

David S. Caudill

Introduction

I wish to compare the critiques of legal ideology given in reformational philosophy and in the Critical Legal Studies movement (CLS). Contemporary critical legal scholarship, as embodied in CLS, inherits as an attempted *ideologiekritik*, the problems of defining what ideology is, escaping or otherwise accounting for its own ideology, and establishing the usefulness of its critique of ideology. For some of these critics, the recent confrontation between creationists and evolutionists in the courts has served to illustrate the inevitable operation of ideology or worldviews in legal processes and institutions.

Similarly, while reformational philosophy is not usually associated with the critique of legal ideology, legal culture (including the creation-evolution dispute) betrays the effects of those fundamental beliefs—or motives or perspectives—that reformational philosophers do in fact seek to disclose and discuss. In this philosophical framework *Ideologiekritik* becomes a project characterized by self-critical discourse between and about competing views of the world. Consequently there are parallels between these approaches that can usefully be compared and contrasted.

The Critique of Legal Ideology

CLS is a loose-knit collection of left-leaning scholars and their recent writings and is nowadays a fixture in North American jurisprudence.[1] Although assessments of the movement's academic and practical value vary,[2] one of the most significant contributions of CLS is its restatement of theoretical controversies in terms of commitment and ideology.[3] From the viewpoint of CLS scholars, traditional appeals to universal principles grounded in human rationality provide no real foundations for legal scholarship. Indeed, rationality itself appears to be historically and culturally situated.[4] Such a perspective, I hope to show, can best be understood as a type or style of ideology critique.

Albeit problematic, we may distinguish between the conditions of theoretical thought, common to all analysis, and the necessary presuppositions or prejudices that characterize various thinkers and philosophies. Likewise, a distinction is useful between the universal structures of society and the shared ideas, motivations, beliefs, and assumptions that give a particular society direction and that justify or legitimize a society's historically variable institutions. The latter can be viewed as the elements of a worldview or ideology.[5] When such ideological elements are disclosed in a critical analysis, the goal is not to overcome myths by the "light" of "reason," but to identify the starting points for theory and practice that can only be revised or replaced by another ideological framework. Therefore, a conception of ideology as something to be eliminated through "enlightenment" or "emancipation" signals a failure of self-criticism on the part of the ideology critic.

The self-critical conception of the critique of ideology has as its goal the disclosure of hidden assumptions for purposes of communication and further criticism.[6] The power of ideology is that shared ideas become entrenched, appear to be natural or "given," replicate themselves, are legitimated by cultural institutions such as legal systems, operate as boundaries to human thought, are formative of consciousness, and through all of the above become a dynamic force independent of other social, political, and economic influences. The critique of ideology serves, in its various versions, (i) to "unfreeze" the ideological framework by recreating the tacit value system, (ii) to disclose the arbitrary element of belief that constitutes the given world, and (iii) to expose tensions or contradictions within a worldview notwithstanding the defense mechanisms (such as "common sense") that make recognition of the worldview difficult.

Roberto Unger, a founder of CLS, distinguishes "routine disputes" that occur within a "formative context" from "revolutionary struggles" about the context itself. The distinction is crucial to the present study, because the biases and prejudices identified in the critique of legal ideology are not those of misinformed or bigoted judges. Rather, the subject of criticism is the collective belief system reflected in the opinions of even those judges perceived to be most brilliant and fair. The question is always why a society considers a decision brilliant or fair: what beliefs constitute the perception that a legitimate law has been properly applied for justifiable reasons by an appropriate authority? The discourse is removed from a context where all those adjectives have assumed meanings to a consideration of the assumptions themselves.

In popular parlance of CLS, all of law is politics: there is no political neutrality in law-making and adjudication. Bias—not the personal bias of legislators and judges, but the ideological "tilt" discernible in any social context—is inevitable. Ronald Dworkin's distinction between justified and unjustified bias is an attempt to find a basis for choice where such bias is inevitable. His search (and a judge's search) for fundamental *principles* that reflect the background rights or political morality of litigants has resulted in a conception of law that is both impressive and attractive. Yet radical theoreticians are already asserting that Dworkin is still not critical— he draws his principles from the very framework that the critique of ideology wants to question. In a sense, the analytical efforts of Dworkin and CLS are not mutually exclusive. That is, Dworkin and his colleagues are working within, or "tinkering with," the existing culture and legal system, while the radical critics are attempting to disclose, in a fashion that the positivist considers impossible, the ideological framework "from the outside."

The Enemy Within: What is Ideology?

The critique of legal ideology appears in two forms in CLS literature. The self-critical version can be identified as modest, descriptive and *methodological*, as opposed to the competing version that appears confident, judgmental and *normative*. The primary goal of the former is communication, while the latter's goal is to overcome the false consciousness supporting a ruling class. Both styles of ideology critique might view the other as failing to be critical. The normative critic perceives the descriptive exercise that dissolves the link between domination and ideology as vague, directionless, and relativistic. Why search for a belief-system—or worldview or interpretive grid—that may not exist when it is obvious that social relations of domination are hidden in our language and life irrespective of shared beliefs? Conversely, the methodological critic perceives an unwillingness on the part of the normative critic to acknowledge his or her own ideology. Turning the previous question around, why search for illegitimate power structures in society before submitting one's own standards or values to the critical process?

Because disclosure and acknowledgement of one's own, or one's society's, belief-system can lead to expansion of options and genuine choice, I maintain that the modest approach to ideology retains a critical bite. After all, the methodological critic will have goals and standards, perhaps identical to the normative critic's; the difference is that the methodological critic recognizes that his or her goals and standards are beliefs and must be defended. Nevertheless, the objection that a modest ideology critique is not critical is only one barrier to the development of such an approach. The problem of defining ideology remains: perhaps our culture is characterized by its diversity and not by a belief-system.

The dilemma appears to be partially solved simply by narrowing the critique of ideology to the field of law. Here, "ideology" may be viewed as the collective beliefs and assumptions of a society concerning law and the legitimacy of its demands. Significantly, in CLS parlance, people not only support a legal system by believing in it, but law also provides or represents to society a picture of order and ordinary social reality. Law, therefore, operates to justify or legitimize other social structures.

Even while the problem of vagueness appears to be receding, however, another difficulty in the modest critique of ideology arises:

> Theoretically, . . . through what processes is legal ideology transmitted from the specialist arenas of legal discourse to install itself in popular consciousness? . . . Empirically[,] is there any evidence that the population in general or some particular section . . . is influenced by the ideological products of the legal process?[7]

Some CLS scholars propose, given time, to demonstrate empirically the ideological tilt in American law. Such efforts may prove fruitful, but they must be seen as a "domesticated" version of CLS.[8] After all, CLS is in part constituted by its rejection of mainstream sociological research methods. More to the point, any purported empirical investigation of law, for CLS, always take place within an ideological framework that is rarely admitted or exposed.

Refining the Critique

Three features emerge as requirements for the development of a critique of legal ideology. First, the term "ideology" must be defined with sufficient precision to give the critique meaning and direction. In CLS, the field of inquiry is limited to legal institutions and processes, and the relationship between law and shared beliefs or consciousness can be explored theoretically and empirically in future literature.

Second, a critique of ideology must strive to be self-critical. A genuinely radical critic holds in abeyance his or her own social values and political preferences, to the extent possible, in the process of belief-disclosure. The methodological strand of CLS scholarship is, in this respect, preferable to the normative critique because no particular approach to law is—initially—privileged.

Third, and finally, the goals of communication and awareness must be complemented by the practical, competitive, and transformative efforts of the critic. This emphasis is a response to the objection that a modest ideology critique is directionless and hopelessly relativistic. Throughout CLS literature, the disclosure of hidden or marginalized options is aimed at emancipation and enlightenment of society.

The Creation/Evolution Dispute Revisited

In June, 1987, the latest chapter of the legal controversy between proponents of evolutionary theory and of creation theory, concerning the place of each in public school education, was closed. Louisiana's balanced treatment law (requiring that creation-science be taught alongside the topic of evolution), carefully drafted to withstand the constitutional challenge that it was an establishment of religion, was overturned by the U.S. Supreme Court in *Aguillard v. Edwards.*[9] Predictably, responses to the decision vary. Stephen J. Gould, a Harvard biologist and geologist, echoes the scientific establishment when he writes, in his recent article criticizing the (dissenting) minority opinion of Justice Scalia, "we all rejoiced."[10] Wendell Bird, the Atlanta attorney who argued the case before the Court on behalf of the State of Louisiana, continues to seek legitimacy for creation-science in a new two-volume book surveying criticism of evolution and Darwinism by non-creationists.[11]

Does the U.S. Supreme Court's opinion represent more than just a blessing for evolutionists and a disappointment for creationists? Apart from the obvious "religion" of the creationists, is there in *Aguillard* an ideological dispute? The case does not seem to involve a political power struggle, except indirectly if one views the outcome as a blow to the growing cultural clout of fundamentalist Christians. On the surface, the case also does not involve social domination or class oppression. One might conclude that CLS would not be concerned at all with this revival of the creation/evolution controversy.

Nevertheless, the critique of legal ideology purports to deal with all of the law's institutions and processes. And, notwithstanding the absence of traditional leftist concerns, *Aguillard* did evoke a response from four scholars commonly associated with CLS (Gary Peller, Peter Gabel, Betty Mensch and Alan Freeman) in a trilogy of articles in *Tikkun.*[12] Their work is especially helpful in drawing out the practical implications of ideology critique.

Peter Gabel argues, from an almost romanticist perspective, that the scientific way of looking at things—detached, objectifying—leads to a tragic, impoverished experience of the world.[13] While Gabel's friends "regard the creationists as a bunch of nut-cases," it is the scientist who, in Gabel's analysis, "appears slightly crazy for suppressing" intuitive knowledge.[14] Gabel makes it clear that his

> aim is certainly not to defend the creationist credo that the Bible must be taken as literally true. . . . But the creationists have been able to touch that dimension of people's ordinary experience that sees life in all its forms as expressive of some in-dwelling and miraculous beauty and goodness, and that knows with a certain intuition that this in-dwelling presence must be at the heart of any true knowledge of the world. . . . There is something correct and admirable in their refusal to accept the hegemony of science as a privileged source of truth.[15]

Gabel is even sympathetic to the rigidity of the creationists in their insistence that the Bible is literally true. He understands such rigidity as a defensive reaction to our cultural insecurity, "fostered by centuries of the dominance of scientific ideology," that we have no "capacity to claim any direct knowledge of spiritual truth that would reveal" what is good or how we should live.[16]

Freeman and Mensch are also sympathetic to fundamentalist Christians who "feel disaffected from America's orthodoxy of secularism."[17] The authors believe, however, that fundamentalists have "forced scientists to confront the shallowness of their traditional claims to intellectual authority." Science, for Freeman and Mensch, "is rooted in the culture within which it operates, and its underlying presuppositions are always part of that social context." Again, without defending the creationist platform, the authors treat the evolutionists as well as the creationists as members of self-referencing, interpretative communities.[18]

Finally, Gary Peller recognizes creationism a "part of a developing rhetoric of resistance against the reigning ideology of the South."[19] The establishment in the southeastern United States—those with political and economic power—also control education;

biology classrooms may represent one battleground for the class struggle between those served by the official ideology and working-class whites.[20] Like Gabel, Freeman and Mensch, Peller views creationism as a potential challenge to changeable social institutions and ways of thinking that have become rigid and seemingly unchangeable.

Peter Gabel, several years ago, identified four potential approaches in attacking the Supreme Court under Chief Justice Burger.[21] One can condemn the results of the decisions—for example, by claiming the decisions hurt the poor and help big corporations. Next, one might criticize the Court's faulty legal reasoning, indifference to precedent, simplistic constitutional interpretation, and/or "abdication of its proper role as the principal formulator of a national political morality to rectify inequalities."[22] Third, one may argue that the Supreme Court is engaged in a right-wing political program hidden by ideological justifications that mask the politics at work.[23] In the fourth approach, Gabel's choice, the Supreme Court's role is exemplified not by harmful results, poor reasoning, or a hidden political agenda, but by its legitimation of the present social order.[24]

> The objective of the Supreme Court is to pacify conflict through the mediation of a false social-meaning system, a set of ideas and images about the world which serve today as the secular equivalent of religious ideology in previous historical periods.[25]

Unlike those who focus on the *influence* of cultural bias on the law, Gabel sees the Supreme Court as reshaping and confirming a worldview-producing "illusions about the justness of the existing order."[26]

Removing Gabel's analysis from its political context, both sides in *Aguillard* might have been concerned that the Supreme Court's ideology, the universe of ideas shared by a majority, would not permit their arguments to be heard. The conflict would then be interpreted according to and assimilated into an existing web of social-meaning, a ruling ideology. Proponents of balanced treatment perhaps feared that the scientific establishment and "secular humanists" had already co-opted the Justices. Similarly, opponents of the Act might have worried that President Reagan and the "Moral Majority" already had unwitting insiders on the highest bench, vigilant for assaults on the nation's religious heritage. These analyses presume that a fantasy of the cultural imagination—whether scientism or creationism—was to be legitimated in, *Aguillard* and reconstituted as something legal and right by some mystifying constitutional analysis.

Admittedly, there is little likelihood that CLS will do more to assist fundamentalist Christians in their attack upon evolutionist ideology. Yet the feeling among creation-scientists that the odds are against them when they approach the courts, because they represent an unpopular viewpoint, is one shared by victims of class or race bias. Likewise, the desire to look behind a carefully reasoned opinion for the marks of established belief-structures is shared by any scholar engaged in the critique of legal ideology.

Reformational Philosophy
The philosophical perspective associated with Herman Dooyeweerd (and his followers) is, at certain points, strikingly similar to CLS. In Dooyeweerd's epistemology, theoretical thought always begins with pre-theoretical suppositions accepted, of necessity, by faith. Such an analysis proved useful in classifying and understanding various western philosophers according to their *religious* starting points. Moreover, Dooyeweerd's work inspired his disciples and revisionists to move beyond the preoccupation with "great thinkers" and to explore the role of collective, pre-theoretical assumptions in culture.

Faith and the Ideologiekritik
Beginning with the view that religious beliefs are best characterized as central, formative motives or forces in society, rather than theological or moral precepts consciously adopted by their holders, reformational philosophers have identified belief systems that appear to unify and direct various social structures, including legal processes. In the attempt to define "ideology," such religious beliefs are not only seen as determinative prior to disclosure, but as subject to evaluation and change after disclosure. Bob Goudzwaard, for

example, in his *Capitalism and Progress* (1975), argues that confidence in progress constitutes a foundational belief in our consumeristic society. Self-criticism is implied in such a perspective, since social life *and* social criticism are characterized by faith, either Christian or otherwise. Moreover, reformational philosophers have rarely been passive in their disclosure of the religious motivations in theory and culture. Indeed, the Christian worldview is conceived of as an all-encompassing project with implications for each discipline of academia and every aspect of social life.

CLS adherents and scholars associated with reformational philosophy thus share common methods of belief-disclosure and common goals of open communication regarding worldviews. These similarities should not, however, eclipse the vast differences that appear when one inquires into the transformative visions of each movement. On the one hand, CLS is inspired by Marxian ideals of freedom and human autonomy; the Marxian tradition can be quite hostile to the "oppressive" Christian emphasis on service ("servanthood") to God. Reformational philosophy, on the other hand, is a distinctly Christian perspective, viewing the world as God's creation and confessing genuine freedom only in Christ; Marxian ideals of human freedom and autonomy represent, from this biblical standpoint, distorted visions of the world. The stage is thus set for discourse between proponents of antithetical ideologies, although some will attempt a synthesis between Christianity and Marxism.

Aguillard Reconsidered

For Dooyeweerd and his followers, science, including natural science, begins with pretheoretical assumptions or beliefs that are not scientific and are often not acknowledged. When a set of beliefs becomes institutionalized in a scientific discipline, the framework appears natural, factual, common-sensical; contrary views appear non-sensical or perhaps "religious." In the *Aguillard* series of judicial opinions, leading from the trial court through the Court of Appeals to the Supreme Court, creation-scientists were typically characterized as academicians who permitted religious belief to direct and infect their biological theories. Conversely, evolutionists were seen by most of the judges as fact-finders bereft of religious bias. Irrespective of the scientific legitimacy of either popular evolutionary theories or so-called creation-science, reformational philosophy would teach us that this ideal of a fact-based, non-religious science is a myth.

The significance of *Aguillard*, or any judicial opinion, in this context is the power of law to support or legitimize belief-structures in society. The brief filed by the Rutherford Institute (the "Institute"), a Christian organization of lawyers, in support of Louisiana's balanced treatment law was particularly oriented to the issue of freedom of thought.[27] Most of the other briefs filled with the Court were predictable—various scientific and educational organizations argued for evolution as genuine science and against creation-science as disguised religion; the State's brief appealed to the Court to recognize the shortcomings of evolutionary theory as well as the difference between creation-science and the religious doctrine of creation. The Institute brief, however, asked the Court to direct its attention away from the scientific dispute—an endless and ever-changing debate—and toward the ideological controversy—a more accurate description of the case.

Starting with the familiar distinction between fact and ideology, the Institute argued that government alternates between its role as arbiter of factuality (as with an allegation of fraud in securities regulation) and as the observer of ideological controversy (as with an allegation that political speech has been silenced). The political theory that shaped the free speech clause of the First Amendment to the Constitution "assigns government a role outside of ideological controversy."[28] Majoritarian pressures on the government, however, may operate to narrow the definition of ideology and contract the area of First Amendment protection.

> The obvious danger is that too broad an understanding of "factuality" will license the government to step in as enforcer of truth, to place the power and prestige of government behind a particular view, and thereby to undermine substantially freedom of thought in a particular area.[29]

The Court, apparently, was not willing to so recast its analysis. Throughout the majority opinion, the religion behind creation-science was continually contrasted with science of evolution. From the perspective of reformational philosophy, the Court's distinction between science and religion fails to recognize that religion—in the sense of fundamental pre-commitments—is not limited to organized world religions, and science—establishment or otherwise—is not without a religious aspect.

Conclusions

The critique of legal ideology constitutes an attempt to disclose the hidden belief-structures that underlie and give meaning to legal processes and institutions. Ideology critique is by definition disruptive—comfortably established standards and rules, generally accepted factual "data," and common sense are revealed as tentative and socially qualified. Knowledge is suddenly reduced to the propaganda of one's own history and culture.

In this secular age a confession of Christian faith is for many an admission of unscholarly bias. Christian scholarship is thus viewed as tainted, and is often marginalized and rendered powerless. After all, one might ask, how can one be scientific and religious at the same time? That question, I have suggested, is representative of a tradition of thought that ignores the religious or ideological aspect of all science.

Scholars associated with Critical Legal Studies have also felt the sting of a dogmatic and uncritical culture that, ironically, marginalizes certain perspectives as too dogmatic and uncritical. Yet in little more than a decade, CLS has become a "movement" in the realm of legal scholarship. CLS is being discussed and criticized, even though it is not yet clear to many what the movement is about or where it is going.

I have argued that CLS can be conceived of as an ideology critique, and that two variations of that critique appear in CLS literature. The first, normative critique retains at every turn a picture of oppression and liberation, and those fellow-travellers who both long for praxis and have little use for abstract theorizing will find the normative critique admirable. However, if the goal of the critique is to disclose contingent legal conceptions that have been reified so as to appear natural, then the normative critic's conceptions of oppression and vision of liberation must also be called into question.

The second, methodological strand of CLS critique, I believe, is far more compelling. While a vision of social transformation will be important to any useful theory of law, the timing, or staged analysis, of the methodological critique leads to a more critical, and self-critical, analysis. The methodological critic at least attempts, initially, to identify and hold back his or her own ideology until a framework for discourse, or open communication, has been constructed.

Thus, in my view, the problem that is partially solved in CLS scholarship is not oppression and illegitimate hierarchies, but the problem of marginalized discourse and the disappearance of alternative visions of life. As a critique of ideology, CLS can only hope to provide a forum for non-establishment voices—to level the playing field—so that a meaningful debate concerning human values and social goals can begin.

Such a conception of CLS is consistent with my own understanding of the goals of reformational philosophy. While some may feel that I have domesticated CLS in order to make the analogy, I am fully aware that the ultimate goal of CLS is not academic dialogue. Scholars associated with CLS are variously inspired by Marxian notions of changing (and not just interpreting) the world (and its oppressive class structures) and by neo-Marxian visions of emancipation; CLS writings betray a persistent concern for human alienation and misery. Likewise, Reformational philosophy is driven by a biblical vision of creation by God, the fall of humanity, and redemption in Christ. The point is that prior to the needed practical suggestions as to how to improve social institutions or eliminate human suffering, one cannot privilege either one's own views or the current dominant worldview.

Particularly in the Calvinist perspective, religion is not a private matter, but is something that is reflected in all of culture. Individuals, families, social institutions and government each exist in relation to, and in faithful or unfaithful response to, God and His Word. One finds here a concern for reformation of all of society and obedience to God in all areas of life.

Some have pointed out, however, that the record of Christianity in ameliorating social conditions . . . is not a particularly proud one. The main traditions in Christianity tend to be conservatistic.[30]

Contemporary Christian scholars must work in the shadow of the fact that non-Christian traditions are often first to expose evil and begin working on solutions. At the same time, liberation movements inspired by Marxism or neo-Marxism have given rise to repressive regimes. Yet another similarity between CLS and the Reformational Philosophy appears—both have skeletons in their closets. The hope is that the various critical traditions can learn from past mistakes and learn from one another. The critique of ideology, at its best, is a method of disclosing hidden dogmatism (in one's own belief-system and in the belief-systems of others) so that various competing viewpoints will then be open to learn from each other.

The inevitable charge of nihilism that follows any attempted critique of ideology is misdirected. Such a charge is based upon several false assumptions about the debate that follows an acknowledgement that we are all believers. The first is that people will no longer have confidence in any laws, values, and goals once the foundations of social order and progress are shown to be religious or ideological. The second is that the various, competing viewpoints will not be able to agree on any common grounds for discussion, analysis and research. Finally, those fearing nihilism assume that no one will be able to convince another to change viewpoints.

I have attempted to show the reactionary character of these assumptions. Scholars in the two critical traditions discussed in this essay are confident in their analyses, willing to discuss alternatives, and hopeful that a consensus can be reached in order to improve society. And yet, there is no universal common sense, or rationality, to which members of a culture can appeal to settle disputes that arise concerning legal processes and institutions. There are, of course, ideas about what in law is rational or common-sensical, as well as ideas about what is good, just and legitimate. Such ideas will be regularly introduced, and then accepted or rejected by individuals and social groups, depending upon whether the ideas are consistent with the individual's or group's changeable and transparent beliefs about the world. This is one lesson of the critique of legal ideology: confidence in a purported neutral rationality is revealed as yet another ideology.

Notes

1. See R. Unger, *The Critical Legal Studies Movement* (1986); M. Kelman, *A Guide To Critical Legal Studies* (1987).

2. See Price, "Taking Rights Cynically: A Review of Critical Legal Studies," vol. 48, *Cambridge Law Journal,* 271 (1989).

3. Some leftist legal scholars prefer not to emphasize "ideology." Anthony Chase praises Franz Neumann's argument "that 'power' rather than 'ideologies and beliefs' should be at the center of analysis." See Chase, "The Left on Rights," vol. 62, *Texas Law Review,* 1541, 1552 (1984). Peter Gabel dislikes labelling the "contestation of meaning [of rights] an 'ideological struggle,' to the degree that the term implies a battle of disembodied ideas over what legal concepts ought to mean 'conceptually,'" for it is "rather an ontological struggle over opposing ways of being that determine what these concepts do mean in their qualitative, lived dimension." See Gabel, "The Phenomenology of Rights-Consciousness and the Pact of the Withdrawn Selves," vol. 82, *Texas Law Review,* 1583, 1589 (1984).

4. See Singer, "The Player and the Cards. . . .," vol. 94, *Yale Law Review,* vol. 1, 63 (1984); see also Boyle, "The Politics of Reason. . . .," vol. 133, *Univ. of Pennsylvania Law Review,* vol. 85, 690 ("Our ideas of rationality are themselves incoherent, authoritarian, or politically tilted."), and 715-16 ("It seems as though we must challenge not only liberal legalism but our very notion of rationality.") vol. 1 (1985).

5. See generally, *Stained Glass: Worldviews and Social Science* (P. Marshall, S. Griffioen and R. Mouw, eds. 1989). This volume contains important essays on the notion of worldview in Christian scholarship. I have especially relied on the essays by Albert Wolters, James Olthuis, and Jacob Klapwijk.

6. "What now is the fruit of this transcendental critique. . . .? It can pave the way for a real contact of thought among the various philosophical trends." H. Dooyeweerd, *A New Critique of Theoretical Thought*, vol. I, at 70 (D. Freeman and H. de Jongste trans. 1989). See also Boyle, note 4 above, at 737: "It is actually useful and liberating to find out about the philosophical structures behind the richly textured justifications for 'the way things are' in every area of social life."

7. Hunt, "The Theory of Critical Legal Studies," vol. 6, *Ox. J. L. Stud.* 1, 12 (1986).

8. See Nelken, "Beyond the Study of 'Law and Society'? . . . ," 1986 *Am. B. Found. Res. J.*, 323, 325.

9. 107 S. Ct. 2573 (1987) (Louisiana balanced-treatment law held to be an establishment of religion).

10. Gould, "Justice Scalia's Misunderstanding," *Nat. Hist.*, Oct. 1987, at 16.

11. W. Bird, *The Origin Of Species Revisited: The Theories of Evolution and of Abrupt Appearance* (1989).

12. *Tikkun* is a new magazine that describes itself as a "bi-monthly Jewish critique of politics, culture and society." Gabel serves as Associate Editor.

13. Gabel, "Creationism and the Spirit Nature," *Tikkun*, Nov./Dec., 1987, at 55.

14. Id. at 55, 57.

15. Id. at 59.

16. Id. at 62.

17. Freeman and Mensch, "Religion as Science/Science as Religion: Constitutional Law and the Fundamentalist Challenge," *Tikkun*, Nov./Dec. 1987, at 71.

18. Id. at 69.

19. Peller, "Creation, Evolution, and New South," *Tikkun*, Nov./Dec., 1987, at 72.

20. Id. at 74, 75.

21. See Gabel, "The Mass Psychology of the New Federalism. . . ," 52, Geo. Wash. Law Review, 263-64 (1984). Burger was Chief Justice of the U. S. Supreme Court in recent years, and has now been replaced by Chief Justice Rehnquist.

22. Id. at 263, citing Fiss and Krauthammer, "The Rehnquist Court," vol. 186, *New Republic*, 14 (1982).

23. Gabel, note 21 above, at 263-64, citing Comment, "Cases that Shock the Conscience. . . ," vol. 15, *Harv. C.R.-C.L. L. Rev.* 713 (1980).

24. Gabel, note 21 above, at 264.

25. Id. at 265.

26. Id. at 264.

27. *Brief Amici Curiae* of the Rabbinical Alliance of America, the Catholic Center, the Free Methodist Church of North America, the Committee on Openness in Science, and the Honorable Robert K. Dornan, William E. Dannemeyer, and Patrick L. Swindall in Support of Appellants, *Edwards v. Aguillard*, (U. S. 1986) (No. 85-1513).

28. Id. at 8. The theory "denies government the authority to interfere in the competition among ideas." Id.

29. Id. at 10.

30. Hart, "Introduction," in *Hearing And Doing: Philosophical Essays Dedicated to H. Evan Runner* (J. Kraay and A. Tol., eds., 1979), 3.

Von Mises' Economic Reductionism

Bruce Clemenger

Introduction

The practical and theoretical breakdown of post-second world war
Keynesianism has not yet ushered in a successor. But one of the most
important results has been the influence of the Austrian economic
school in the policies of Reagan and Thatcher. While Friedrich von
Hayek is the best known proponent of this school, even winning a
Nobel Prize, yet the "Dean" of this school is Ludwig von Mises.[1]
Mises' stress on the freedom of the individual and his ardent defense
of the free market and private property have caused his approach
to become increasingly popular among business leaders, politicians
and conservative Christians. Mises sought scientifically to establish
the proper nature and significance of economic science. He
developed a general science of human action in order to situate
economics within the sciences and to provide it with an epistemological foundation. He hoped that such an exposition of
economics would expose the fallacies of both interventionism and
socialism and provide a rational and scientific defense for liberalism,
the political doctrine which he considered to be the practical result
of correct economic theorizing. In this essay I will argue that Mises'

stress on individual economic activity systematically ignores the place of other features of human life and ends up in denying that freedom consists in anything other than acting as a rational accumulator.

Praxeology
In order to provide an adequate foundation for economics, Mises developed a general science of human action of which economics is considered to be one branch. This science, which he calls praxeology, arises from the realization that action is the result of the subject consciously aiming at an end. This orientation to results makes all action rational. The purpose of an action does not make an act rational, that the action is purposeful makes it rational. As all actions are performed by individuals, the individual is the primary given for the science of human action, and hence Mises believes that human cooperation and social action can only be understood in terms of individual rational action.

Mises did not think that the study of human action could be undertaken in an empirical way because each action is determined by the end sought, and ends, being chosen subjectively, cannot be studied theoretically.[2] As well the nature of human action is determined by a priori categories which are "the mental equipment of the individual that enable him to think and . . . to act."[3] These categories are presupposed in the ability of humans to reason and are the products of the logical structure of the human mind which allows us to grasp the causality in nature. They enable us to be cognizant of the relations between cause and effect and to make sense out of empirical knowledge. As the purpose of action is subjectively chosen, the only aspect of action subject to analysis is the selection and appropriation of means necessary to attain the desired end. The ability of man to act rationally is presupposed by Mises and is considered self-evident; it requires no further analysis or explanation.

Through the selection of means, individual rational action ascribes value. In reality there are no ends or means, there are only things and things have no value in themselves. Value is not an inherent quality nor is it imputed to a thing via labor. The value of a thing is determined by its perceived usefulness in attaining an end. The designation "end" or "mean" is a purely subjective one. A thing only becomes a means "when human reason plans to employ it for the attainment of some ends and human action really employs it for this purpose,"[4] and conceptions such as goods, commodities, and wealth only have meaning in reference to action. Mises does not deny that valuations are often adopted from the individual's social environment. He admits that the "immense majority of people take their valuation from the social environment into which they were born . . . " and that few "have the power to deviate from the traditional set of values and to establish their own scale of what appears to be better and what appears to be worse."[5] However, Mises insists on considering valuations solely on an individual basis as it is at the personal level that these valuations affect human action. Thus the foundation for economics, praxeology, is restricted to the study of individual rational action. Human action is reduced to the activity of a rational individual who ascribes value in the pursuit of ends. The influence of community, culture, morality or religion can only be understood in terms of subjectively chosen ends which are considered to be beyond the realm of analysis.

Economics

The development and application of a subjective theory of value broadened the scope of economics to include all human activity as it changed the focus of economics from the study of wealth to the study of exchange.[6] In specifying the scope of economics, Mises contrasted it to the study of human action (praxeology) and the study of market phenomena (catallactics). Economics provides the link between the two as it is concerned with the exchange aspect of all human action and its influence in the determination of exchange ratios within a market economy. Exchange is undertaken to improve one's situation. When inter-personal exchange occurs, each individual considers the good obtained as more valuable than the one traded. Thus the cost or price paid for the good obtained is less than its subjective value for that individual. The price paid is referred to by Mises as the objective exchange value and it is this which serves as the unit of calculation. In calculating the individual does not measure the value of a thing or a group of things, rather he calculates the value of the services he expects those things to render him. The private ownership of goods is requisite for the valuation of goods and for the process of calculation. If the means of production are not exchangeable, their relative values cannot be established and knowledge of relative values is necessary to determine the most efficient use of available means for the attainment of a given end.

As fundamental economic categories are involved in every action, economics is a science which studies all action from an economic point of view. In such economics the value of a thing is reduced to its calculated value which is determined by its usefulness in attaining a given end and private property becomes a necessary factor in this process. On the basis of the foundation provided by praxeology, the focus of economics is understood in terms of rational calculating individuals engaged in the acquisition of means, and then the analysis of social phenomena becomes dominated by the reduction of human action to the economic.

Social Cooperation
Mises understands society in terms of the actions of rational individuals: society is nothing more than the "concentration of individuals for cooperative effort,"[7] it "exists nowhere else than in the actions of individual man."[8] It is the "total complex of mutual relations" which results from concerted action and it is erroneous, argued Mises, to speak of society as having "autonomous and independent existence."[9] The latter is the view of "holistic" or "metaphysical" interpretations which perceive society as an "entity living its own life, independent of and separate from the lives of various individuals, acting on its own behalf and aiming at its own ends which are different from the ends sought by the individuals."[10] Since such a conception of society presumes an "antagonism between the aims of society and those of its members," in order to establish a basis for social harmony, it must integrate these divergent aims. Mises believes science need not resort to an idea of superhuman intervention, that of Lord, *Weltgeist* or history, to explain the reality of society and social cooperation. The basis of society and

social cooperation is provided by the higher productivity which results from a division of labor.[11]

The division of labor is described by Mises as a law of nature and it is the recognition and investigation of this law that provides us with knowledge which enables us to improve our condition. The individual is not required to sacrifice his own interest for the sake of cooperation, rather cooperation is the product of the individual's pursuit of his own interest. And if cooperation requires the individual to sacrifice his own interest, he is compensated by the greater returns possible under the division of labor. Any sacrifice is only "apparent and temporary" as a smaller gain is foregone in order to reap a greater one. The sacrifice one makes is merely "provisional" and there is no basis for a conflict of interest between the individual and society. Mises concluded:

Once it has been perceived that the division of labor is the essence of society, nothing remains of the antithesis between individual and society. The contradictions between individual in principle and the social disappears.[12]

There need be no agreement among individuals concerning subjectively chosen ends to ensure cooperation. Society is not an end, but a means which enables us to attain the ends which we wish to attain. Material needs, in that they are necessary for the attainment of higher ends, are means required by all and it is this common interest plus the advantages of the division of labor which binds us together in society. Thus in his analysis society is strictly an economic union; it has no other meaning than this. The ordering structure within the economic union is the market.

The Market

The market is a process which is "actuated by the interplay of the actions of various individuals cooperating in the division of labor."[13] In a market economy, the market is "supreme" as it "alone puts the whole social system in order and provides it with a sense and meaning."[14] The market directs the actions of individuals through the process of economic calculation which results in the formation of relative prices. This price structure, which is "the totality of the exchange as established by the interaction of those eager to buy and those eager to sell," indicates what consumers desire.[15] For the producer prices are the "mental tools of economic planning."[16] By producing and selling goods which consumers desire, the producer acquires the means by which he can pursue his own ends. As Mises summarized it, "The market directs him and reveals in what way he can best promote his own welfare as well as that of other people."[17] The market process adjusts the actions of the individual to the "requirements of mutual cooperation."[18] The market, by facilitating economic calculation of relative prices, is the sole guide and arbiter in the pursuit of subjectively chosen ends.

Mises felt the pursuit of profit was a sufficient motivation for social cooperation. He refutes the idea that the market economy must be formed on the basis of both the ownership of private property and on moral principles as he feels the latter would restrict the utilization of private property. He believes moral principles restraining greed or vice are not necessary to ensure the maintenance of social order. The imposition of moral principles affecting human action is one way in which the value judgments of some are imposed on everyone and as such it is a form of interventionism. Economic factors, as circumscribed by Mises, are all that is necessary for the functioning of the social order and all that is required for the maintenance of social cooperation is that individuals do not infringe "upon the persons of their fellow men and upon the right of private property."[19] It is in everyone's best interest that these two principles are abided by, and the sole function of the government is to ensure that they are adhered to. This is the task of liberalism.

Liberalism
According to Mises, the nature and function of the government is properly prescribed by the social system which it is required to maintain. Since the social system, and consequently the government, is a means and not an end in itself, Mises considers the selection and determination of each to be issues best addressed by economists. Though the market system has given the world a higher standard of living, Mises realized that even a beneficial system cannot function

without the support of public opinion. Common men "do not conceive any ideas, sound or unsound" wrote Mises, "they only choose between ideologies developed by the intellectual leaders of mankind."[20] As he felt economists were the best qualified to determine the suitability of a system of social cooperation it was incumbent upon economists to "conceive sound social and economic theories" and to make "these ideologies palatable to the majority."[21] So long as people understood what their rightly understood interests were, Mises believed that liberalism could maintain the requirements necessary for social cooperation and the unhampered operation of the market. Thus questions of political theory are best answered by economists. Indeed the political realm is effectively dissolved into the economic as liberalism is the political doctrine which results from the "application of theories developed by praxeology and especially by economics to definite problems of human action within society."[22]

Though it is the product of a scientific analysis of human action, liberalism itself is not neutral with respect to ultimate ends. The common goals with which liberalism is concerned are material and concern the preference of "life to death, health to sickness, nourishment to starvation, abundance to poverty."[23] It is liberalism which instructs us on how to act in regard to these desires. "It does not promise men happiness and contentment" he writes, "but only the most abundant possible satisfaction of all those desires that can be satisfied by the things of the outer world."[24] Liberalism does not deny the validity of man's pursuit of higher or more noble values, but it recognizes that the pursuit of such ends still require material goods which are necessary to life. Whether material welfare is considered an end in itself, or merely a means to another end, it is commonly sought by all and this pursuit is the basis of social cooperation. Liberalism does not say everyone ought to seek material welfare; rather it recognizes that everyone does in fact seek it. Public goals are merely economic means common to all people and what is not common to all is excluded from the public sphere. The public realm is constituted by material considerations.

There is no basis in liberalism for the implementation of interventionist policies. Governments interfere in the operation of the market in order to correct what the government considers to be defects in the system. Thus government interventionism is no different from socialism, or moral and religious interference, and it is rejected by Mises for the same reason. Interventionism is the imposition of one person's or group's subjective value judgments on the whole society. Mises felt such interference was a direct challenge to the freedom and liberty of the individual as it does not allow the individual to use his property freely in the pursuit of his own ends. In undertaking a course of interventionism, the government "moves beyond its role as preserver of private ownership and production against violent encroachment and interferes with the operation of business by means of orders and prohibition."[25]

Justice
Mises rejects any attempt to organize social cooperation in accordance with some supposed eternal or absolute notion of justice. He feels an appeal to such a notion would be ineffectual if there was disagreement concerning the proper understanding of justice as, he believes, there would be no way of establishing the truthfulness of one conception as opposed to another. Mises not only feels such a notion is unnecessary for the maintenance of social cooperation, but he believes that an absolute notion of justice does not exist.

> There is no such thing as an absolute notion of justice not referring to a definite system of social organization. It is not justice that determines the decision in favour of a definite social system. It is on the contrary, the social system which determines what should be deemed right and wrong. There is neither right nor wrong outside the social nexus.[26]

Whatever preserves social cooperation is just and right. All action detrimental to social cooperation is unjust. The nature of social cooperation, hence the role of government, is not determined by a notion of justice but the attainment of the subjectively chosen ends of the individual. The only valid "standard of justice" and the "sole guide of legislation" is social utility and social utility is determined by the ability of individuals to acquire the means necessary for the attainment of their individually selected ends.[27]

As long as everyone recognizes that social cooperation is of benefit to them in preserving their own ends, then the problem of maintaining social cooperation can "be discussed without reference to judgments of value."[28] The idea of justice and the formulation of laws protecting social cooperation do not conflict with an individual's subjective scale of value because they are concerned with the provision of means, not the selection or attainment of ends. The idea of justice, conceptions of right and wrong, and societal laws are only means contributing to the maintenance of social cooperation.

Religion

Mises considered liberalism to be neutral with respect to religion. As liberalism affirms what is common to all ideologies, liberal policies maintain social cooperation in the pursuit of an improved material well-being. Liberalism does not conflict with religion, rather it provides necessary requirements for the pursuit of religious ends. This neutrality can be maintained so long as religion does not "pretend to interfere with the conduct of social, political, and economic affairs."[29] Conflict only arises when religion, through the imposition of its valuations, hampers the market process and social cooperation.

Interference with the realm of social cooperation is beyond the proper scope of religion as Mises perceived it. Religion enjoins upon man a certain mode of individual conduct. But it does not assert anything with regard to the problems of social cooperation. Just as liberalism allows the individual freedom to pursue his own interests as long as he does not interfere with the operation of the market, likewise liberalism provides the basis for everyone to hold freely any religious belief insofar as those beliefs do not disrupt social cooperation and the market process.

Mises believed that liberalism, by distinguishing between church and state, is able to establish peace between the various religious factions and gives to each of them the opportunity to "preach the gospel unmolested."[30] Liberalism opposes all forms of "theocracy" which attempts to "organize the earthly affairs of mankind according to the contents of a complex of ideas whose validity cannot be demonstrated by reasoning"[31] and "all endeavors to silence the rational discussion of problems of social welfare by an appeal to religious intervention or revelation."[32] Liberalism enables the market to direct human action in the most efficient pursuit of material welfare and it allows men to pursue higher ends unmolested by the subjective valuations of others in society. As social welfare is considered only in economic terms, extra-economic considerations are considered irrelevant.

Evaluation
The isolation and analysis of an aspect of complex phenomena is an essential part of any study. However, if the relevance of other aspects are ignored and the conclusions of the analysis are not reintegrated with insights drawn from other disciplines, then the analysis will be biased towards this one aspect and will remain one-dimensional. This results in a diluted perception of the role and significance of the aspect under distorted perception of the phenomenon being studied.[33]

Mises developed the general science of human action to provide economics with an epistemological foundation. Though he said economics was only one of several branches of human action, he considered economics to be the "best elaborated" branch and he confined his analysis to economics.[34] He did not explain what the other branches might be nor how they would relate to economics within the framework of a general science of human action or in the study of individuals or social phenomena. Thus human action as presented by Mises is not a general science as such, but merely a philosophic framework which provided his conception of economics with a philosophical basis. It provides no fundamental link between economics and other disciplines. The failure to provide other aspects such as the political, social, or religious dimensions of human activity with a similar foundation results in the nature and scope of the other aspects being determined by the economic aspect in the application of the science of human action to human behavior and social phenomena. Not only is economics "divorced" from other disciplines, it dominates them.[35]

According to Mises, concepts of justice and liberty as well as the place and role of government and religion are determined by the form of social cooperation adopted by society and the form of social cooperation is selected strictly on the basis of economic expediency. Notions of right and wrong and the idea of justice are merely utilitarian precepts which are useful in conforming man's behavior to the requirements of social cooperation. Liberty and freedom are conditions of the structure of the market which allows individuals to pursue their own interests by serving others. The function of political society and government is to maintain, through force or the threat of force, the system of social cooperation. Religious beliefs and practices are tolerated only insofar as they do not interfere with the economic process. Thus, as a consequence of Mises' analysis of human action and society strictly in terms of the economic aspect, moral values are given content only in relation to the economic structure of society and the political and religious spheres are already prescribed by the requirements of the economic sphere.

Not only are there questions about the relation of the economic aspect to other aspects, but in Mises' theory, the economic sphere itself is limited in scope by his presuppositions about the nature and purpose of human action identified in praxeology. The economic calculating characteristic of the individual becomes the essence of the human character. A person's course of action is directed by a rational calculation of the most effective utilization of means necessary for the attainment of a given end. Mises derives this view of rational economic man from what he considered to be a self-evident understanding of human action based on a priori categories. However this conception of man was first developed within the framework of a specific form of social cooperation.[36] It was within the context of a developing market economy that this conception became tenable and it is such an understanding of human action and rationality which is presupposed in the development of praxeology.

Similarly, the nature and role of society is also determined by requirements of rational economic man. The structure of society, specifically the form of social cooperation utilized by the society, is determined on the basis of its effectiveness in maintaining the necessary conditions for free exchange between individuals. Society is a means; it is a vehicle for the individual's pursuit of his own interests. Society is merely the arena of action for Mises' economic man and thus it is reduced to being a function of the requirements of Mises' economic man, the calculating entrepreneur.

The predominance of economic considerations in Mises theory also has prescriptive implications for the selection of ends, something he wants to argue is subjective and beyond the realm of theory. He claims that science does not prescribe the ultimate ends man should pursue and that economics is prescriptive only concerning the selection of means. The determination of what is an end, thus what constitutes a means, is considered to be subjective. Yet what one person may consider an end, another may consider a means to an end. Mises avoids this dilemma by restricting his analysis to the means which he believes are common to all ends. Economics indicates what is the most effective way to provide these material needs and this effectively restricts one's subjective valuation to selection of only those ends which do not prescribe how they ought to be attained. A person is free to determine what ultimate ends he or she wishes to pursue but the pursuit of these ends is prescribed by economic science. The process by which an end is attained cannot itself be considered an end. A desire to live life according to a certain notion of justice or a set of religious values which will affect action in the marketplace cannot within Mises' framework be considered ends. They can merely be notions which conform man's actions to the requirements of social cooperation and they are themselves determined by the form of social cooperation employed. Meanwhile the selection of the appropriate form of social cooperation is, in Mises' opinion, best left for economists to determine.

He does not believe the individual is necessarily able to perceive correctly what his properly understood interests are. Economists can do so, and it is their task to supply the appropriate ideologies. Though he acknowledges that the ultimate choice between systems of social cooperation is made by public opinion, he believes that only economists can determine which system is in the best interest of all individuals.[37] The implication is that the ends people choose may not be in their own best interest. Though ends are held to be subjectively chosen by the individual, and are irrational and beyond the realm of science, yet it is economic science which prescribes what is in the best interest of the individual. What constitutes a means is prescribed by what is common to the attainment of all ends, and the appropriate ends to be sought are those which are consistent with the form of social cooperation and political ideology prescribed by the conclusions of economic science. Political issues are reduced to questions of economics and are best addressed by economists. Thus the prescriptive nature of economics restricts the freedom of the individual to choose a desired end.

As a result of Mises' attempt to provide a scientific defense of liberalism, economic science became hegemonic and prescriptive. Man is reduced to and is required to be a rational calculating entrepreneur. Society is considered to be merely a means which facilitates this pursuit, and is required to conform to Mises' model of society. The individual must relegate all except material needs to the private realm of life. In the name of freedom all other options are forbidden.

Notes

1. H. W. Spiegel writes: "If purely theoretical work, undiluted by empiricism and free of mathematics, and methodological and political individualism were the hallmarks of the Austrian School, no one confirmed this tradition in a more forthright and uncompromising fashion than Mises." *The Growth of Economic Thought* (Durham: Duke University Press, 1971), 543. See also John P. East, "American Conservative Thought: The Impact of Ludwig von Mises," *Modern Age*, Fall, 1979.

2. He wrote: "It is impossible to reform the sciences of human action according to the pattern of physics and the other natural sciences. There is no means to establish an a posteriori theory of human conduct and social events. History can neither prove nor disprove any general statements in the manner in which the natural sciences accept or reject a hypothesis on the grounds of laboratory experi-

ments." Ludwig Von Mises, *Human Action*, (London: William Hodge, 1949), 30.

3. Ludwig Von Mises, *Ultimate Foundations*, (Toronto: D. Van Nostrand Co., 1962), 12.

4. *Human Action*, 42.

5. Ludwig Von Mises, *Theory and History*, (New Haven: Yale University Press, 1957), 22.

6. When value was understood as being a characteristic of a good, being either intrinsic to the good or imputed to the good via human labor, then economists would focus their attention on the production or distribution of wealth. By applying a subjective theory of value to economics, the economic principle becomes the "fundamental principle of all rational action" and therefore all rational action may be considered as "an act of economizing." Ludwig Von Mises, *Epistemological Problems of Economics*, (Toronto: D. Van Nostrand Co., 1960), 148.

7. *Human Action*, 232.

8. Ibid., 143.

9. Ibid.

10. Ibid., 145.

11. He referred to the division of labor as the "great cosmic principle of becoming." *Ultimate Foundation*, 126.

12. Ludwig Von Mises, *Socialism,* (New Haven: Yale University Press, 1951), 299.

13. *Human Action*, 258.

14. Ibid.

15. Ibid.

16. Ibid., 209-10.

17. Ibid., 258.

18. Ibid.

19. Ibid., 720.

20. Ibid., 860

21. Ibid.

22. Ibid., 153

23. Ibid.

24. Ludwig Von Mises, *Free and Prosperous Commonwealth* (Toronto: D. Van Nostrand Co., 1962), 4.

25. *Human Action*, 148.

26. Ibid., 717.

27. *Theory and History*, 54.

28. Ibid., 52.

29. *Human Action*, 155.

30. Ibid., 157.

31. Ibid., 155.

32. Ibid., 156.

33. For a philosophical analysis of the irreducibility and fundamental interrelation of the aspects or modes through which we experience reality, see Herman Dooyeweerd's *A New Critique of Theoretical Thought*, 4 vols., (Amsterdam, Paris, Philadelphia: Presbyterian and Reformed, 1953-1958). The consequence of such a narrow focus on modern society is analyzed by Bob Goudzwaard in *Capitalism and Progress*, (Toronto: Wedge; Grand Rapids: Eerdmans, 1979). Goudzwaard describes it as "funnelling" (chapter 18).

34. Ibid., 3

35. Mises mentions sociology as another branch of praxeology but he did not elaborate the aspect of human action which sociology would study.

36. Describing the concept of man in seventeenth-century liberalism, C. B. Macpherson provides an accurate description of Mises' view of man. He writes, "The individual was seen neither as a moral whole, nor as a part of a larger social whole, but as an owner of himself. . . . The individual, it was thought, is free inasmuch as he is proprietor of his person and capacities. The human essence is freedom and dependence on the wills of others, and freedom is a function of possession. Society becomes a lot of free equal individuals related to each other as proprietors of their own capacities and of what they have acquired by their exercise. Society consists of relations of exchange between proprietors. Political society becomes a calculated device for the protection of this property and for the maintenance of an orderly relation of exchange." *The Political Theory of Possessive Individualism*, (Oxford: Oxford University Press, 1977), 3.

37. He felt that the challenges facing economists were particularly acute. Men like J. M. Keynes, Bertrand Russell, Harold Laski and

Albert Einstein "could not comprehend economic problems." Ludwig Von Mises, *Notes and Recollections* (South Holland: Libertarian Press, 1978), 63.

Reconceptualizing Economics:
The Contributions of Karl Polanyi

David Woods

Introduction

Economic activity functions within a social environment. While this appears to be an obvious fact of everyday life its implications for economic analysis are not always so easy to draw. The truth is that the social context of economics can be interpreted in a variety of ways.

In this paper I shall look at how the social context of economics has been interpreted by the economic anthropologist Karl Polanyi.[1] His notion of the "social embeddedness" of economic life leads him to consider the different ways in which economic activity can be institutionally organized in any society. His approach is therefore at odds with the underlying individualist methodology in the orthodox neoclassical economic paradigm. This methodology conceptually abstracts individuals from the social relations within which they live and implicitly makes the assumption that the essence of individual behavior can be understood apart from the reality of human society. This is reflected in its concentration on the characteristics of an abstract rational individual. The starting point within Polanyi's theoretical framework, by contrast, is the institutional structures within which economic life functions.

I shall in particular focus on the link between this individualist methodology and the widely accepted definition of economics as the science of scarcity. This idea received its most definitive statement in Lionel Robbins' influential 1932 treatise on economic science.[2] I shall outline Polanyi's diagnosis of the methodology underpinning this widely accepted idea that economics is concerned with the scarcity dimension of life and consequently also, by doing so, consider his critique of the notion that scarcity is a universally applicable economic concept.

My interest in such fundamental questions in economics flows from a desire to understand the economic meaning of God's call to humanity in the first chapter of Genesis to "be fruitful and multiply."[3] In the New Testament this economic theme of being fruitful is picked up again many times by Jesus (for instance in the Parable of the Talents) as he re-echoes our calling to be good stewards of creation. I hope that an understanding of the underlying issues in Polanyi's debate with economic orthodoxy will help to elucidate more fully what it means for people to use fruitfully the resources with which they have been entrusted.

Since economic activity operates within a social environment, what it means to be fruitful needs to be grasped in the context of human relationships. A Christian understanding of economic life in society should be informed by the central New Testament theme of "the Body of Christ." Pointing to the variety of gifts possessed by the members of the Christian church at Corinth, Paul emphasizes that each and every person is an essential part of the whole body.[4] Interdependence is as intrinsic to human society as is the individuality of its various members. Each individual relies upon the contributions of others, just as what they can offer is needed too.

The challenge for the Christian theorist is to grasp the meaning of economics, and to interpret what it means to be fruitful, in the context of human interdependence. An important question is whether the Robbinsian idea of economics as the science of scarcity provides an adequate understanding of economics in this regard.

Polanyi's work in economic anthropology is important because his concept of the social embeddedness of economic life and his institutionally oriented methodology help to enlighten these issues.

Social Embeddedness and Institutional Methodology
The social embeddedness of the economy is one of the key concepts in Polanyi's thought. In *The Great Transformation* Polanyi elaborates the thesis that an economy is naturally embedded in the society within which it functions. He describes how the "laissez-faire" experiment in nineteenth century Europe attempted to make the economy autonomous and thus divorce it from society by transforming economic relations into a system of self-regulating markets. Since economic processes are naturally embedded in the wider society, Polanyi sees this phenomenon as having been an historical aberration. More than this, however, it was perverse; the end result of the laissez-faire ideology was to turn society into an extension of the market. In order for a system of markets to be self-regulating all economic elements had to be organized along market lines. Land and labor, which are the constituent components of economic activity as well as being part of the basic fabric of any society were transformed into saleable commodities and thereby society itself became subject to the sway of economic forces. This is what Polanyi means by "The Great Transformation."

In *Trade and Market*[5] the focus shifts from economic and social history to economic theory and economic anthropology. The concept of social embeddedness points to the fact that economic life functions within social institutions and norms that are more than economic. This is particularly evident in non-capitalist societies. Religious ceremonies, political events and other kinds of social activities may perform important economic functions. Among the Huron Indians of Ontario in Canada, for example, a substantial redistribution of furs and other kinds of wealth took place as part of a reburial ceremony which occurred every ten or twelve years.[6] A religious ceremony thus served a significant redistributive function in their society.

Even in advanced industrial societies where there are discernable economic institutions (such as business firms) separate from activities and institutions that tend to be thought of as non-economic, the so-called economic institutions are themselves a configuration of many different elements ecological, technological and social. While businesses are economic in focus they are also more than economic in their character and make-up. Business life is shaped by social and cultural norms that prescribe appropriate ways of interacting with others as employees and consumers, while its smooth operation in a complex economy depends on a suitable legal framework. Business firms themselves are made up of individuals with particular needs, gifts and skills using available material and technological resources.

Since economic activity is always embedded in the society in which it functions, Polanyi talks about economic systems as socially instituted.[7] The particular kinds of economic relationship and styles of economic behavior are a consequence of how economic activity has been instituted in any given society. Economic life has to be understood in terms of the institutional structures within which it functions.

An implication of this is that there is no natural or necessary kind of economic behavior that is intrinsic to economic relationships as such, nor is there a natural or necessary species of economic institution that characterizes economic activity at most times and places. Compare this with Adam Smith's contention that people are natural traders with a universal "propensity to truck, barter, and exchange,"[8] the start of a long tradition in economics that has tended to see armslength exchanges between individuals as the paradigmatic economic relationship and markets as the main economic institution.

Polanyi distinguishes three basic kinds of economic relationship (including armslength market exchanges), which he sees as alternative "forms of integration" for organizing the economic process. The three basic types are referred to as reciprocity, redistribution and market exchange.[9] Reciprocity is about "movements between correlative points of symmetrical groupings," such as reciprocal exchanges of gifts on specified occasions or at particular ceremonies. Redistribution denotes the movement of goods towards a center and out of it again, such as the payment of taxes to a center of authority which then redistributes the money and goods to necessary projects and dependent groups, as well as to pay its agents. Market exchange refers to "vice-versa movements" taking place as between buyers and sellers under a market system.[10]

It should be noted that although in some formal sense market exchange might appear to be the same as reciprocity in that they both involve a two-way movement of goods (or goods, services and money), there are important differences. First, whereas in a market the two parties are free whether or not to contract an exchange of goods, the necessity for a reciprocal movement of goods, for example in a gift exchange, is largely predetermined by social norm and by parameters, such as the giving of presents on certain occasions such as at Christmas. In addition, the setting of the market provides for the possibility of higgling-haggling in arriving at a competitive rate of exchange mutually acceptable to both parties, whereas reciprocal movements are usually on an approximate scale of equivalence reflecting a social consensus as to what is appropriate. Finally, whereas the two-way movements of goods in a market are clearly and closely connected to each other, reciprocal movements of goods may be separated in time and may not even be between the same two parties.

Although Polanyi talks about his three forms of integration as ways whereby the movement of goods is integrated with social institutions, he does not interpret the concept of "goods" in an inflexible manner to mean simply material objects. To some extent his understanding of economic processes includes also the movement and use of services.[11] Nor indeed is the "movement" of goods interpreted to mean simply their transportation and their circulation among people. Polanyi makes it clear that the movement of goods includes also the process of production (in which goods shift from a lower to a higher order in terms of their usefulness to the consumer),[12] and indeed his threefold classification of economic relationships can be as easily used to analyze production activities as much as it can the simple distribution and circulation of goods.[13]

Polanyi emphasizes that the presence of reciprocity, redistribution and market exchange as forms of economic relationship depend on certain kinds of institutional structure being present. Reciprocity assumes the presence of symmetrically arranged groups; redistribution depends on there being some measure of "centricity" in the group, such as an allocative center; and market exchange presupposes a system of price-making markets.[14]

If it were not for these structural parameters then individual acts of reciprocity, redistribution or exchange might take place but they could not genuinely integrate the economy in the sense of producing an economic system.[15] Individual acts of barter occur in primitive societies organized largely around reciprocity and redistribution, but unless a system of price-making markets exist, these acts of barter will remain just that: sporadic acts of barter. They will not tend to create an exchange economy. Similarly in capitalist market societies acts of reciprocity often occur within families and voluntary groups but they will never tend to lead to an economy based on reciprocity since businesses are just not institutionally organized on those lines.

Consider, by way of contrast, Adam Smith's account of the birth of a capitalist market society at the start of Book One of *The Wealth of Nations*. Smith takes us back to that "rude state of society," prior to the division of labor, in which exchanges are seldom made. At this stage of society "every man provides everything for himself" and looks completely after his own needs.[16] But gradually people are led out of a sense of their own self-interest to begin specializing in occupations for which they have a particular talent or skill. What they produce over and above their own requirements they exchange for goods which they are less adept at making.[17] Later with the increasing complexity and scale of production it becomes necessary to store up a stock of goods of various kinds (i.e., a stock of capital) sufficient to maintain workers, and to supply them with the materials and tools of their work, during the process of production, carrying them over until such time as what they are manufacturing can be sold.[18] Thereby the capitalist enterprise is born.

It should be noted however that in such a modern capitalist market economy, characterized by a complex division of labor, a myriad of exchange transactions, the accumulation of capital, economic growth and wealth creation, does not develop because of anyone's intentional design. The division of labor is "not originally the effect of any human wisdom, which foresees and intends that general opulence to which it gives occasion."[19]

It is the consequence rather of Nature's having given to each individual a "trucking disposition." Market oriented self-interest leads people to specialize and implicitly to cooperate with each other. The free actions of money-making individuals therefore create prosperity for all even though that was never their intention.

In Smith's analysis there is the idea that the inner dynamic of capitalism is to be found not in the institutional environment, nor in a distinctive cultural ethos, nor even in the necessity that individuals work together somehow, but in the characteristic behavior and predispositions of individuals. For Smith, we might say, the "trucking disposition" is the seed from which market capitalism eventually grows. For Polanyi, by contrast, capitalism is the product of a society where economic activity has been institutionally organized around a system of price-making markets.

Smith's approach can be seen as the beginning of a long tradition in economics which assumes that models of the economy must be constructed from the actions of its autonomous constituent individuals and their characteristic propensities. Consider the individual maximizers, each with their own preference functions and initial endowments, so beloved of introductory microeconomic textbooks. This theme will be pursued further below when the scarcity assumption and Robbins' underlying model is discussed in the context of the contrast between these two approaches, the individualist and the institutional.

Returning to Polanyi we can see that, by focusing on how economic activity is instituted within any society, he is placing himself at odds with the dominant individualist methodology in economics. Polanyi's underlying premise is that economic activity is inherently a social process in which people interact with each other at the same time as they transform the natural environment.[20] In consequence his methodology of economics starts with society and social institutions. He writes:

Institutional arrangements, such as symmetrical organizations, central points and market systems . . . seem to represent a mere aggregate of the same personal patterns the eventual effects of which they are supposed to condition. The significant fact is that mere aggregates of the personal behaviors in question do not by themselves produce such structures. Reciprocity behavior between individuals integrates the economy only if symmetrically organized structures, such as a symmetrical system of kinship groups, are given. But a kinship system never arises as the result of mere reciprocating behavior on the personal level.[21]

The same logic applies for individual acts of barter and a market system, as we saw above.

Some commentators have criticized Polanyi for playing up and emphasizing altruistic tendencies, particularly in his study of primitive societies. But this would appear to be a fundamental misunderstanding of his approach.[22] Polanyi is not saying that individuals in primitive societies are somehow morally superior to the members of a market society. Nor is he seeking to explain the workings of primitive societies (or indeed any others) from the moral dispositions of its constituent individual members. David Kaplan writes that:

Polanyi is not concerned with "innate" economic propensities, or for that matter with the behavior of individuals qua individuals at all. What does concern him is institutionalized behavior.[23]

Patterns of economic behavior differ from society to society and these reflect neither innate moral traits, nor any other kinds of (given) individual predispositions, but the different structure of socioeconomic institutions.

Having therefore examined Polanyi's notion of the social embeddedness of economic life, and his institutionally oriented methodology of economics, we shall now go on to investigate the Robbinsian idea of economics as concerned with scarcity and discuss how Polanyi's critique of this conception of economics flows from his alternative starting point and methodology.

Critique of the Scarcity Assumption

It has been a widespread assumption among mainstream economists at least since Lionel Robbins' authoritative 1932 *Essay on the Nature and Significance of Economic Science* that the human economic situation should be seen primarily as a confrontation of individuals with scarcity. In this treatise Robbins demonstrated convincingly to fellow Anglo-Saxon practitioners that economics should be regarded as the science of scarcity.

Robbins contrasts this position with that of economists who circumscribe their subject as "the study of the causes of material welfare."[24] He argues that this limits the analytical scope of economics too greatly. For Robbins economics is fundamentally about the allocation of resources among alternative uses. The necessity of making choices in the use of resources is the key to whether an activity has economic relevance. There is therefore no logical reason for economists to restrict themselves to looking only at how resources are used to meet material ends. This gives privileged status to a certain class of ends for no particular reason.[25] Indeed, since it is often the case that there is a conflict of resources between material and non-material ends (at the very least in terms of how people use the resource of time), one would be left with an incomplete understanding of economic processes if economics had to confine itself to analysing the use of resources in relation only to material ends.[26]

Robbins outlines three conditions which must be satisfied for an economic dimension to be present.[27] First, there must be more than one end, these ends being arranged in an order of priority. Second, the means to satisfy these ends must be limited and not sufficient to satisfy them completely. Third, the means must be capable of alternative uses. When all three conditions are met then an activity can be studied using economic tools, since for Robbins economics is "the science which studies human behavior as a relationship between ends and scarce means which have alternative uses."[28]

In practice it may be that all three conditions are not always satisfied. One may find that some resources are not in fact scarce. There is, for instance, a comparative abundance of air compared to our need for it, and so in general air is not scarce and therefore has no economic significance in Robbins' framework. Robbins however concludes by asserting his belief that *"scarcity* of means to satisfy ends of varying importance is an *almost ubiquitous* condition of human behavior"[29] [my emphasis].

Polanyi's critique of the idea that scarcity is the defining concept in economics turns on the distinction he makes between *scarcity* and *insufficiency*. These two concepts are somewhat similar but it is important that they should not be confused. Scarcity assumes the presence of insufficiency, but insufficiency does not in itself imply scarcity.

Polanyi criticizes the relevance of the postulate of scarcity by arguing that it makes two assumptions. It assumes, first, that means are insufficient, and second, where they are insufficient, that the insufficiency induces choice.[30] As we shall see, these two assumptions roughly correspond, respectively, to Robbins' second condition (insufficiency of means to satisfy ends), and to his first and third conditions (alternative uses of means of satisfaction of diverse ends).

With respect to the first assumption, insufficiency simply refers to whether or not there is enough of a particular resource to go round, that is to meet people's needs for it at a certain time. Is there, for example, enough food to feed people over a certain period? The presence of insufficiency therefore depends on how abundant a particular resource is, as well as on the level of wants that people have for that resource, given the society in which they live. Thus for instance water and air are not generally commodities that people are short of, though water may be insufficient for people in areas of drought, and clean air may be in short supply for modern city dwellers.

Moving to the second assumption, Polanyi's argument is that the presence of insufficiency, purely of itself, has no behavioral implications. Insufficiency leads to rational economizing behavior only where choice arises out of that insufficiency:

> For the insufficiency to induce choice there must be given more than one use to the means, as well as graded ends, i.e., at least two ends ordered in sequence of preference. Both conditions are factual.[31]

But as a matter of fact, *there may be no choice* of how means may be used. A resource may only be able to be used in one fixed way because of the physical characteristics of a good, such as the manna in the Old Testament which rotted after one day; because of the state of technology; or because society ordains that things must be done a certain way or otherwise places constraints on how resources of various kinds can be used. The cow, for instance, is a sacred animal in India and even though people are poor it cannot be exploited like other animals. And where in human society there exists a strict division of labor, either on the basis of social position, race or sex, human labor cannot be freely allocated as is possible in a pure capitalist society. The existence of these factual constraints on how means may be used seriously limits the scope of validity of Robbins' concept of scarcity.

Although interestingly Robbins himself refers to these same assumptions as being implicit in the concept of scarcity,[32] the inference he draws from this differs sharply from Polanyi's conclusion. Looking at a situation where insufficiency exists but not choice, Robbins writes that:

Nor is the mere limitation of means *by itself* sufficient to give rise to economic phenomena. If means of satisfaction have no alternative use, then they may be scarce, but they cannot be economized. The manna which fell from heaven may have been scarce, but if it was impossible to exchange it for something else or to postpone its use, it was not the object of any activity with an economic aspect.[33]

Where the preconditions of insufficiency and choice are not both satisfied at the same time then, for Robbins, there is no economic aspect in which economists can properly take an interest. For Polanyi, by contrast, it is precisely because he believes that economic activity does exist even in situations (such as the above) where there is no scarcity, that scarcity cannot possibly be the defining characteristic of economics. Economic categories are relevant for instance in describing how goods are distributed within a society and move to their final destination even where these goods do not have alternative uses.

In a capitalist society both the insufficiency condition and the choice condition are satisfied and economically there can be said to be a continual state of scarcity. People are never able to consume as much as they seem to want, while the near universality of commodity status allows almost everything to be freely bought and sold for money by individuals who can both use and dispose of resources without restraint.

Scarcity is a relevant economic concept when people actually experience their economic situation as one of scarcity. This is obviously the case in a capitalist society (as seen above) and so tends also to hold in contemporary democratic mixed capitalist economies to the extent that they approach the capitalist ideal. But in a noncapitalist society scarcity might also be experienced, and can therefore be a relevant economic variable, when a famine or flood leads to critical shortages which directly affect people's behavior by causing either a partial or complete breakdown of normal modes of living.[34]

The important point in all this is that whether scarcity exists in a particular situation in the sense that Polanyi defines it as insufficiency leading to choice, is an empirical question and a matter of degree rather than an a priori given. In understanding economic life what is important is not how people would behave if they lived in some kind of Robinson Crusoe "state of nature," but rather how they do actually behave given the culture and society in which they live and the institutional economic parameters that it sets for them.

In focusing on the abstract individual, the model of economics as scarcity developed by Robbins is individualistic in its underlying methodology. It attempts to understand the situation facing individuals and individual behavior apart from any society in which such individuals might be thought to live and apart from any particular form of social relationships.

Polanyi's approach, by contrast, is more relational as noted previously. He emphasizes that economic resources are always used in a social and cultural context of one kind or another. People work with tools, natural resources, and goods of various kinds, and in conjunction with other persons, in the context of social parameters that affect the shape, color and nature of these economic relationships.

Consequently the cultural and institutional context of economic activity therefore affects the extent to which people experience themselves as not having enough of any resource, and the extent to which they are able to use resources in alternative ways. In assessing the significance of scarcity, and its relevance for individual behavior, the economist or economic anthropologist needs to investigate subjective perceptions, needs, rights and abilities, and how far these are impacted on by, and dependent upon, social and economic institutions and cultural forces. Rather than seeing scarcity as a universal quality which can be deduced by a priori reasoning, Polanyi points us to investigate its actual importance by looking at the extent to which people do actually experience their situation as one of scarcity.

Apart from its individualistic methodology there are two other important implicit assumptions which can be distinguished in the Robbinsian paradigm of economics as the science of scarcity. The first is the underlying philosophical model of economics. The second is the narrow conception of the human person.

As to the first, Richard McKenzie writes in *The Limits of Economic Science* that:

> Neoclassical economics is, in the main, wedded to "Robbinsian" maximizing behavior, which posits a fundamental distinction and conflict between the internal subjective world of the individual and the external objective world in which the individual pursues personal goals. . . . The "economic problem" emerges when the individual pursues subjectively established interests by objective external means. "Economizing behavior" is, almost by definition, the individual's natural response to the personal "problem" that emerges.[35]

The underlying philosophical model is of an isolated individual ego seeking to achieve subjective goals, in conflict with the external objective world.

As to the second assumption, there is implicit in the Robbinsian model a very specific and narrow conception of the individual who is in conflict with the external world. The individual human agent is seen as a kind of logical operator, a rational self manipulating the objective world. Although the "internal subjective world" of the individual (referred to by McKenzie) may be a complex place of feelings, images and ideas, it is the logical structure of the relationship between subjective and objective worlds that is presumed to matter in any analysis of economic phenomena.

A consequence of this exclusive preoccupation with logical structure is that the individual's relationship with the objective world is conceived of as one-dimensional. Moreover since the logic in question is a kind of mathematical logic, what is being assumed is that the human economic relationship between resources and needs can be modelled as largely quantitative in form. The concept of scarcity, for example, with its idea of "limited" resources in conflict with "insatiable" wants, reflects this one-dimensional, quantitative understanding of economic processes. The implication of the Robbinsian notion that economics is the science of scarcity is that the primary analytical focus of economics is quantitative in this sense.

Such a reduced perspective is, I believe, an integral part of the Robbinsian approach to economics. In order to fence off an area in which economic laws can be studied according to purely objective principles of analysis it is necessary to reduce the economist's scope of vision. The many social norms, individual values and other subjective elements which bear upon the formation of human goals and the development of economic means must be excluded from its proper realm of analysis. Subjective and objective features are separated so as to create a defined area in which objective economic laws can be studied.

The ingenious *ceteris paribus* assumption is used to take tastes, technology, the kinds of goods produced, and human abilities as "givens." This implies that, for instance, the formation of tastes and the development of technology are not seen as part of the internal domain of economics. For Robbins, economic analysis is the study of how given resources and a given catalogue of technology can most effectively be used to satisfy given wants. The complex and ever-changing nature of wants, technology, skills, social institutions, re-sources and human abilities are ignored. Together these entities are all frozen at a particular point in time. With this assumption the theoretical structure of economic life is reduced to a scarcity-focused relationship between means (resources) and ends (wants).

The problem with this economic paradigm is that it leads to a too narrow understanding of economic activities which tends to downplay broader qualitative dimensions. How might we attempt to characterize these broader components of the internal structure of economics which are neglected in an exclusive focus upon scarcity?

The first important aspect to be noticed is that of the formation of resources and the development of working abilities and skills. In Robbins' paradigm it seems to assume that physical resources and labor inputs are given in a finished and usable form, i.e., as so many units of L1, L2, L3 . . . and L11 which can be plugged into a production function. In practice however all of us, as stewards of ourselves and of the earth, have a vital (entrepreneurial) role to play in identifying what are usable resources and in converting them into a manageable form, as well as in uncovering and developing our own gifts and abilities.

A second important component of economics is the preservation of resources and the maintenance of working capacities. Any economic unit, such as a business firm, has to ensure its continuity of operation from period to period by replacement of material inputs used up in production, by putting aside enough resources for the depletion of capital, and by arranging for continuity in personnel with appropriate levels of skills. Similarly any society has to provide for its future by the education and training of tomorrow's workers, by ensuring that renewable resources are replaced as they are used up, and that nonrenewable natural resources are not depleted too fast.

A third component of economics is the directing of resources to the meeting of human priorities and needs. Needs as well as resour-ces develop over time. In each period needs must be identified as such by economic agents and appropriate economic goals deter-mined to meet them. Finally appropriate resources have to be found and brought together so that the goals can be achieved. Robbins nevertheless seems to talk about "resources" and "means" inter-changeably as though the two concepts are almost equivalent and as if resources are somehow already means. But it is only through human economic activity that resources *become* means to certain ends. It is only through the economic process that they become means to the meeting of human needs.

These three dimensions of economic activity focus therefore on the formation, the preservation, and the goal-orientation of resources. In practice these different dimensions of economics interconnect with each other. They also overlap with the scarcity dimension (whose focus seems to be about making the best with limited resources.) If (following Polanyi) we use the term "economizing" to describe economic activity directed narrowly and exclusively towards the overcoming of scarcity, then (to make the contrast) we might follow the Christian economist Bob Goudzwaard in designating economic activity in its broader and more opened up sense as "stewardship."[36] Accordingly the four economic elements[37] reviewed above might be thought of as together constituting the meaning of stewardship.

A possible objection to such an understanding of economics is that the formation, preservation and goal-orientation of resources might only be *sub*dimensions (rather than *equal* dimensions) of economics. The core meaning of economics, it might be argued, is to be found in the overcoming of scarcity: other dimensions are only economically relevant to the extent that they contribute to the overcoming of scarcity.

However this line of reasoning appears to be flawed since, even if there were unlimited physical resources and no shortage of time, it would still be necessary to develop resources and identify human needs. In such an imaginary situation *appropriate* goods and services would still need to be produced and, for this purpose, appropriate resources would therefore also be required. Furthermore it would still be necessary to insure the continuity of economic processes.

What particularly emerges from this discussion of the various functions of economic life is the centrality of the human role and the many different human qualities involved in economic activities. The great diversity of relevant human resources needs to be recognized in economics. This includes qualities such as creativity, imagination, technical skills, empathy, communication, management and organization. The notion of the individual person as a logical operator is therefore far too narrow. Economic analysis has to recognize the importance of subjective features in economic activity as well as its objective aspects.

These subjective features do not however figure prominently in Polanyi's analysis as vital characteristics of economic activities. Possibly the reason is that Polanyi tends to focus on economic processes through the entry point of goods and the different ways that they move. To be sure, neither his concept of "goods" nor his notion of "movement" display rigid or narrow interpretations. But it may be that the metaphor of movement, expressing as it does a quality that can be applied as much to material objects and animals as it can to human beings, conceals some of the subjective human qualities involved in economic relationships. It perhaps obscures the breadth of human resources which participate in economic activities.

Conclusion

Polanyi's work in economic anthropology is important and interesting because his idea of the social embeddedness of economic life, as well as his institutionally oriented approach, are so different from the individualist methodology characteristic of orthodox neoclassical theory.

The present paper has focused upon the link between this individualist methodology and the notion of economics as being the science of scarcity. Polanyi's critique of this conception of economics emphasizes the social context in which economic resources are used. Scarcity may be a relevant economic concept in some circumstances but may not make sense in others. It is important to consider empirically the different ways in which economic activities are institutionally organized in any society. Rather than seeing scarcity as the defining characteristic of economics, Polanyi's model seeks to provide alternative categories which show how economic activities can exist and function even without the presence of scarcity.

Polanyi's fundamental premise is that economic activities are socially embedded. His conception of economics is therefore at odds with the idea of scarcity which seems to be inspired by an underlying picture which abstracts from the reality of human society and in which the individual ego is in conflict with the external world. Polanyi sees that through economic activity people necessarily interact with each other at the same time as they transform their natural environment. Polanyi's basic categories therefore describe fundamental types of economic relationship between people.

Finally I have attempted to characterize the various important component dimensions of economics in addition to scarcity. These dimensions I describe as being concerned with the formation, preservation[38] and goal orientation of resources. Seeing the internal structure of economics in this way, rather than as primarily about the individual ego's confrontation with the external world, helps us to grasp how economic processes are embedded within human society and social relationships.

Notes

1. Karl Polanyi's important publications include *The Great Transformation*, (Boston: Beacon Press, 1957); *Trade and Market in the Early Empires: Economies in History and Theory*, edited with Conrad M. Arensberg and Harry W. Pearson (New York: The Free Press, 1957); and *The Livelihood of Man*, edited by Harry W. Pearson, (New York: Academic Press, 1977).
2. Lionel Robbins, *An Essay on the Nature and Significance of Economic Science*, (London: Macmillan, 1935, 2nd edn.).
3. Genesis, chapter 1 verse 28.
4. See chapter 12 of Paul's first letter to the Corinthians.
5. *Trade and Market* is a collection of essays emanating from a collaborative group project at Columbia University in the 1950s. Polanyi's overview essay (chapter) in this volume is probably the most succinct introduction to his theoretical approach to economic anthropology and the comparative study of economic systems.
6. See Bruce G. Trigger, *The Huron Farmers of the North*, (New York: Holt, Rinehart and Winston, 1959), 105-12.

7. See particularly *Trade and Market*, chapter 13, "The Economy as Instituted Process."

8. Adam Smith, *An Inquiry into the Nature and Causes of the Wealth of Nations*, edited with introduction and notes by Edwin Cannan, (New York: Random House, 1937), 13.

9. See *Trade and Market*, 250-55.

10. Ibid., 250.

11. This is particularly so in his last volume, *The Livelihood of Man*.

12. *Trade and Market*, 248.

13. Thus, for example, production within a conventional capitalist enterprise is organized around the principle of market exchange; employees and businesses have an arms-length contractual relationship with each other in which labor is exchanged for monetary reward. By contrast, a large hunt in an early society organized around a tribal or kinship grouping, and in which the catch is either divided afterwards among the members themselves or used for some common purpose, would be said to be structured along redistributive lines.

14. *Trade and Market*, 250.

15. Ibid., 251.

16. *The Wealth of Nations*, 259.

17. Ibid., 15.

18. Ibid., Book Two: "Introduction."

19. Ibid., 13.

20. See his concept of the "substantive meaning of economic" in *Trade and Market*, 243.

21. Ibid., 251.

22. See, for instance, Scott Cook's essay "The Obsolete 'Anti-Market' Mentality: A Critique of the Substantive Approach to Economic Anthropology" in Leclari & Schneider, eds., *Economic Anthropology*, 213.

23. Kaplan, "The Formal-Substantive Controversy in Economic Anthropology," *South-Western Journal of Anthropology*, vol. 24. no. 3 (1968): 233-34.

24. Robbins, op. cit., 4.

25. Ibid., 6.

26. Ibid., 11.

27. Ibid., 12-15. In fact Robbins talks about four conditions. What I have done is to amalgamate his first and fourth conditions.

28. Ibid., 16.

29. Ibid., 14-15.

30. Polanyi et al., op. cit., 246.

31. Ibid., 246.

32. Robbins, op. cit., 12-15.

33. Ibid., 13

34. Terence Hopkins, "Sociology and the Substantive View of the Economy" in Polanyi et al., op. cit., 290.

35. Richard B. McKenzie, *The Limits of Economic Science: Essays on Methodology,* (Boston: Kluwer-Nijhoff Publishing, 1983), 42-43.

36. See Bob Goudzwaard, *Capitalism and Progress: A Diagnosis of Western Society,* translated and edited by Josina Van Nuis Zylstra, (Toronto: Wedge Publishing Foundation, 1979), 211f.

37. "Four" includes the scarcity dimension.

38. In fact the need to preserve and reproduce resources over time (as opposed just to using a given stock more efficiently in the present) seems to be ignored in Robbins' discussion more because his analysis abstracts from the ongoing process of time than because it abstracts from social relationships.

"Is Not This Kind of Fasting I Have Chosen?"[1] Simone Weil's Life and Labor

Johanna Selles-Roney

In a photograph taken of her class at the Lycee Henri IV in 1926,[2] Simone Weil is distinguished from her male classmates by an intensity of gaze and an air of somewhat amused detachment. Weil, who graduated from the prestigious "Ecole Normale" in 1931, spent her brief thirty-four years engaged in a passionate search for truth. In many ways, she began this quest from a privileged position—the comfort of a middle-class home, parents who placed a high value on superior education, and the advantage of the best schools and teachers. She struggled with limited success to free herself from these advantages and place herself in a position to understand life from the point of view of the humblest laborer.

Weil's fascination with labor[3] was a consistent theme in her life and consequently offers a key to understanding her thought.[4] Her reflections on the subject are marked by the application of a philosophical method which was rooted in the nineteenth-century voluntarist, *spiritueliste* line of French philosophy.[5] Labor was more than a central theoretical concern; her life demonstrated a practical fascination with the existence of an ordinary laborer, whether in industry, agriculture, or other work. She demonstrated an early interest in this theme; as a student at the Ecole Normale she wrote two published pieces on the subject.[6] Her perseverance in understanding and experiencing manual labor overcame both physical limitations and the scepticism of those who were offended by her lack of regard for the social norms which, had she observed them, might have restricted her quest.[7]

Theoretical Explorations, 1931-34
In the early thirties Weil developed a rudimentary theoretical framework which conditioned the direction of her later work on labor. During these years she taught at three different lycées for girls in Le Puy, Auxerre, and Roanne and also participated in the labor movement, which at that time was struggling with the question of unity.[8] At this point she still supported a revolution which would be executed by the trade unions. This "real" revolution required workers who had appropriated knowledge and had thereby abolished the division of labor into intellectual and manual work, which Marx had originally described. The first step towards removing this distinction was to give the workers the ability to handle language, especially written language.[9] The workers should not have contempt for intellectual culture but should appropriate it for themselves. The true revolution implied taking possession of language, which would free workers from domination by intellectuals. According to Weil, the abolition of the degrading division between intellectual and manual work was a viable goal; to this end, she gave classes to miners on weekends in French and political economy.[10]

During the early thirties, however, Weil became disillusioned with both the trade union movement and with party politics. In the article "Prospects" (1933),[11] she proposed that the individual worker, as opposed to the collectivity, was the supreme value. The work of the individual could gain greater value by opposing specialization and by helping the laborer to understand "his" work.[12] Neither the "right" nor the "left" had properly addressed the issue; the focus needed to be shifted to the worker:

We want to get back to man, that is to say, to the individual, the power which it is his proper function to exercise over nature, over tools, over society itself; to re-establish the importance of the workers as compared with material conditions of work.[13]

Weil's pessimistic view of the possibilities of revolution to usher in a new and just social order was based on her understanding of the failure of the Russian revolution, the defeat of the German working-class movement, and her experience with the French working-class movement.[14] Both the American and the Russian systems had generated productive systems characterized by a oppressive bureaucracy. Marx had recognized the power of bureaucracy to oppress, particulary in the form of the bureaucratic and military machine of the state. Marx had, however, located the problem of the separation of spiritual forces of labor from manual labor in the operation of capitalist economy. By contrast, she believed that in any economic system the existence of a managerial class or a bureaucratic caste guaranteed the existence of an oppressive system, and furthermore, once a social stratum recognized that it had this kind of power, it did everything possible to preserve "that monopoly until the very foundations on which it rests have been undermined by the historical process."[15] Previous regimes such as feudalism, capitalism, or the Greek system, even though oppressive, seemed to be free and happy in contrast to the new form of oppression brought about by the power of war, which would give the state a role in production and consequently increase bureaucracy.[16] The oppressive power of bureaucracy had an innate tendency to reproduce itself and to maintain its hold on society. The social order was seen as a collective structure which allowed little room for individual voluntary agency.[17] In the face of this consuming bureaucracy, Weil claimed that our goal should be to focus on the individual as the supreme value, to oppose increasing specialization, and to give manual labor dignity. She was unclear, however, about how this change in focus could occur, given the power of the collectivity to suppress individual action. Her understanding of the process of social change and the actions of the individual underwent further revision after her factory experience and conversion, but the framework of her thought, namely the focus on the dignity of the individual's labor, would remain consistent throughout her life.[18] At this point though, Weil had not developed a proper basis for a re-evaluation of the dignity of labor.

An important document which emerged from this period was her "Reflections on the Causes of Liberty and Social Oppression" (1934).[19] This essay was not published until after her death, but Weil and others realized the importance of what she jokingly called her "Testament."[20] The article "Reflections" comprised her final critique before she undertook a complete immersion in the life of a laborer. Her position, previously characterized as a rejection of immanence, included a continued grappling with the thought of Marx, which partly demonstrated the extent of his influence on her thinking, but also gave her a point of contact from which to express dissatisfaction with Marxism.[21] The critique of Marx facilitated her later quest for transcendence beyond Marx, and established her reputation as an original thinker.

According to Weil, Marx had failed to observe that modern techniques oppressed laborers. She accused Marx of holding to a "religious" faith in the power of technique to free humans from the curse of work. But this faith only gave employers the means to crush workers, by making them subject to historical progress. Rather than blindly believing in the power of productive forces to liberate workers from oppression, she called for a critical examination of unlimited increase in production and technical progress.

Marx's materialist method whereby "social existence is determined by the relations between man and nature established by production" was the only sound basis for historical investigation.[22] She differed with Marx, however, in her belief that neither technical progress nor the abolition of private property would relieve oppression since "the abolition of private property would be far from sufficient in itself to prevent work in the mines and in the factories from continuing to weigh as a servitude on those who are subjected to it."[23] Her understanding of Marx's materialist method led her to accuse him of a failure to question how the machinery oppressed the workers, independent of the direct ownership relations and power relations in the workplace. The failure of the application of the materialist method was, therefore, situated in the absence of inquiry about the relationship between social oppression and the system of production. Marxists were correct in finding that the economic organization of social life was at the root of social oppression. However "they have failed to inquire into exactly *which* aspects of economic organization are central to this connection and which are not."[24] According to Weil, the organization of work in the form of the power relations within the workplace is distinct from the social relations of production and is a more important factor than the latter in determining the oppression of the worker.[25]

Weil's criticism of the notions of progress and unlimited growth was directed at the optimism which was a legacy of both scientific and Enlightenment thought.[26] Weil restated the problem by analyzing the factors which affected technical progress: the utilization of natural resources; the rationalization of labor; the coordination of effort in time; mechanization; and automation. Despite the generally held belief that progress would improve the conditions of labor, Weil cautioned that "no technique will ever relieve men of the necessity of continually adapting, by the sweat of their brow, the mechanical equipment they use."[27]

The speed of technical progress in the 1930s produced a frenzy which brought about the notion that work "might one day become unnecessary."[28] And in the social sphere, Marx's view that the "higher stage of communism" reflected the final stage of social evolution was in fact utopian thinking.[29] Yet revolutionaries died in pursuit of this utopian vision or the "equally utopian belief that the present system of labor could be placed by mere decree at the service of a society of free and equal men."[30] The term revolution was meaningless, unless it would abolish social oppression. Weil believed that Marx had not carried his analysis far enough to see that the system of production in the form of large industry reduced the worker to being a "mere instrument" in the hands of employers. It was useless to hope that technical progress would alleviate the individual burden by obliterating "the double burden imposed on man by nature and society."[31] The real question, according to Weil, was whether production could be organized in a different way, even though it would not alleviate the "necessities imposed by nature and the social constraint arising therefrom, would enable these at any rate to be exercised without grinding down souls and bodies under oppression."[32]

The relations between "man" and nature established by production had to be considered in terms of the problem of power. Once society was divided into those who commanded and those who executed, all of social life became governed by the struggle for power. Marx rested his analysis on a struggle for subsistence which Weil saw as only one factor in the larger struggle for power. To reinforce this conclusion, Weil re-read history from "primitive" cultures to "advanced" cultures and claimed that technical progress only transferred the cause of human servitude from the forces of nature to the caprices of those in power.[33]

Despite the evidence of slavery everywhere, humans continued to dream of liberty; Marx's communism was one variation on that theme. Having a perfect ideal in mind helped one to hope for and eventually to realize a less perfect liberty. Liberty as an ideal did not presume the abolition of necessity, since the presence of necessity in the world was tied to the need to work. For Weil the struggle against necessity gives our lives meaning and allows us to attempt to attain liberty.[34]

Central to her idea of free society was the use of individual mind.[35] The definition of a free society depended on the congruence between thought and action wherein the most fully human civilization would have manual labor as its pivot, providing the individual with a feeling of worth.[36] The relationship between thought and action would be tested during her factory experience, and cause to her re-evaluate the sources of liberty and human dignity.

In her depiction of an ideal society, work was organized in such a way that bonds between the workers were formed. The heroic model of a fisherman battling the elements and the craftsmen of the Middle Ages more closely approximated her ideal than the modern factory worker.[37] Despite the weaknesses of the essay, she had accurately questioned the harmful effects of technology on the worker and the dangers of dependence on a belief in progress.[38] Using Marx's materialism to focus on the problem of labor, she attempted to analyze the relationship between the organization of the workplace and the workers' ability to achieve a congruence between thought and action. Her spiritual path would lead her to take this initial concept of oppression and liberty and transform it by her understanding of the depths of affliction and the possibility of divine grace.

The Factory Experience, 1934-35

Weil requested a leave from teaching in 1934 to fulfill her desire to work in a factory.[39] The problem, as she understood it, was how to reconcile the organization of industrial society with the conditions of work and life suitable to a free proletariat. Perhaps the actual experience of working conditions would suggest a solution to the problem of organization.[40] She informed the ministry of education that she intended to study the relationship of technology to culture; a relationship that was marked by the oppression of "man by man" and "man by machine."[41]

She kept detailed notes of the factory experience in a journal.[42] The most astonishing thing about the humiliation generated by the factory system was the fact that it passed largely unchallenged.[43] By the end of her experience in the factory, her attitude had changed from submission to acceptance. This acceptance of suffering as necessary would become transformed into a spiritual exercise in the latter phase of her thought, and prepare her for the experience of being "between two realities."[44]

In 1941 she wrote an article entitled "Factory Work"[45] based on her experience of factory life during 1934-35, demonstrating that the memory of the work had not faded in the intervening years. The details of factory oppression which had filled her journal in the form of quotas and hours worked were replaced by prose which reflected Weil's spiritual phase. She had begun to analyze social life in the light of her personal belief in two distinct realities, namely an earthly and a transcendent one, and she attempted to relate the existing world to a transcendent vision.

Instead of the alienation generated by the modern workplace, a factory should "be a place where, for all the inevitability of physical and spiritual travail, working people can taste joy and nourish themselves on it."[46] In 1934 she had observed that liberty did not mean the absence of necessity, because necessity in the case of labor helped a person to exercise self-discipline and self-conquest.[47] By 1941 she continued to believe that labor was inevitable; however, the purpose of that labor, in her new vision, was not only an inevitable aspect of necessity, but it gave the worker access to spiritual joy and nourishment.[48] The factory needed reform and reorganization to allow the worker to benefit from the spiritual possibilities offered by labor, without in the process being completely crushed by the factory system.[49] Individual thought and action, an important feature of her conception of liberty in her early thought, remained a consistent theme in her writing.[50]

Metaxu: Between Two Realities, 1936-43

Weil travelled to Spain to observe the Spanish Civil War but an unfortunate accident prematurely ended her stay. During 1936-37, she took another leave from teaching and used her time to reflect on the workers' problems. Travel in Italy led to the second mystical experience where "something stronger than I compelled me for the first time to go down on my knees."[51] Her writings of this period refer to Christ's suffering as the model for human suffering. This growing sense of spiritual reality did not cause her withdrawal from social and political concerns. She was, however, disappointed in the union movement and in politics; by 1938 her writing focused on subjects such as colonialism and pacifism.

While attending services at Solesmes, she had the third mystical experience, even though she had been stricken at the time with devastating headaches. The experience helped her to perceive a connection between love and affliction: "This experience enabled me by analogy to get a better understanding of the possibility of divine love in the midst of affliction."[52] Being broken but not crushed by the external world implied a submission to purposeful suffering. Where could the individual find purpose in the suffering of factory life? This question, which challenged Weil's new metaphysical understanding, demanded an answer which would address the daily experience of a worker.

The last years of her life[53] represent the final stage of the development of Weil's theology of labor characterized by necessity and affliction, but mediated by creation, beauty, and love. She wrote to a friend that she felt "an ever increasing sense of devastation, both in my intellect and in the centre of my heart, at my inability to think with truth at the same time about the affliction of men, the perfection of God, and the link between the two."[54]

Earthly reality, as she interpreted it, was ruled by necessity which is evidence of the absence of God. Individuals must experience a process of "decreation" which destroys the ego. By consenting to suffer one brings about the absence of God (expiatory suffering).[55] The bringing about of the fullness of the absence of God (redemptive suffering) occurs when an innocent soul suffers affliction and submits to it.[56] Daily life and labor on earth remained crucial to the salvific process. Throughout the last years of Weil's writing, she attempted to connect her spiritual vision with concern for the lives of ordinary laborers and the culture which surrounded them.

The acceptance of two distinct realities, immanent and transcendent, altered Weil's original belief in work as cruel slavery resulting from the fall. Work, in her later view, was imbued with dignity by means of a spiritual root—not because work was redeemed by Christ, but because work allowed the operation of grace through affliction. Work offered the opportunity to direct oneself to the good, but the organization of the workplace and the effects of management and technology could still destroy the sacred in the individual.[57] The afflicted cried out and asked why they had to suffer, but only God could deliver the eternal part of the soul, which is that part which consents to love in the absence of God. The rest of the soul is at the mercy of other persons. An individual injured or destroyed through the actions of another can no longer aspire to the good, a situation which is a sacrilege to the sacred in a person.[58] She believed that the workplace, as well as society, needed to recognize its obligation to remedy every ill which could potentially destroy the soul and body of any human.[59]

In *The Need for Roots* she described work as the point of contact between this world and the world beyond. Both the agricultural and the industrial worker had access to the intermediary nature of work.

She wrote: "Consequently labor and death, if man undergoes them in a spirit of willingness, constitute a transference back into the current of supreme good, which is obedience to God."[60] The experience of work, carried out in an atmosphere of joy and freedom, allows the mind to develop higher forms of thought which reveal truth. Thus, Weil envisioned a civilization founded upon the spiritual nature of work.[61] This ideal civilization would give "the very strongest possible roots in the wide universe" as opposed to a state of almost total uprootedness.[62]

Rather than eliminate the suffering inherent in the world, Weil placed it within a model of obedience provided by antiquity. The passivity of inert matter showed perfect obedience to God, and the beauty of the world also projected "the radiance of this perfect Obedience."[63] In the beauty of the world, "harsh necessity becomes an object of love," leading the individual to a more perfect understanding of God.[64] Through joy, the beauty of the world penetrates the soul, and through suffering it penetrates the body; both are required to know God. An individual must team to appreciate the "obedience of the universe to God."[65] A more direct and daily opportunity to suffer and practice obedience, to decreate, and allow for the descent of grace, was available to every worker through the experience of physical labor which is, in itself, a daily death.[66]

Conclusion
The object of social reform was not the abolition of work, but rather the integration of work into a framework which offered the worker the experience of necessity and affliction. Consenting to necessity in the daily experience of work is a means of loving God and also of recognizing the universality of human suffering[67] which in turn leads to love and compassion for one's neighbor and a recognition of the sacred in all humans.[68]

Weil's reading of Plato underlies her understanding of divine justice and divine love. The judgment of God, which is human salvation, is revealed through human suffering. The action of supernatural grace is presupposed by the presence of love in the soul, awakened by the beauty of the world. Joan O'Donovan notes that, for Weil, "salvation by the beauty of the world is the heart of the

Greek understanding of divine providence as we have inherited it in the thought of Plato, the Pythagoreans, and the Greek Stoics."[69] The consent to necessity and the love of God is also a recognition of the universality of human suffering.[70] Although the experience of work with its supernatural locus directs one's attention to the other world, Weil integrates the power of this world, and of human community to meditate between the two. Liberty, in this sense, is not a flight from harsh necessity, but an opening of the human to the truth, which is a descent of grace. The quality of attention required for the descent of grace stands in stark contrast to the image of modern persons making their own reality, exercising their will. This contrast, based as it is on a synthesis of Platonic thought and elements of Christianity are what drew George Grant to the writings of Simone Weil, as a basis for a critique of modernity.[71]

Weil's understanding of the centrality of suffering and the necessity of affliction directly affected her view of the workplace. Her vision was not anti-technological,[72] but called for a responsible development of technology, in such a way that the worker could understand the process, as opposed to being a blind operator. She did not believe in infinite progress or unlimited development, and called for a critical understanding of social change.[73]

Furthermore, her vision calls others to not only try to hear the cry of the afflicted, but to enter into suffering at the foot of the cross. The centrality of the theme of suffering and the image of Christ crucified places compassion at the forefront of Weil's social vision. As Simone de Beauvoir remarked, "I envied her for having a heart that could beat right across the world."[74] The type of work which offered opportunity for the experience of affliction, inverts the hierarchy of valued work, giving the assembly line worker a greater opportunity to experience divine grace than the bureaucrat, or factory owner. The absence of God from creation does, however, limit Weil's view of the possibility of redemption of all work, whether waged or otherwise. The model of Christ on the cross acts as an example of how one suffers, but offers little consolation or assurance. The gnostic basis of this vision directly countered any notions of divine providence.[75] There is a tension as well between the balance of a perfectly passive subject, open to the descent of grace but not exercising the will. The subject must want, yet not will, must choose but not order, and in this waiting, carry out the laboring process.

Weil called all those who labor to create a workplace and a society which valued labor as rooted in a spiritual process. The application of her vision is a return to "a consciousness of principles,"[76] and a development of conditions necessary for the disclosure of our society which challenges "self-validating progress."[77] The conditions of labor can effect such a complete destruction of the soul that there is no possibility of redemption. The damage can not be limited to the hours spent in the factory, but can destroy all possibility of future redemption. Although Weil's predominant image for dispossessed labor was that of the factory worker, one might well ask whether soul-destroying labor can only be understood in relation to the modern industrial organization of labor, or whether it could also be extended to all work in oppressive conditions, ranging from the production of knowledge in academe, to the migrant worker of western societies. By undervaluing certain kinds of work, by focusing change on wage reform alone, or by underestimating the damage done when one works in conflict with one's values or conscience, the conditions of work continue to oppress the individual. But only in those who are able to be fully human can the necessary decreation take place and therefore the workplace or a society which dehumanizes people removes from them the possibility of experiencing necessity, affliction and the love of God.

The need to analyse and to reform the way a society labors is directly related to the individual's ability to be both fully human and to reach spiritual understanding. The integration of politics, society, the family, education, and work reflected how Weil connected work to the rootedness of a culture. This recognition, written as a plan for post-war reconstruction in France, was intended to rebuild society with a renewed sense of the value of manual labor. Yet both the diagnosis and the prescription for change were applicable to the other modern industrialized societies, which had lost both the potential for humanity and spirituality in the frenzy of production and "progress." Weil stood alone from the intellectual currents of her time in projecting this challenge. Her critique of Marxism enabled her to question some fundamental notions at the heart of Western culture, such as faith in science and progress, which in turn inspired an examination of the real causes of oppression. At the time, few recognized the profound nature of her analysis. Weil's own quest for transcendence shaped the nature of her inquiry and led to a vision for modern civilization that, although idealistic and flawed, attempted to restore wholeness to those broken by oppression, and dignity to those chained by injustice.

Notes

1. Isaiah 58:6. I gratefully acknowledge the comments and suggestions by Richelle Wiseman on earlier drafts.
2. Simone Pétrement, *Simone Weil: A Life,* (New York: Schocken, 1976). Weil was one of a handful of women students at the Ecole, since the school had only allowed women to enter in 1924.
3. In this paper I use "work" and "labor" interchangeably, since Weil did not follow the distinction that Hannah Arendt explored in *The Human Condition,* (Chicago: University of Chicago Press, 1972), 131.
4. There is such a close link between Simone Weil's life and her theoretical development that in this article, the two will be presented together. This approach is rooted in the attempt by feminist history to recover life stories and restore the wholeness between life and theory. This approach integrates the individuals' journals, diaries, and letters as well as their formal writings.
5. See *Formative Writings 1929-1941: Simone Weil,* Dorothy Tuck McFarland and Wilhelmina Van Ness, eds. and trans., (Amherst: University of Massachusetts Press, 1988), 6-7. Weil was taught this line of thought by her teacher Alain, who had been influenced by Jules Lagneau, who in turn was influenced directly by Descartes, but through the revisions of Maine de Biran. Weil constantly revised her thought and this tendency, in addition to the absence of a mature body of thought, should caution the reader from making too strict an interpretation of her meaning. See also, David McLellan, *Utopian Pessimist: The Life and Thought of Simone Weil* (New York: Posiedon Press, 1990), especially chapter 2.

6. Weil, "Concerning Perception, or the Adventure of Proteus," and "Concerning Time," in *Libres Propos*, New Series, No. 5 (1929): 237-41; and No. 8 (1929): 387-92. See Pétrement, *Simone Weil*, 61. Weil's interest in labor was more than theoretical; she actively sought first-hand experience of labor, digging potatoes and accompanying fishing expeditions. She was unsuited to physical labor, however, by a lack of physical dexterity and a tendency to suffer severe headaches.

7. Weil consciously rejected those elements of her biography which she believed interfered with her quest. On the complex subject of her attitude to her Jewish ancestry, see Robert Coles, *Simone Weil: A Modern Pilgrimage*, (Reading, MA: Addison-Wesley, 1987), chapter 3. The question of attitudes towards her sex deserves further investigation since the subject is complicated by Pétrement's problematic treatment of this aspect. See Pétrement, *Simone Weil*, 28 for an awkward discussion of the "natural" need to express one's feminine nature, a need which was absent in Weil and thus by implication, "unnatural." Pétrement's obvious discomfort with Weil's habits of dress, and her description of Weil's behavior as "manly" reflects a historical judgment that needs reconsideration. Weil's style was partly inspired by a lack of interest in mundane matters and probably was partly a response to the liberating climate among the few female students at the Ecole Normale. On the latter, see for example, John Hellman, *Simone Weil: An Introduction to Her Thought*, (Waterloo: Wilfrid Laurier University Press, 1982), 10-15. See also Stan Miles, ed., *Simone Weil: An Anthology*, (Essex, England: Virago Press, 1986), 1-68; and J. P. Little, *Simone Weil: Waiting on Truth,* (Oxford, New York, Hamburg: Berg, 1988), 11-12. The issue of gender is addressed by Mary Dietz, *Between the Human and the Divine: The Political Thought of Simone Weil*, (Totowa, N.J.: Rowman and Littlefield, 1989).

8. There were two main bodies, the Confederation Generale du Travail (C. G. T.), Confederation Generale du Travail Unitaire (C.G.T.U.). Pétrement summarizes the differences between the two main unions by explaining that the C. G. T. advocated separation between political parties and trade unions, whereas the C. G. T. U.

favored affiliation between the trade unions and political parties and especially the communist party. See Pétrement, *Simone Weil*, 83.

9. Pétrement, *Simone Weil*, 88-89.

10. Weil's activities on behalf of the unemployed townspeople at Le Puy did nothing to endear her to the school authorities. Experiences such as these and, for example, her visit to a mine during which she used an air hammer, led to a lifelong preoccupation with the impact of technology on the worker's life.

11. Weil, "Are We Heading for the Proletarian Revolution?" in *Oppression and Liberty*, (Amherst: University of Massachusetts Press, 1973). Originally published in *La Revolution proletarienne*, No. 158 (25 August 1933), and reprinted in *Oppression et Liberte*, (Paris: Gallimard, 1955).

12. Note that Wilhelmina Van Ness observes in the preface to *Formative Writings 1929-1941* that Weil's style adheres to conventions that are now regarded as hopelessly sexist, but that in her writings "mankind" and "man" stand for all humanity. Weil refused to divide the human race along sex lines, or to extend privileges to any one except the oppressed. See Preface, xiii.

13. Pétrement, *Simone Weil*, 176.

14. See Miles, *Simone Weil*, 15. A revolution wherein there is a sudden reversal of the relationship between forces is impossible, because it would mean a "victory of weakness over force." History offers slow transformations which do nothing but "grind beneath them the unfortunate race of human beings." Weil, "Reflections," 77-78.

15. Weil, "Prospects. Are We Heading For The Proletarian Revolution?" in *Oppression and Liberty*, 14. Weil's reading of social change deserves more attention in terms of its relationship to the social thought of Durkheim and Weber, as well as Marx.

16. Weil, "Prospects," 17-18.

17. See Jeffrey Alexander, *The Classical Attempt at Theoretical Synthesis: Max Weber*, (Berkeley, Los Angeles: University of California Press, 1983); and Roger O'Toole, *Religion: Classical Sociological Approaches*, (Toronto: McGraw-Hill Ryerson, 1984). See also, Wolfhardt Pannenberg, "Christianity, Marxism and Liberation Theology," *Christian Scholars Review* 18, 3 (March 1989): 215-26.

18. The article provoked anger from readers who were offended by her pessimism. One of those readers was Leon Trotsky who reacted sharply to Weil's criticism. Pétrement observes, however, that there was a sharp change in Trotskyist policy in the summer of 1933 and attributes this shift to Weil's influence, see Pétrement, *Simone Weil*, 176.

19. Weil, *Oppression and Liberty*, 37-124.

20. Pétrement, *Simone Weil*, 204. In this same year Weil decided to withdraw from political action to search for a deeper analysis of oppression which would draw her to a source outside of the immanent polarities of modern France to a supernatural source. Weil's "Testament" is divided into four parts, entitled "Critique of Marxism," "Analysis of Oppression," "Theoretical Picture of a Free Society," and "Sketch of Contemporary Social Life." The first two parts are characterized by criticism and analysis and the last two sections outline Weil's ideal against which she measures the state of contemporary social life.

21. The Marxism which Weil criticizes is the Marxism of the European Communist parties in the 1920s and 1930s, especially that of the French Communist Party. This Marxism is called "orthodox Marxism" by Blum and Seidler, a view which was dominant during the Second International, and filtered for Weil through the canon of orthodox Marxism, such as *Capital, German Ideology, Communist Manifesto*. See Lawrence A. Blum and Victor Seidler, *A Truer Liberty: Simone Weil and Marxism,* (New York and London: Routledge, 1989), 30. It should be noted that Weil's engagement with Marx is based on a reading which is selective and interpretive, a reading which Weil also applied in her understanding of history, and of the Bible, resulting in her rejection of the Old Testament and her total disdain for the Roman empire.

22. Weil, "Reflections concerning the Causes of Liberty and Social Oppression," in *Oppression and Liberty*, 71.

23. "Reflections," 46.

24. Blum and Seidler, *A Truer Liberty*, 39-40.

25. Ibid., 38.

26. See Bob Goudzwaard, *Capitalism and Progress,* (Toronto: Wedge Publishing Co., 1979); Egbert Schuurman, *Technology and* *the Future,* (Toronto: Wedge Publishing, 1980); and H. Van Riessen, *The Society of the Future,* (Philadelphia: Presbyterian and Reformed Publishing Co., 1952).

27. Weil, "Reflections," 52.

28. Ibid., 54. One could argue that Weil is creating a polemic here which is not based on an accurate reading of Marx. In the *Economic and Philosophic Manuscripts of 1844,* Marx examines the situation of alienated labor, not the end of labor itself. See, *The Marx-Engels Reader,* Robert Tucker, ed., (New York, London: W. W. Norton, 1978), 80. McLellan notes, however, that *Oppression and Liberty* was published before Molitor published the *Economic and Philosophic Manuscripts of 1844.* In *Utopian Pessimist,* McLellan observes that "the radical mind/matter dualism that she inherited from Descartes through Alain meant that any neo-Hegelian reading of Marx was unacceptable to her." (79).

29. "Reflections," 54.

30. Ibid., 55.

31. Ibid., 56. According to Blum and Seidler, *A Truer Liberty,* 49, the real difference between Marx and Weil on this point is that Marx believes that "free" labor can only take place outside of the realm of necessity, whereas for Weil, it is only when work directly faces necessity that it is free. McLellan, *Utopian Pessimist,* notes that the linking of Marx's materialist method with the myth of progress led her to over-simplifications. For example, she glossed over the distinction between a mode of production and a technique of production, adopted uncritically Rousseau's view of a pre-industrial golden age, and appeared "downright absurd on some of the reasons she gives for the impossibility of capitalist expansion," 78.

32. Ibid., 56.

33. Ibid., 83. There are similarities in the way both Simone Weil and Hannah Arendt "read" human history, studying the relationship between nature, humanity, and labor from ancient to modern times. The similarities and differences between the two interpretations of history merit further research.

34. See Blum and Seidler, *A Truer Liberty,* 84-97. The conception of liberty which Weil developed here is rooted in a Kantian framework, in which liberty is tied to an inner quality. She appropriated Kant's

sense "of moral capacity" as a source of human dignity in order to criticize what she understood as Marxism's conception of freedom. Weil's reading of liberty at this stage tried to combine Marx's view of oppression with a Kantian ethical system, a reading which Blum and Seidler attribute to her misunderstanding of the weight of dialectic in Marx and its dependence on Hegel's critique of Kant.

35. When a person works, he or she as a thinking being is in direct confrontation with nature. See Peter Winch, *Simone Weil: "The Just Balance"*, (Cambridge: Cambridge University Press, 1989), 101. For a description of how Weil took the Kantian notion that we must exercise freedom in our thoughts and actions and used this idea to challenge both the liberal and utilitarian traditions in Western thought, see Blum and Seidler, *A Truer Liberty*, 109.

36. Ibid., 106. The question remains how different Weil's view of labor is from that of Marx, since for her labor gives rise to self worth, and for Marx, labor is process of objectification of the species life wherein "man duplicates himself not only, as in consciousness, intellectually, but also actively, in reality, and therefore he contemplates himself in a world that he has created." See *Economic and Philosophic Manuscripts of 1844*, 74.

37. This model was influenced by the intellectualism and independence of thought which was a legacy of her academic training. See Hellman, *Simone Weil*, 32. The tone of her utopian vision has been attributed to a combination of her extreme individualism with her extreme intellectualism. Further, McLellan traces the points of similarity with Rousseau concerning her idea of an individual sharing a pact with the universe, the contrast of slavery and freedom, the centrality of manual labor, and the role of education. She had, however, no social theory of political change, and neglected political factors such as "different state forms and the impact of, for example, electoral practices," McLellan, *Utopian Pessimist*, 91.

38. See Hellman, *Simone Weil*, 32. Weil failed to link the mode of appropriation of surplus and the development of bureaucratic oppression; in her terminology she mixed bureaucratic class and social caste, technology and bureaucracy, and she made technocracy a new mode of production. The result is a "phenomenological account" strong in description but weak in "analysis and explanation." Mc-Lellan, *Utopian Pessimist*, 82.

39. Pétrement claimed that the plan was partly motivated by the impasse Weil had reached in her theoretical development. For a discussion of her work experiences, see George Abbott White, "Simone Weil's Work Experiences: From Wigan Pier to Chrystie Street," in *Simone Weil: Interpretations of a Life*, G. A. White, ed., (Amherst: University of Mass. Press, 1981), 137-80.

40. Pétrement, *Simone Weil*, 204

41. Ibid., 205. She rented a room near the factory and began work as a power press operator. During the year she was laid off and worked in three different factories, was injured and experienced hunger, illness and exhaustion. The humiliation endured during Weil's factory experience marked her forever with the feeling of being a slave. This perception coincided with the realization that slavery was a consequence of the material conditions and machinery of work.

42. Simone Weil, "Factory Journal," in *Formative Writings 1929-41*, 149-226. See also "Factory Work," in *The Simone Weil Reader*, George Panichas, ed., (New York: David McKay, 1977), 55-72, and "Journal d'usine," in *La Condition ouvriere* (Paris: Editions Gallimard, 1951), 45-145. The almost obsessive attention to detail does not disguise the crushing sense of failure she experienced as she failed to meet deadlines, and was devastated by blinding headaches. She observed a lack of sympathy between workers and commented on the special problems faced by women workers. See "Factory Journal," 159.

43. One day while riding on a bus, Weil realized that she felt she had no right to be there and that she felt like a slave. The depersonalization effected by the workplace had almost completely deprived her of a sense of self; see "Factory Journal," 211. She noted that "You kill yourself with nothing at all to show for it, either a subjective result (wages) or an objective one (work accomplished), that corresponds to the effort you've put out. In that situation you really feel you are a slave, humiliated to the very depths of your being." "Factory Journal," 194.

44. After the factory experience, Weil travelled to Portugal and there had the first mystical experience on her path to Christianity. While watching a village festival Weil suddenly realized that Christianity was "pre-eminently the religion of slaves, that slaves cannot help belonging to it, and I among others." See Weil, *Waiting on God*, Emma Craufurd, trans., (New York: Putnam, 1951), 66-67.

45. Weil, "Factory Work," 53-72.

46. Ibid., 66.

47. Weil, *Oppression and Liberty*, 84.

48. See also, Little, *Simone Weil: Waiting on Truth*, 1, 18. Joy is a sign that manual labor is made for us; and lowering the status of manual work in the way that a modern factory does is a sacrilege.

49. The most important part of the problem of work was time and rhythm. She did not advocate the elimination of monotony since tedium characterized earthly reality. Humans had been thrown out of eternity; our journey required this painful travel through time. Yet our vocation was to master time, and this had to be "kept inviolate" in every human. There is a parallel between uniformity and variety as it is manifest in days and seasons or in its hold on the peasant's labor. The factory removes one from this natural rhythm and leaves the worker isolated from either past or future by the ticking of a clock, which has no relationship to eternity. See Weil, "Factory Work," 69-70.

50. See also Winch, *Simone Weil*. Blum and Seidler (*A Truer Liberty*, 179) observe that Weil's recognition through the factory experience that oppression does not necessarily lead to revolt, was a break with Hegelian tradition, which assumed the necessity of struggle against oppression as the core of historical process.

51. Weil, *Waiting for God*, 68.

52. Ibid., 68.

53. The invasion of France forced the Weil family to flee to Vichy and then to Marseille. Weil wrote constantly during this period and also fulfilled a dream to work as an agricultural laborer. The family sailed to New York in 1942, where Weil was desperately unhappy until she was able to sail to England to join the war effort. She worked for the Free French in London and wrote *The Need for Roots*. Weil became ill with tuberculosis, was hospitalized in April,

1943, and died in August of the same year. Her death is discussed elsewhere by Coles, *Simone Weil,* chapter 2, and Dorothy Tuck McFarland, *Simone Weil,* (New York: Frederick Ungar, 1983), 163

54. Weil to Maurice Schumann, 1943, in *Seventy Letters,* Richard Rees, ed., (London: Oxford University Press, 1962), 178.

55. "Il y a trois especes de douleur. La douleur inutile (degradante). La douleur expiatrice. La douleur redemptrice (celle-ci est la privilege des innocents). Nous constatons que Dieu inflige toutes trois." Weil, *Cahiers,* II, (Paris: Plon, 1972), 110.

56. For a discussion of Weil's religious thought, see Johanna Selles-Roney, *The Spirituality of Labour: Simone Weil's Quest for Transcendence,* (Toronto: Institute for Christian Studies, 1983), especially chapter four. See also Wayne Sheppard, "The Idea of the Absence of God in Simone Weil," Ph. D. diss., McMaster University, Hamilton, Ontario, 1982.

57. Weil, "Draft for a Statement of Human Obligations," in *Selected Essays, 1934-1943,* trans. Richard Rees, (London: Oxford University Press, 1962), 219-27.

58. Ibid., 221.

59. Weil, *The Need for Roots,* Arthur Wills, trans., (New York: Harper, 1971), 300. According to Blum and Seidler (*A Truer Liberty,* 192), the problem, as she saw it after her factory experience, was how to progress from total subordination to a mixture of subordination and cooperation.

60. Weil, *Need for Roots,* 300.

61. Ibid., 96.

62. Ibid., 98.

63. Ibid., 301.

64. Weil, "The Love of God and Affliction," in *The Simone Weil Reader,* Panichas, ed., 445.

65. Ibid., 449.

66. See also Clare Benedicks Fischer, *The Fiery Bridge: Simone Weil's Theology of Work,* (Ann Arbor, Mich.: University Microfiims, 1979).

67. See Joan E. O'Donovan, *George Grant and the Twilight of Justice,* (Toronto: University of Toronto Press, 1984), 84-85.

68. Ibid., 85.

69. Ibid., 81. See also, McLellan, *Utopian Pessimist,* chapter 9.

70. Ibid., 85.

71. Bernard Zylstra, "Philosophy, Revelation and Modernity: Crossroads in the Thought of George Grant" in *George Grant in Process*, (Toronto: Anansi, 1978), 148-52.

72. Technological changes in the workplace have changed the conditions of labor in a way that Weil could hardly have imagined in the 1940s. Yet she did anticipate that technology's ability to free the worker was matched by its power to enslave. For an exploration of the connections between Marxism and computers, see David Lyon, "Modes of Production and Information: Does Computer Technology Challenge Marxist Analysis?" *Christian Scholars Review* 18,3 (March 1989): 238-45.

73. See, for example, Paul Marshall, *Thine is the Kingdom*, (Basingstoke, England: Marshall, Morgan and Scott, 1984), especially chapter 4, and *Stained Glass: Worldviews and Social Science*, edited by Paul Marshall, Sander Griffioen, and Richard Mouw, (Lanham, Maryland: University Press of America, 1989).

74. Quoted in Pétrement, *Simone Weil*, 51.

75. The gnostic basis of her understanding of Christianity is explored by McLellan, *Utopian Pessimist*, 195-200.

76. Eric Voegelin, *The New Science of Politics* (Chicago: University of Chicago Press), 1.

77. Goudzwaard, *Capitalism and Progress*, 195.

Index